Reading Borges after Benjamin

SUNY series in Latin American and Iberian Thought and Culture

Jorge J. E. Gracia and Rosemary Geisdorfer Feal, editors

Reading Borges after Benjamin

Allegory, Afterlife, and the Writing of History

Kate Jenckes

State University of New York Press

Published by
State University of New York Press, Albany

Printed in the United States of America

For information, address State University of New York Press,
194 Washington Avenue, Suite 305, Albany, NY 12210-2384

Production by Ryan Morris
Marketing by Michael Campochiaro

Library of Congress Cataloging-in-Publication Data

Jenckes, Kate, 1969–
Reading Borges after Benjamin : allegory, afterlife, and the writing of history / Kate Jenckes.
p. cm. — (SUNY series in Latin American and Iberian thought and culture)
Includes bibliographical references and index.
ISBN-13: 978-0-7914-6989-7 (hardcover : alk. paper)
ISBN-13: 978-0-7914-6990-3 (pbk : alk. paper)
1. Borges, Jorge Luis, 1899–1986—Criticism and interpretation. 2. Benjamin, Walter, 1892–1940—Criticism and interpretation. I. Title. II. Series.

PQ7797.B635Z7373 2007
868'.64—dc22 2006012811

10 9 8 7 6 5 4 3 2 1

For Wolf Sohlich, who taught me that reading matters

Contents

Acknowledgments

As with any life project, this book would not have been written if it were not for the help, support, and inspiration of a number of teachers, friends, and colleagues. Alberto Moreiras and Brett Levinson deserve a special acknowledgment for their generosity and encouragement from beginning to end. Roland Greene, Ken Calhoon, and Leonardo García-Pabón helped tremendously with an early draft of the project. Irving Wohlfarth and Gary Wihl provided valuable comments toward the end. Lisa Chesnel and Ryan Morris have my profound gratitude for their help and patience at the production stage. Large portions of the book were conceived in Chile, and would not have been written without the participation of Federico Galende, Elizabeth Collingwood-Selby, Pablo Oyarzún, Willy Thayer, Carlos Pérez, Nelly Richard, Adriana Valdés, and Juan, Julia, and Joaquín. Lara Galloway, Jan Mieszkowski, Sharon Larisch, Teresa Vilarós, Gareth Williams, Cristina Moreiras, Santiago Colás, Patrick Dove, David Johnson, Bruno Bosteels, Adriana Johnson, Horacio Legrás, and Oscar Cabezas provided friendship and guidance of varying sorts. Thanks to my parents, who are an unending source of strength and support. And finally, to Thom, whose love and wit shape my ongoing sense of life.

Portions of chapters 1 and 3 appeared in the *Latin American Literary Review* and the *Journal of Latin American Cultural Studies*. It is with their permission that these texts are reprinted here.

Introduction

> El tiempo es aquí lo único que sobra, y sobra no al modo contabilizable de los relojes, sino al modo en que sobran, enteras, la vida y la historia.
>
> —Elizabeth Collingwood-Selby, "Un retrazo en la escritura"

> The concept of life is given its due only if everything that has a history of its own, and is not merely the setting for history, is credited with life.
>
> —Walter Benjamin, "The Task of the Translator"

In "The Task of the Translator," Walter Benjamin suggests that life should be thought in relation to literature and language rather than nature. For him, life thought in terms of nature is conceived as discrete units or "lives," an organic sense of wholeness, and a linear development from birth to death and from parent to child. Literature, on the other hand, cannot be thought in such discrete and linear ways. A book does not live and die autonomously and pass its essence, intact, along to an offspring. Made up of language, it shares words and ideas with other books, with predecessors and contemporaries as well as those that follow it. Transmission of any sort—including translation, intertextuality, and tradition—is never direct and unilateral. Linguistic difference and, as Jorge Luis Borges's story "Pierre Menard" purports to demonstrate, a difference intrinsic to time and writing interrupts any one-way descendance from the original. Indeed, the recognition of such manifold difference infects the very notion of the original, which loses its privileged status as an autonomous work outside of time, and is shown to be part of what Benjamin calls linguistic life and the ongoing life (or afterlife) of artworks.[1]

It is important to remember that Benjamin's somewhat surprising analogy concerns history as well as literary history. His description of history as a kind of life, thought through the "life" of literature and translation, emphasizes both singularity and an interrelatedness that exceeds and interrupts every conception of either autonomy or direct relation. He insists that history is not a setting, a static and immortal universality in which individual lives occur. It is not linear or progressive: the past does not authorize the present nor does the present determine the past. Like the translated work or the precursor, the past exists in time just like its translation or successor. It is both vital and mortal; it is subject to change based on who is regarding it; it can be rewritten in the present but it can also shatter attempts to represent it.

As works such as "Pierre Menard" and "Kafka y sus precursores" indicate, Borges had similar ideas about literary history. His notion of precursors and originals that are invented or rewritten by their successors as well as vice versa is strikingly similar to Benjamin's description of artistic life and afterlife. Like Benjamin, Borges considered life as well as literature to be irremediably temporal, and he viewed time as neither a linear development nor a passive setting, but as an uncertain materiality that both takes us away from ourselves and constitutes our sense of who we are ("Time is a river that takes me away, but I am that river," *Otras inquisiciones* 187).

What is often not acknowledged is that Borges was concerned with history as well as literary history and individual experiences of temporality.[2] His repeated insistence that life and representation exist in time responds to the same questions of singularity and difference and the idea that life always exceeds its representations that Benjamin describes in "The Task of the Translator" as the nature of both life and history. The places in Borges's writing that refute temporal linearity and a stable sense of identity demand that we learn to look for what has been left out of their constructions, both at a level of individual life history and larger narratives, such as national, imperial, or universal history. Paul de Man's distinction that "temporality" denotes a passive unfolding, whereas "history" introduces the possibility of interrupting such unfolding, allows us to understand what is most historical about Borges's writings on time, life, and history (*Aesthetic Ideology* 133). For Borges, as for Benjamin, the past is never dead, but can irrupt in the present and change the way we see the world. Lives and times that are left out of dominant narratives have the ability to interrupt those narratives, forcing us to acknowledge the structures of exclusion on which they are based.

Borges does not always embrace the temporal nature of life and representation. He often portrays himself wishing for a point outside of time on which to ground a sense of himself and the world around him, only to reveal the impossibility of the same. He suggests that he would like, like his rival Carlos Argentino Daneri in "El aleph," to appropriate time's shifting movement and contain it within a totalizing representation (Daneri's lifework is titled "The Earth," and aims to represent the entire planet), but then he admits that the most he can do is piece together a fragmented account that can only gesture to an ongoing sense of time, which includes his own mortality. In his first published collection, *Fervor de Buenos Aires* (collected in *Obra poética*), Borges opens his book at the family cemetery, as if looking for a ground of identity that would legitimate his career as an Argentine writer, but then notices that that ground is a ground of dust and time. He spends the rest of the book sifting through fragments that indicate the limited and contingent nature of any representation of identity and linear time.

This form of pointing to a historicity that can never be fully represented constitutes a kind of *allegory,* in Benjamin's peculiar sense of the term. In Benjamin's understanding, allegory breaks up naturalized concepts of history and life, creating discontinuities through which other times and histories can emerge. Tom Cohen helpfully glosses the term as "allography" or "other-writing," describing it as a practice of writing that, like translation, indicates a difference in language that corresponds to history's ongoing and infinitely singular alterity (*Ideology* 12). Although Borges rejects allegory as an "aesthetic error," he also acknowledges that it merely exacerbates an abstract aspect of language that is impossible to avoid, even in such forms as the symbol or the novel, which purport to represent immediacy and particularity ("De las alegarías a las novelas," *Otras inquisiciones* 153–56). If the symbol, the novel, and allegory constitute "maps of the universe," the symbol and the novel are like Borges's famous imperial map that is spread over the colonized territory, and allegory is perhaps the same map, but ill-fitting and shredding with time, perforated by an otherness that it cannot keep covered. Allegory thus concerns a sense of life that cannot be fully represented, but rather gestures beyond itself to what both Benjamin and Borges describe as the "secrets of history"—that is, a conception of history that can never be appropriated by those who Benjamin calls history's victors.

I do not intend to imply that Borges and Benjamin had identical projects. Their different relationships to the states of emergency that rocked the twentieth century, as well as their political convictions, differentiate them considerably from one another. Benjamin lost his life under persecution from the Nazis, while Borges lost his job at the municipal library under Juan Domingo Perón; Benjamin was an avowed Marxist who believed in the possibility of a social revolution, while Borges was a lifelong skeptic who never expressed faith that the world could change except in the most minute of ways.[3] This book does not intend to give a comprehensive account of the differences or similarities between the two: it is not a strictly comparative book in any traditional sense of the term. Its objective is to explore points of resonance between the two authors around a sense of *life* that is both mortal and ongoing, singular and differential; and a practice of *allegory* or allography that indicates this life as an excess or alterity, and in doing so, interrupts representations that seek to fix it into naturalized narratives of linearity and identity.

The project of reading Borges "after" Benjamin does not mean to suggest, of course, a linear progression or a direct influence. The analyses focus on Borges, with Benjamin's ideas on allegory and historical or life representation intervening allegorically. Although Borges and Benjamin have received ample commentary over the years, this interaction between the two draws attention to aspects of both of their work that have either become stale or have been overlooked entirely. Reading Borges in relationship to Benjamin has the distinct advantage of drawing out ethical and political implications about his considerations of temporality and life that have largely escaped the purview of his critics. Borges was long accused of being a writer of unreality who thought with his back to history. In the last twenty or so years, the emphasis has been on bringing him "back" to history, that is, to place him into a historical and cultural "landscape."[4] Such a tendency has gone hand in hand with international trends of new historicism and the historicist side of cultural studies, critical practices that also latched onto Benjamin, reorienting him away from epistemological questions to focus on things like urban space and popular culture. The readings presented in these pages stress the intimate relationship between language and life, and, in so doing, work to undo the false opposition between literature and history that remains a predominant feature in cultural criticism today.

Perhaps one of the most pronounced differences between Benjamin and Borges is a difference in tone. Borges often acknowledges a wish to escape temporal uncertainty and find refuge in atemporal forms of representation. He repeatedly portrays himself seeking a ground of identity—an enduring sense of self, city, or nation, a solid sense of the past or the present—only to recognize that he is "unfortunately" a temporal being. Alberto Moreiras describes Borges as replacing Lyotardian metanarratives with "mournful intonation" ("entonación desdichada," *Tercer espacio* 129). Such repetition and resignation contrasts considerably with Benjamin, whose writings are not without a certain melancholy, but they are at the same time charged with an anguished sense of hope. This difference, however, is instructive. In spite of his apparent reluctance to accept life's temporal nature, Borges returns to it compulsively, never allowing himself to fall completely for the timeless metaphors that he turns over and over in his hands. Although often expressed with a resigned tone, Borges finds a sense of *life* in such temporal difference: a life that spills over discrete representations of life and death, an ongoing sense of life that rumbles beneath narratives of modernization, nationalization, and universal history. Borges's reluctant acknowledgment of such temporality and his repeated attempts to escape it reminds us that it is not necessary to have a voluntary relationship with time in order to experience its effects on representation. Benjamin would have undoubtedly agreed, hoping that the flashes of history would strike even where least welcome, and that the differences between a messianic materialist and the "feeble artifice of an Argentine astray in metaphysics" (*Otras inquisiciones* 170) might not be so profound.[5]

In the spirit of both authors' fondness for margins and forgotten texts, I have for the most part avoided the more celebrated parts of Borges's oeuvre to focus on texts that represent, often in a "skeletal" way, the questions of life, history, and identity that I have been discussing here. I begin with Borges's first three books of poetry, in which he explores his relationship to the physical and cultural space of Buenos Aires, and his biography of Evaristo Carriego, a poet who wrote about Buenos Aires at the turn of the century. I find these texts especially intriguing because they appear to be invested in establishing a sense of regional identity based on a linear relationship to the past, whether through blood relations and an inherited sense of propriety in the city, or through elective affinities and literary history. This has been the conclusion of the handful of critics who have considered them, in any case—among them some of Borges's most influential readers, including Ricardo Piglia, Beatriz Sarlo, and Sylvia Molloy. Yet Borges's remarks, made on several occasions, that his early poems prefigured all that was to come later, require that we read his early writings about life and the city with an eye to what does not fit in such representations of identity and lineage.

Borges's first books of poems open with the mortal ground of the Recoleta cemetery, and then show him wandering through a city streaked with time and mortality. He tries to find refuge in images of the past, but he is reminded again and again that both he and the city inhabit a temporal world, and are subject to ongoing change and a past that refuses to remain in the past. Language is an unwilling protagonist in this process, providing both the allure of a stable representation of self and city, and inflicting its repeated failure. Borges observes this failure reluctantly in both his own poetry and the cemeteries' sepulchral rhetoric, but ends up calling it an "act of life."

He explores the relationship between life and representation further in *Evaristo Carriego,* which is ostensibly a biography about the eponymous poet, but also includes meditations about life, death, and representation in Buenos Aires. In this book, Borges critically examines the concept of biography, that is, the idea that there could be a definitive writing of life, and he rejects the idea that a regional identity could be represented by such a biographical figure, even if the figure is a famous poet such as Carriego, Whitman, or even (implicitly) Borges himself. Borges's faux biography demonstrates how a single life cannot be properly told and how a regional poet cannot represent a regional identity, but it also addresses the impossibility of representing life in the modern form of the state, which links together individual lives in a general life of the nation. Borges introduces a writing practice—performed by knife fighters and guitar players, among others—that interrupts such privative representations of life and indicates the interpenetration of life and death, self and other that is the basis of life itself, both individual and communal.

In the second half of the book, I shift my focus from questions of life and death in Buenos Aires to a consideration of what is excluded from regional and universal representations of time and history. Borges says of the British conquest of India: "They did not accumulate only space, but also time: that is to say, experiences, experiences of nights, days, terrains, mountains, cities, cleverness, heroisms, betrayals, pains, destinies, deaths, diseases, beasts, happiness, rites, cosmogonies, dialects, gods, venerations" (*Discusión* 43). In *Historia universal de la infamia* (*Universal History of Infamy*), he shows how such subhistories have the potential to "aturdir," disturb or rattle, the dominant narratives. Borges's allegories of these narratives—not strictly "national allegories," which compared to Benjamin's understanding of allegory constitute another form of national narrative, dedicated to representing an albeit unstable totality—point to these active silences and the ways in which they mark the stories that exclude them. Such exclusions can be given a representation and even a sense of identity, as the enumerative list of African American history at the beginning of "El espantoso redentor Lazarus Morell" ("The Horrible Redeemer Lazarus Morell") suggests. Nevertheless, that does not erase the forced silence of the slaves, which to this day can irrupt into North American national narratives.

One of the most important ideas presented in these pages is that it is not enough to bring such excluded elements into representation. Spanish dictionaries can introduce the verb "to lynch" to their vocabularies, as we read in "El espantoso redentor Lazarus Morell," but the horror of lynching can never be adequately represented. Nor should we ignore it simply because it cannot be entirely represented. Rather, Borges seems to suggest that we should try to represent such things, acknowledging at the same time that it is impossible to represent them entirely.

Allegorical or allographical writing must be an ongoing endeavor, pointing to an "other" sphere that is always outside representation, and yet whose silences and exclusions can be traced in the cracks and crevices of language. Translating these silences into dictionary entries, or giving them their own spot in history, may be useful in certain respects, but it also neutralizes the singular force of their alterity, which has the potential to irrupt into what we think we know about the world.

The first three chapters focus on the works I have just mentioned, together with some of Benjamin's most important discussions of history, allegory, and representation. There are also incursions into what I like to think of as the "afterlife" of Benjamin's ideas in the work of Paul de Man and Jacques Derrida. The final chapter puts Borges's work into more direct contact with these thinkers, focusing on the way in which history and life can perhaps best be understood through language, as Benjamin says in "The Task of the Translator." The chapter explores the relationships between power and representation, writing and history, the past and the future, and repetition and difference in a series of essays by Benjamin and Borges, in conjunction with the notions of mourning and materiality as thought by de Man and Derrida. It considers the idea that history appears as a material excess in language, which can either be denied by representation, or elicited as an index of history's "secrets." Benjamin and Borges agree, albeit with different intonations, that representation that seeks to bring the past fully into the present closes itself off to life and history, while representation that acknowledges its limits and excesses opens itself to a living history that includes the most extreme secret of all: the future.

Abbreviations

BENJAMIN

CP	"Central Park"
GS	*Gesammelte Schriften*
I	*Illuminations*
N	"Konvolut N" (in German, in *Passagen-Werk;* in English, in *Benjamin: Philosophy, Aesthetics, History,* ed. Gary Smith)
OGD	*The Origin of German Tragic Drama*
R	*Reflections*

BORGES

D	*Discusión*
EC	*Evaristo Carriego*
F	*Ficciones*
HE	*Historia de la eternidad*
HI	*Historia universal de la infamia*
OP	*Obra poética*
OI	*Otras inquisiciones*

Chapter 1

Origins and *Orillas*

History, City, and Death in the Early Poems

> Aunque la voz . . .
> oficia en un jardín petrificado
> recuerdo con todas mis vidas
> por qué olvido.
>
> —Alejandra Pizarnik

Critics have long argued that Borges was obsessed with the past. His texts have been understood as attempts to escape history, or, especially in the first decade of his career, to impose a mythic ahistoricism on the present. However, a careful examination of Borges's early books of poems—*Fervor de Buenos Aires* (1923), *Luna de enfrente* (1925), and *Cuaderno San Martín* (1929)—suggests that Borges was not interested in rejecting history, but in developing a sense of history that would not be based on linear and progressivist claims. Representations of a nonlinear time, a familiar conceit in his later fictions, appear in these first volumes in the form of a history that does not remain neatly in the past, but which intervenes in the figure of a progressive present represented by the modernization of Buenos Aires. Such an intervention introduces a temporality that is excluded from a historicism that attempts to leave the past securely contained in what Borges calls a sepulchral form of representation. Borges's early books of poems do not exclude history or, as some critics suggest, reject the present for a glorified past, but rather work to open history to something beyond the accumulative present of a progressive modernity. This attention to history by way of an irrecuperable past is what I call, following Benjamin, a melancholic or allegorical relationship with loss, and which, as I will attempt to show in this and subsequent chapters, opens the possibility for a relationship between history, identity, and writing that is radically distinct from a linear and successive (whether progressive or regressive) understanding of history.

Family Trees

In an influential essay from 1980, Ricardo Piglia proposes that Borges's writings are based on a "ficción de origen" ("fiction of origin"), a fact that is most noticeable in his early writings, but which is evident throughout his work (87). Beatriz Sarlo, taking up this idea several years later, observes an "obsession with origins" in Borges's earliest published works, in which he appropriates the past as a means of legitimizing the present and his personal position within that present (*Modernidad* 45). Piglia's argument, later modified to the anachronistic observation that Borges (who was born in 1899) was the last great writer of the nineteenth century, is that Borges establishes his legitimacy as a writer by appealing to the dominant nineteenth-century narratives of national construction. Piglia charges that Borges bases his writings on a myth of origins through which "he narrates his access to the properties that make writing possible [for him]" (87). Unlike his contemporary Roberto Arlt, he does this not as a means of learning how to achieve legitimacy in the Argentine cultural market, but as a "narración genealógica," a narration of his family history that demonstrates his legitimacy as an Argentine writer. Piglia cites as an example Borges's consideration of the fact that many of the street names in Buenos Aires also appear in his family history: "This vain skein of streets that repeat the past names of my blood: Laprida, Cabrera, Soler, Suárez. Names that echo the (already secret) targets, the republics, the horses and the mornings, the dates, the victories, the military deaths" (88).

Piglia argues that Borges bases his entire body of writing on the naming and renaming of figures from this lineage. The result is a family narrative that implies a specific form of both history and language: "The succession of ancestors and offspring constitutes an onomastic index that repeats the structure of a family tree" (87). History is represented in Borges's writing, Piglia suggests, as a linear and successive ordering of names that leads back into a firm foundation, a family tree with its roots securely planted in the ground of the past. The linear structure of history in this description is accompanied by a particular emphasis on the name. The naming of ancestors in Borges's texts, such as the above citation in which he cites the names of the city streets as names that also appear in his own family history, is said to form an "onomastic index," an arrangement of names in which the names are presumed to indicate (*índice*) the past directly, like the branches and trunk of the family tree that lead directly to the ground. However, even in the passage that Piglia cites, the names do not function in this way: the onomastic index of the city is likened to a tangled skein that repeats the author's family names, names that "retumban," echo or resound, with events, dates, horses, and republics. In this example, at least, the solid ground of the past and of the name is not quite as solid as Piglia suggests.

Sarlo builds on Piglia's explanation of Borges's writing as a "fiction of origins." She reads Borges's early texts as the culmination of a *criollista* ideal that aimed to protect what was seen as a properly Argentine space of culture from the new immigrants who had been crowding Buenos Aires since the turn of the century.[1] What she describes as his "obsessive relationship with origins" was a means of establishing a mythic foundation of this culture, which would have excluded those more recently arrived (this was indeed the case with Borges's contemporary Leopoldo Lugones). Sarlo suggests that Borges, having returned in 1921 after several years in Europe, began his published career in Buenos Aires with the double figure of a return, one that was out of reach for the thousands of immigrants who had recently made Buenos Aires their home. She proposes that unlike these immigrants, Borges returned to Buenos Aires with a double sense of origin firmly in place, one that included both his European roots and his Argentine past. He was "a *criollo* man, a man with origin; a citizen of the world, and at the same time of a country that was strictly limited to Buenos Aires" (*Modernidad* 44–45). Enrique Pezzoni describes Borges's enthusiasm for his *criollo* identity in these early years as a kind of fervor: a nearly religious zeal for cultural salvation which, however, was soon transformed into an ongoing coming to terms with the fallen nature of being (*Texto* 72).[2]

Although Sarlo later focuses on the figure of a double inscription or double origin in relation to the cultural-historical site that Borges calls the "*orillas*," referring literally to the edges or limits of the city, she begins with the more central figure of the Recoleta cemetery that appears as the subject of the first poem of *Fervor de Buenos Aires*.[3] She sees this poem as representing a "beginning" in Edward Saïd's sense of the word, in which the differences that establish cultural identity are set forth in the opening of a given work (*Modernidad* 45, 46n). She interprets the fact that Borges begins his first book of poetry with the central cemetery of Buenos Aires as the indication of a poetic and civic ground, a privileged site of belonging where his ancestors lie and where he too will be buried, past and future contained in a single site of "origin": "Lo anterior: escuchado, leído, meditado, / lo resentí en la Recoleta, / junto al propio lugar en que han de enterrarme" ("The anterior: heard, read, meditated, / I felt it in the Recoleta, / next to the very place in which they will have to bury me," cited in Sarlo, *Modernidad* 45).

For Sarlo, Borges's early writings are based on the figure of a return, through which he represents his sense of belonging to a *criollista* cultural space that has its roots in the past. I want to argue, however, that Borges was aware from the outset that no such return is possible, both in the sense that it is impossible to return in time, but also in terms of representation: that is, the fact that there can be no return or recuperation possible in language, which would be the condition of possibility of a *criollista* cultural project.

A Journey of No Return

If after his years abroad, Borges wished that he could return to an older Buenos Aires, he recognized almost immediately that he could not. He acknowledges in his earliest writings that it is not only impossible to return to a point of departure across the Atlantic and over a period of several years, but that a real return or connection to the past is not possible even in everyday existence, from one minute to the next. He describes his return from Europe in "La nadería de la personalidad" ("The Nothingness of Personality"), an essay published in *Inquisiciones* (1925).[4] This emblematic departure is told as a scene of farewell to a friend in Mallorca, with the tacit acknowledgment that the two would probably never see each other again. Of the moment of this farewell and the departure from Europe, Borges says,

> ocurrióseme que nunca justificaría mi vida un instante pleno, absoluto, contenedor de los demás, que todos ellos serían etapas provisorias, aniquiladoras del pasado y encaradas hacia el porvenir, y que fuera de lo episódico, de lo presente, de lo circunstancial, no éramos nadie. Y abominé de todo misteriosismo. (99)
>
> It occurred to me that my life would never justify a full or absolute instant, one that would contain all the rest, that they would all be provisory stages, annihilating of the past and facing the future, and that beyond the episodic, the present, the circumstantial, we weren't anyone. And I abhorred all mysticism.[5]

In the moment of his departure from Europe, site of one of his two origins, and returning to the other "doubly inscribed" origin of Buenos Aires, Borges describes an experience of time in which any return to an origin or even to a previous instant would be impossible. The moment of return is described as a turn into time, in which there is neither a fixed origin nor an end.

In addition to the impossibility of return—to a friend or a country—the experience of time that Borges describes also disrupts any integral sense of self, even in the present. The dissolution or "nadería" of personality indicated by the essay's title is described as an effect of a temporal experience that does not permit any "mysterious" or spiritual sense of self. In a subsequent paragraph, Borges describes how he wanted to "show his entire soul to his friend," but this intention was interrupted "de golpe" by the realization cited above. Sylvia Molloy underscores the fact that the dissolution of personal identity described in the essay occurs facing Buenos Aires: "en una despedida encarada *hacia* Buenos Aires" ("Flâneuries textuales" 490). Borges is not returning to Buenos Aires with one-half of his double origins intact, ready to collect on the other half. He notes that all investments (he speaks of "adobando" his memories: preserving, as with pickles or meat) are annulled by the nature of temporal existence—the episodic, circumstantial, self-annihilating nature of time that he acknowledges, as if for the first time, on his return to Buenos Aires.

His description of time denies the possibility of any real return, whether to a friend or a site of origin, but it does not propose as an alternative a progressive or an exclusively present-based experience of time. The "annihilating" nature of time does not imply that there is not or that there cannot be any relationship with the past. It is just that there is nothing stable in the past that we can return to, nothing that can be preserved ("adobado"), no instant, past or present, that can be "full, absolute, containing of all the rest." The provisory, episodic nature of time allows for neither progress nor return, but neither does it mean that the episodic present is autonomous. Borges's anecdote suggests that the present can be hit, disrupted ("de golpe"), its fullness reduced to nothing ("nadería"). Temporal experience is described as a radically unstable experience, utterly lacking in any form of a ground. The fact that Borges observes this upon his departure from Europe and his return to Buenos Aires suggests that rather than returning to an origin, he is turning toward this experience of time: a turning *in* time and not a turning from time. It is a return in which he experiences the impossibility of any real return, any return to plenitude, anything that would be in any sense "contenedor."

The volumes of poetry that Borges wrote upon his return to Buenos Aires thematize this turn or return. They do not demonstrate a primacy of origins that would ground a sense of identity in the present, but rather show the lack of such a thing and the poet's coming to terms with this lack. To the extent that Borges traces the names and lines of a sense of belonging in the present or the past, he does so to emphasize the unstable limits of both. This is why he moves from the limit between life and death, past and present in the Recoleta cementery, where he begins his poems, to wander the unstable limits of the city's present, the *orillas*. Although Sarlo interprets the figural site of the *orillas* as yet another ground of dual origin where Borges establishes his sense of identity as rooted in the past, on the edges of the city where a simpler life can still be glimpsed, the *orillas* appear in his work as the unstable limit of identity as it exists in time. Borges's hovering on the limits of time and identity in these poems leads him to consider language's limits as well. Language cannot securely represent the past, present, or a sense of belonging against the annihilating nature of time. If Borges wishes for an identity or a temporal space that would be "full, absolute, containing of all the rest" (that is, an origin), the poems show how he disabuses himself of such a wish. They seem to suggest that it is only by acknowledging loss and our own incomplete nature that we can have any experience with time itself, as historical subjects that can relate to a past, present, and future.

Borges and His (Own) Precursors

Before returning to the poems, I want to make some comments on the volumes in question. Borges published numerous versions of his first three books of poetry, with the first of the three undergoing the most revisions.[6] In the prologue to the 1969 edition of *Fervor de Buenos Aires,* he insists that he did not rewrite the book: "No he re-escrito el libro" (OP 17). Rather, he claims to have merely "mitigado sus excesos barrocos, . . . limado asperezas, . . . tachado sensiblerías y vaguedades" ("merely mitigated its baroque excesses, . . . polished rough spots, . . . cut sensibilities and vagueness"). In other words he rewrote it, and he did so a number of times, in such a way that confounds all critical attempts to account for a single text that we can comfortably refer to as *Fervor de Buenos Aires*.

The question is, which version of the book should we read? Should the final version published during Borges's lifetime (in the collection of *Obra poética* from 1977) be considered the definitive version? Or would it be better to return to the original, published in 1923? What should we do with critical essays that were written using versions from the periods in between (such as Sarlo's): are they wrong, to be corrected using a later version of the text? Clearly not. It is as though Borges has represented for his readers the provisory nature of the past in the form of provisory versions of his poetic texts, confounding our critical desire for a single and definitive text.

This problem of literary history resembles the case of the disillusioned lover that Borges relates in "Nueva refutación del tiempo." In that text he describes how the lover who rejects his happy memory because he later found out that his beloved was cheating on him falls into a trap

(OI 176). All states are valid ones, he says: the lover's momentary bliss should not be negated by the later discovery of deception. One state (that of love, or a particular version of a book) is not truer than another, either in a progressive or a regressive sense. Just as the lover should not discount his former happiness because of the later discovery of infidelity, the former versions of a book or poem should not be entirely discounted because of later revisions, but neither can we disregard later versions in a regressive search for the original or definitive text. Borges remarks in *Discusión* that "el concepto de texto definitivo no corresponde sino a la religion o al cansancio" ("the concept of a definitive text corresponds only to religion or fatigue," D 106).

The fact that all versions of *Fervor de Buenos Aires* bear the date 1923 poses a different kind of problem. If we are thinking linearly, and want to compare the early period of Borges's work to his development in later years, or if we are thinking in terms of contemporaneity and what it means that he wrote this book in the sociopolitical or literary-cultural context of the 1920s, what does it mean if we cannot locate the text exclusively in that period because of its multiple rewritings? As Borges himself will say time and again, the idea that time progresses linearly and that there is one time for everyone is false, and this is particularly true or particularly easy to see in the case of literary history. The date of publication always bears an indeterminate relation to the literary text. Borges's tendency to rewrite his texts forces us to confront this indeterminacy, the ultimately unfixable nature of his body of writing. The year 1923, as the designated publication date of a book that Borges wrote three or four times at different points in his life, becomes more like a memory, subject to all kinds of revisions, personal and otherwise, than a fixed date in time. Of course this does not mean that we cannot consider the relationship of Borges's text, dated 1923 (and the subsequent books of poetry dated 1925 and 1929, and similarly rewritten in later editions), to what was going on in the 1920s, or to what the 1920s may have meant in Borges's life. But we should do so with caution, taking the texts dated from the 1920s less as a cultural product from that decade than a lengthy reflection on that period.

I have come to the conclusion that all versions of the poems dated from the 1920s are valid, and simultaneously so. The simplicity of some of the earlier versions of the poems does not invalidate the more sophisticated nature of some of the later versions, and vice versa. It is not necessary, nor even always possible (the early editions are difficult to find), to read the different versions, but to the extent that we do, it is better to consider the strange web of texts that has come down to us in their shifting totality than to try to order and eliminate certain versions and figure out which ones to privilege. That privileging occurs by default, based on the later texts that are more available to us, which is also the way that Borges intended for it to be. We read primarily the latest versions, with hints of the earlier texts peeking through, either due to citations of those versions in critical texts or out of a curious look at an earlier edition.

Finally I want to say about my reading of *Fervor de Buenos Aires,* and to a lesser extent *Luna de enfrente* and *Cuaderno San Martín,* that I am always in some sense reading them as texts that, as Borges said on several occasions, prefigured in a "secret" sort of way the rest of his work.[7] This is another reason why I believe it is important to consider the different versions of the texts and not stick to just one, since if *Fervor de Buenos Aires* in some sense influenced or was an expression of what came later, then certainly what came later also had its influence on it, much as Borges says of creative precursors in "Kafka y sus precursores." Just as each author "creates his own precursors," Borges has also created, and recreated numerous times, his own precursive texts (OI 109). Here, as in many other places, it is impossible to distinguish origin and copy, originality and influence. Furthermore, regarding Borges's statement that *Fervor de Buenos Aires* prefigured his later work, it is commonly accepted that this book—in its various manifestations—is remarkably inferior to some of his later work, particularly the fictions. Even though I think it safe to say that Borges was a far better narrator than he was a poet, as he himself admits in the epigraph to his *Obra poética,*[8] my objective here is to read the early poetry with an eye to the complexity of the best of his later work. This is not always easy to do, since some of the poems are quite trite, but I have come to believe that the triteness that is left in the later versions (the worst of it is edited out) is left as a curiosity, one of Borges's collector's items, that provides an ironic commentary on a *criollismo* that is ultimately left without a ground to stand on.

Sepulchral Rhetoric

As we have seen, Sarlo argues that the first poem of *Fervor de Buenos Aires* serves to establish an ideological ground on which Borges will assert his sense of identity and cultural legitimacy. She suggests that "La Recoleta" represents not only Borges's line of belonging to the past, but also to the future: it is the place of his ancestors and also the "place in which they will have to bury me." It is a ground, then, that would be fundamentally "contenedor," representing not only Borges's and the city's origins, but also a conception of history that is determined by the ground from which it comes and to which it will return. In this interpretation of the poem, the cemetery serves as a nearly literal representation of what Piglia has termed an "onomastic index." However, I want to propose that the poem reveals that the ground that Borges contemplates in the Recoleta cemetery is no more stable than the one that Piglia describes. And if the cemetery leads the poet to consider a certain figure of history that is rooted in the past and going toward a knowable end, it is one that he ultimately rejects.

The poem begins with the kind of reverence one might expect before a monument to the ground of history. It describes a "we" who upon entering the cemetery, slow down and lower our voices in reverence for the "certainties" of death.

> Convencidos de caducidad
> por tantas nobles certidumbres de polvo,
> nos demoramos y bajamos la voz
> entre las lentas filas de panteones,
> cuya retórica de sombra y de mármol
> promete o prefigura la deseable
> dignidad de haber muerto. (OP 21)[9]
>
> Convinced of decrepitude
> by so many noble certainties of dust,
> we slow down and lower our voices
> between the slow rows of pantheons,
> whose rhetoric of shadow and marble
> promises or prefigures the desirable
> dignity of having died.

Our certainties about death are the result both of our own desire to imagine a peaceful and dignified end to mortal time and the cemetery's own "rhetoric," which promises and prefigures this desirable end. And yet in spite of the grandiose solidity of the cemetery's rhetoric, the representation of death as a solid entity is on shaky ground. Shadows punctuate the marble's solidity in what amounts to a rhetorical device of contrasts, although its description, a "retórica de sombra," suggests that it is also based on the very thing the pantheons hope to conceal. But the real problem, the poem tells us, is that the grandiloquence of the cemetery, the aspiration to solidity, is based on dust. The rhetorical certainties that we find so convincing are "certidumbres de polvo."

The rhetoric of the cemetery, the poem continues, "el desnudo latín y las trabadas fechas fatales" ("the naked Latin and the engraved fatal dates") of the epitaphs, works to hide this dust, which is the dust of history. The cemetery's representation of history is of a "historia . . . detenida y única" ("detained and unique history"), written in the cemetery's "lentas filas" ("slow rows") as an opposition between "mármol" and "flor." It is a representation that contrasts permanence with the ephemeral, a frozen image of history with what the poem calls "los muchos ayeres de la historia" ("the many yesterdays of history"). The rhetoric of the "lentas filas de panteones" also represents linear time, the sepulchral lines of progressive history, which "promises or prefigures" death as a definite end ("fin").

Convinced by this discourse, we accept its teleology and desire the promised end. But this is an error: "Equivocamos." We can desire a solid ground and a definitive end, but for us "sólo la vida existe" ("only life exists"). This may sound like a naive assertion, but it is more complex than it first appears. The cemetery space aims to fix past lives into an eternal representation in death, submitting the ongoing nature of time to an unchanging spatial organization, but life, like death, cannot be detained in such a form of representation. The poem suggests that space and time are parts of life, "formas suyas," as is, surprisingly, death. They are tools that we use to understand the world, but like our own lives, they are mortal, and they extend and disperse in ways that we can never quite control or anticipate. Life in this poem both escapes and invades the cemetery's ordered space: it is asleep in the ivy that climbs the cemetery's walls, filtered in the tree's shadows, aloft on the wind, and infused in an "alma que se dispersa en otras almas" ("soul that disperses into other souls," OP 22).

The poet remarks that it is hard to imagine such uncontained and expansive life coming to an end, but life is nevertheless haunted by thoughts of death: not in the contained way that the cemetery tries to represent it, but as an "imaginaria repetición [que infama] con horror nuestros días" ("imaginary repetition that infames our days with horror"). The possibility of death disrupts or "infames" our temporal life in a repeated encounter with mortality that contrasts significantly with the cemetery's neat representation of a dignified end, the promise and prefiguration of detained time. One such imaginary repetition is the occasion for this poem, the poet's visit to the cemetery where he assumes he will be buried. Repetition resonates in the name "Recoleta," and is doubly stressed in the earlier version of the poem that Sarlo cites: "Lo anterior: escuchado, leído, meditado, / lo resentí en la Recoleta, / junto al propio lugar en que han de enterrarme."[10] Here the poet "resiente"—resents or feels with pain, but also feels or perceives again ("re-siente")—an anteriority, at the site that in a later edition of the poem he comes to call "el lugar de mi ceniza" ("the place of my ash"). The ash in the final line of the final version repeats the "dust" with which the poem began, the ash or dust upon which our "certainties" of life and death are based, and to which they will, as the familiar funereal refrain reminds us, return. The repetitive nature of death infames and provokes horror because it does not stop, it does not reach an end "detenida y única" which can be represented in the sepulchral rhetoric of the cemetery, but is always ongoing and multiple, like the "muchos ayeres de la historia."

This repetitive, incomprehensible death, which is also life ("sólo la vida existe"), is part of a historicity that is greater than individual, biographical histories. The cemetery's structure or rhetoric is intended to represent a linear and finite form of history, and also to fix in stone the identities of the individuals buried within its walls; that is to say, to contain the life and death of a person in a name. The cemetery is an onomastic index par excellence. Yet rather than accepting or defending this structure, Borges reveals its limits, indicating a history that is not contained by the engraved names or the "fechas fatales," and he begins his poems, rather than on the solid ground of his own origins, resolved to "listen to, read, or think" an anteriority that is not comprehended by this kind of sepulchral rhetoric.

The theme of a sepulchral rhetoric reappears several times throughout the poems. In *Fervor de Buenos Aires,* three poems after "La Recoleta" name the theme in their titles: "Inscripción sepulcral" ("Sepulchral Inscription"), "Inscripción en cualquier sepulcro" ("Inscription on Any Sepulcher"), and "Remordimiento por cualquier muerte" ("Remorse for Any Death"). As I will discuss at the end of this chapter, Borges later returns to the theme in *Cuaderno San Martín* in which he includes another poem on the Recoleta cemetery and a poem on the other major cemetery in Buenos Aires, La Chacarita.

"Inscripción sepulcral" is dedicated to the poet's great-grandfather, and has been used as evidence of Borges's founding of his poetry in the past,[11] but if we read the poem in light of the representation of sepulchral rhetoric in "La Recoleta," the poem's significance changes slightly. The poem is a eulogy, but what it eulogizes, the last line tells us, is a bit of ash ("Ahora es un poco de ceniza y de gloria," OP 29). The echo of the title later in the volume as "Inscripción en cualquier sepulcro" seems to disrupt the clarity of the name's inscription in the former poem's epigraph. "Inscripción sepulcral" is dedicated to the poet's great-grandfather, Colonel Isodoro Suárez, but the later poem suggests that such funerary specificity is futile, since all lives blend into one another after death. Rather than indicating a clear sense of identity ("un índice onomástico"), the name is made to reveal its clumsy materiality: it becomes a relic, like the "desnudo latín" of the Recoleta's inscriptions. The "temerarious marble," we are told in "Inscripción en cualquier sepulcro," risks little more than the name against the "todopoder del olvido" ("omnipotence of forgetting"), but even that soon disintegrates, and we are left with the title's indifferent adjective,"cualquier," "any" or "whichever" (40).

The inscriptions in *Fervor de Buenos Aires* move from the name, in "Inscripción sepulcral," to the disintegration of the name in "Inscripción en cualquier sepulcro," to a strange kind of remorse in "Remordimiento por cualquier muerte." Contrary to the objective of commemorative inscription that seeks to mark the past as property against the all-powerful flow of time, the "remordimiento" in this latter poem is for a kind of theft that a progressive idea of time inflicts on the past or on time itself. The poem functions as a kind of antisepulchral inscription, because rather than trying to capitalize on the past by keeping it fixed and significant for the present, it points out that by ignoring the past or by burying it in contained sites, we are actually denying ourselves access to the future. The poem reads,

> Como el Dios de los místicos
> de Quien deben negarse todos los predicados,
> el muerto ubicuamente ajeno
> no es sino la perdición y la ausencia del mundo. (38)
>
> Like the God of the mystics,
> whom all predicates would deny,
> the ubiquitously foreign dead man
> is nothing but the perdition and absence of the world.

The "ubiquitously foreign" dead man, who is also death itself ("el muerto no es un muerto: es la muerte") represents a loss or absence that must be recognized in life. The present robs this absence when it ignores the past: a past that is not restricted to the orderly rhetoric of a cemetery, but which is an "absent presence" in daily life, in the colors, syllables, and patios previously occupied by the dead. Having robbed time, and greedily trying to keep the present for ourselves ("nos hemos repartido como ladrones / el caudal de las noches y de los días"), our only means of establishing a relationship to the future is by reconnecting to this lost past, by opening up the present to its absence. The indeterminacy of the dead, who cannot be named by either names or predicates and who do not remain in a single point in time, paradoxically represents an access to the future: the dead or death itself is "ilimitado, abstracto, casi futuro" ("unlimited, abstract, almost future"). Our selfish attempts to keep all of time for ourselves has the nefarious effect of closing off not only our connection to the past but also to time in general. Attention to the dead that still live among us is one way of reconnecting with time, allowing us to reestablish a relationship with the unpossessable realm of the future.

"Remordimiento por cualquier muerte" indicates a relationship to both time and language that is opposed to the Recoleta's rhetoric. Rather than language that is presumed to contain its represented object, the remorse described by this poem concerns the uncontainability of death, as well as its absent presence in any language that tries to name it. Like the predicates that do not suffice to refer to it, but are the only things that we have, so too our thoughts may belong to the dead, occupied by its ubiquitously strange presence ("Aun lo que pensamos / podría estar pensándolo él"). Such an occupation requires that we reconsider any conception of the present as property, as something properly "ours," as well as any understanding of representation as something that is able to recall or re-present things from the past for a proper sense of the present.

Life Possessions

In his essay "On Some Motifs on Baudelaire," Benjamin explains how the understanding of historical experience in the modern era is based on a particular idea of life or lived experience (*Erlebnis*). He notes that from the end of the nineteenth century to the first decades of the twentieth, philosophy could be classified as "life philosophy," a category that describes the attempts to establish a concept of "true" experience that was removed from the shock experience of modern, metropolitan life. This concept of life is situated as far away from the present as possible, and is based in the ahistorical world of myths, a pastoral relation with nature, and a poetry that pitted an eternal concept of life against the increasing changes of the modern world. The concept of lived experience is not just restricted to philosophy, Benjamin avers, but describes a constitutive aspect of modern historical consciousness. He relates "lived experience" to Freud's understanding of consciousness as a means to protect against stimuli, and thereby to a form of experience that has been sterilized of the shocks of the modern world and processed into something that the psyche can comfortably bear. Direct stimulation representing too great a threat to the psyche, what we think of as experience is always already filtered through the screen of consciousness and presented to us as a coherent object.

One of the objectives of this protective consciousness is to order lived experience into a particular kind of historical structure: "Perhaps the special achievement of shock defense may be seen in its function of assigning to an incident a precise point in time in consciousness at the cost of the integrity of its contents. This would be a peak achievement of the intellect; it would turn the incident into a moment that has been lived

(*Erlebnis*)" (I 163). Life or lived experience is ordered into a linear, "empty" concept of time, which functions as an additional defense for the psyche. Past experience is kept in the past, safely contained for indexing by what Benjamin, following Proust, calls "discursive, volitional memory" (186). *Erlebnis* refers above all to an experience of the present that leaves the past behind, comfortably ordered into a sense of history, and in which the future is conceived as a mere extension of the present. The "concept of lived experiences" ("Begriff des Erlebnisse," GS 1.2.615) offers an appearance of wholeness: the universe is conceived as a coherent whole ("Begriff" means concept but also grasp or comprehension) held together by the figure of human life at its center. Outside stimuli are filtered for shock and are internalized into this concept of life experience. Memories are included in this internalizing process. This is the sense behind the German word *Erinnerung:* memory is brought into consciousness and inventoried as what Benjamin calls "dead possession," something dead or past that is a possession of the living (CP 49).[12]

Emancipation from the "Begriff" of experience would require a relationship with the past that has not been incorporated into a linear and anthropocentric conception of history. This other kind of experience is called *Erfahrung,* which Benjamin describes, against the life philosophers, as the more poetic of the two kinds of experience. *Erfahrung* describes experience that has not been personalized for comfortable use by an autonomous subject. It is experienced as bits and pieces that break through into consciousness, and which cannot be fully incorporated into an appearance of organic wholeness. It concerns a realm of experience that does not grasp a concept of life or a coherent sense of the present. As something that cannot be perceived consciously and directly, *Erfahrung* also presents a problem for representation. It is not at the disposal of voluntary and spontaneous recall, but lies outside the comfortable grasp of memory or representation. This does not mean that this kind of experience cannot be remembered or represented, but it cannot be integrally incorporated into the concept of ongoing *life*.

Against what Benjamin calls "the self-alienation of the person who inventories his past as dead possession" (CP 49), there exists a need to insist on a different kind of deadness, a different kind of past. This is the task, for Benjamin, of the melancholic allegorist. Rather than a concept or "Begriff" that interiorizes memory "at the cost of the integrity of its contents," the melancholic brooder (*Grübler*) practices a "Zugriff," a "firm, apparently brutal grasp" on the fragments that lie in his hand (CP 46; GS 1.2.676). Rather than the usual understanding of melancholy as the denial of the passing of time, Benjamin understands melancholy to be a way of resisting a progressive concept of life in which "things just go on" (CP 50). The melancholic's strong grip on the pieces of the past is a way for him to interrupt "the course of the world," and to reveal that what appears to be a single and comprehensive course is in fact fragmentary.

Allegory is an attempt to represent such a process. The allegorist looks to the fissures in the "catastrophe" of ongoing life, and works toward a "destruction of the organic and living—the extinguishing of appearance" (CP 41). Allegory resists a concept of life as a *Begriff* that attempts to file away the pieces of the past to fit its progressive picture of the present. It holds on to the pieces of experience (*Erfahrung*) that are not sterilized and ordered into a progressive, "living" sense of history: "That which is touched by the allegorical intention is torn from the context of life's interconnections: it is simultaneously shattered and conserved. Allegory attaches itself to the rubble" (38). Melancholic allegory involves a relationship to the past that aims to open a "temporal abyss (*zeitlichen Abgrund*) in things," which the *Begriff* of progressive history attempts to sew up so it can move on (CP 47; GS 1.2.679).

Benjamin's explanation of modern allegory is perhaps best exemplified in Baudelaire's poem "Le cygne." The poem concerns the poet's distress at the changing face of Paris, and also invokes the question of loss in general, including "anyone who has ever lost something they will not recover (*retrouve*)" (Baudelaire 107–8). The poem begins at a site of death, a nearly dry riverbed that connects the poet to Andromaque's ancient grief, and in which the swan of the poem's title, a symbol of music and poetry, tries in vain to bathe itself. The poet invokes Andromaque, Hector's widow, as a figure who refused to give up her mourning for her dead husband even when pressured at the cost of her life to marry anew, to get on with things, as Paris itself seems to be doing: "la forme d'une ville / Change plus vite, hélas! que le coeur d'un mortel" ("the shape of a city / Changes faster, alas! than a mortal's heart").[13] Neither Andromaque nor the poet is seduced by the new: both keep a firm, although not necessarily voluntary, grip on the past. Andromaque, in spite of being encouraged or even obligated to go on with life, remains "bent in ecstasy" over Hector's empty tomb. The poet observes the changes to Paris but sees beneath its gleaming surfaces the pieces and "blocs" of the old city: "Paris change! Mais rien dans ma mélancholie / n'a bougé! palais neufs, échafaudages, blocs, / Vieux faubourgs, tout pour moi devient allégorie, / Et mes chers souvenirs sont plus lourds que des rocs" ("Paris is changing! But nothing in my melancholy / has changed! New palaces, scaffolding, blocks, / Old suburbs, everything becomes allegory for me, / And my dear remembrances are heavier than rocks").

Freud famously argues that melancholy is a dangerous form of grief, because in it the shadow of the lost object falls upon the ego, provoking paralysis (249). Yet at the same time he admits that what the melancholic does not want to let go of is in the last instance quite ambiguous, perhaps not even an object. "It must be admitted," Freud writes, "that a loss has indeed occurred, without it being known what has been lost" (245). The object of Andromaque's mourning, for example, is an absent one and casts no shadow, or is nothing *but* shadow: she mourns leaning over an empty tomb. Rather than mourning for a particular lost object, one that "cannot be lost because it was never possessed" (Agamben, *Stanzas* 20), it is as though she mourns loss itself, or perhaps even the lack of a place for loss in the life she is told she must get on with. What she and the poet, in his different way, hold on to is not the past as "dead possession," but a refusal to accept such a conception of the past, or a history that presses forward, rendering the past dead and irrelevant to a present concept of life. The empty tomb and the blocks that refuse to budge are pieces that resist the sovereignty of the notion of progress. They are rocks that will not wash away in the river of history. Paradoxically, Andromaque's refusal to cease mourning is not a refusal to forget a particular object, but an insistence on the necessity of forgetting in a world that tries to forget forgetting itself. Bent over the empty tomb, Andromaque struggles to mark her husband's loss on her own terms, to allow his death to live on as another side to life.

This holding on to loss *as* loss (and not as an attempt to repossess a lost object) is the objective of allegory. Timothy Bahti highlights one of Benjamin's distinctions between nineteenth-century and Baroque allegory: "In the nineteenth century melancholy displays a different character than it did in the seventeenth. The key to the earlier allegory is the corpse. The key to the later allegory is *Andenken*" (224). The figure of "Andenken"—memory or remembrance, but with the root word "Denken," which means thinking or thought—contrasts with the more immediate experience of death in the Baroque, in which the corpse or skeleton represented in a more visceral form the loss of what once was. In the nineteenth century, it is understood that what "was" was never possessed. Memory does not fall on a decaying body, a fallen representation of what was once whole, but concerns the absence of such a sign or, rather, the sign of such an absence: the empty tomb, or what Bahti calls the "signe" of "Le cygne" (222). In neither the nineteenth century nor the Baroque does melancholy represent an attempt to recover the lost object as possession, to resuscitate the corpse and internalize it (*Erinnerung*) into a life concept, but rather attempts to hold up its absence to life, in what Bahti calls "the unremembering memory (*unerinnernde Andenken*) of loss" (224).

As I have mentioned, "Erinnerung" describes a form of memory that internalizes the past, incorporating it as an integral component of *Erlebnis*. Benjamin writes that one of the special characteristics of consciousness is to situate each remembered component of lived experience "in a precise point in time," as though on a time line (I 163). This allocation of the remembered incident places it into a structure where it can be retrieved at will, like a library archive or like the "onomastic index" of a cemetery layout in which the dead are mapped out with dates and names. Paradoxically, Benjamin calls the destruction of this structure a historical act (I 162). He says that Baudelaire's introduction of "blank spaces" into the apparent integrity of life characterized his work as "historical." This attribution implies that the life concept as it is organized along a time line is consequently *not* historical. By trying to internalize everything and make it part of an integral concept of life, this kind of structure denies the existence of anything outside itself, including history. Breaking up the "organic interconnections" of a progressive life concept and holding on to the resulting fragments and spaces is a way of opening up room for history, like writing or thinking that "remembers unremembering." By allowing loss to be a part of memory, allegory maintains the other as other, and invites the dead to interrogate "life."[14]

As I have tried to suggest in the first part of this chapter, Borges is more interested in what does not fit into the interiorizing structures of memory and language than in holding on to the past for the purposes of self-legitimation. His poems do not work to create protective structures in which to house identity or a familial sense of legitimacy, as the rhetoric of cemeteries attempts to do, but rather work to acknowledge language's incapacity to contain the objects it tries to name and to maintain them in a fixed point in time. He is poised in these poems to listen to and read an anteriority ("Lo anterior: escuchado, leído, meditado") that repeatedly escapes any firm determination. His poetics of re-turning begins with the indication of a past that cannot be named or claimed, either for himself or for language. Rather, through language he wants to open the tombs of the past and introduce the nonground of time (*Abgrund* or abyss) to a present that either wants to ignore the past altogether, or as in the rhetoric of the Recoleta, to entomb it.

Melancholic Fervor

Borges's Buenos Aires is a world that is traversed by shadows and disturbances, wounds and edges. The city is always on the brink of dissolution or loss, and remembrance and representation are continually threatened by dismemberment. Borges represents himself walking around Buenos Aires and picking up fragments of memory and experience. As he tries to order these fragments, he repeatedly encounters a temporality that interrupts the attempt to construct any structure of containment, whether of his own subjectivity, the identity of the city, or an autonomous past or present.

"El tiempo está viviéndome" ("Time is living me") Borges acknowledges in one of his poems (OP 72). His life is not only something that is in time, but is actually "lived" by time. What this means, however, is something of an enigma. In the poem "Final de año," Borges writes that "The enigma of Time" is not just the sobering idea that we are all mere drops of water in Heraclitus's river, that time flows on and subjects us to "infinitos azares" ("infinite chances"), but that in spite of this, we have a relationship with the past: the startling miracle that "perdure algo en nosotros" ("something remain[s] in us," 35). It is a wonder that we have any relationship with the past at all, and yet we do. The dead that our concept of a linear and progressive life "robs" have a way of sticking around in spite of the fact that they may not have any voice in our world. The past does not endure as dead possession, but as a mute reminder of what our ongoing concept of life does not include. As the years rush on, and the calendar pages flip by, "perdur[a] algo en nosotros: inmóvil, algo que no encontró lo que buscaba" ("something remains in us: immobile, something that did not find what it was looking for"). This is an aspect of time that is not included in the "symbolic detail" ("pormenor simbólico") of calendar time that at the end of the year adds a number to indicate that we have advanced another year. The poem suggests that we are irremediably in time and cannot return to the past, but the past is something that time does not leave behind, and something remains in it that continues to search ("buscar") in a way that disrupts any sense of a contained and autonomous present.

The poems are full of motifs that represent this kind of return, elements that are not settled into a completed past and are still looking for what they have not yet found. The past never appears as whole, but tends to be recalled in pieces, fragments that the poet's "ignorancia no ha aprendido a nombrar ni a ordenar en constelaciones" ("ignorance has not learned how to name or order into constellations," 23). Paratactic lists of remembered objects recur throughout the poems, manifestations perhaps of the "imaginary repetitions" cited in "La Recoleta." An example of such a list appears in "Líneas que pude haber escrito y perdido hacia 1922" ("Lines I Might Have Written and Lost Around 1922"), the final poem of *Fervor de Buenos Aires,* in which the structure of the poem is based on an enumeration of discrete objects, scenes, and memories:

Silenciosas batallas del ocaso
en arrebales últimos,
siempre antiguas derrotas de una guerra en el cielo,
albas ruinosas que nos llegan
desde el fondo desierto del espacio
como desde el fondo del tiempo,
negros jardines de la lluvia, una esfinge en un libro
que yo tenía miedo de abrir
y cuya imagen vuelve en los sueños,
la corrupción y el eco que seremos,
la luna sobre el mármol,
árboles que se elevan y perduran
como divinidades tranquilas . . . (59)

Silent sunset battles
in final suburbs,
always ancient defeats of a war in the sky,
ruinous dawns that reach us
from the deserted depth of space,
as though from the depth of time,
dark gardens in the rain, a sphinx in a book
that I was afraid to open,
and whose image returns in dreams,
the corruption and the echo that we will be,
the moon on marble,
trees that grow and last
like quiet divinities . . .

The elements that he invokes are familiar motifs in Borges's writing: books from the familial library, the childhood garden, sunsets in the extreme reaches of the city ("últimos" in the temporal as well as spatial sense, before the city is too built-up to see the horizon). The poem presents familiar images of Borges's past, but it does not present the past as a coherent picture. Like the strange title, the past itself seems to have been written and lost, or perhaps lost and then written. The paratactic structure of the poem and the disparate nature of the items invoked represent the past as pieces that poke into the poet's memory, useless pieces that do not get washed away in the movement of time, like the rocks and "old suburbs" of Baudelaire's poem. They do not represent anything whole, and they do not function as a ground for ideological identification. The recollection is made up of echoes and broken memories, the movement of time leaving everything "corrupt" in the sense of "together but broken" (*cor-ruptus*). Based on later descriptions of these things, we might associate the garden and the books as belonging to the Borges family household, but here they do not belong to anyone. The gardens belong to the rain ("jardines de la lluvia"); the book arguably belongs to the sphinx who represents for the poet an oneiric authority. Other things are so distant that they belong to nobody: sunsets in distant suburbs, "always ancient" defeats, even distant races that, without knowing it, engendered him ("los sajones, los árabes y los godos / que, sin saberlo, me engendraron"). Yet these things, although "lost" and perhaps belonging to no one but time (like the poem itself), do not completely disappear. They return from the depths of time, like the sphinx, to interrogate the poet's present sense of identity.

At the end of the list of disparate memories and distant elements, the poet asks himself, "¿Soy yo esas cosas y las otras / o son llaves secretas y arduas álgebras / de lo que no sabremos nunca?" ("Am I those things and the others / or are they secret keys and arduous algebras / of what we will never know?") This question ends the poem and the volume. Am I these things, do these memories, elements, distant occurrences add up to be me? Can they be incorporated into a solid sense of self? It is a question of *Erinnerung* or *Andenken,* interiorizable memory or always external "thought." The "arduous algebras" or "secret keys" that may not open to anything fully knowable describe a conception of language that is not presumed to contain its object. That Borges poses this question at the end of his first volume of poems with no answer to follow but the end of the page and the end of the book, leads us to consider that the question—and the poem, and perhaps the entire collection—is one of the secret keys to which he refers, posing a question for which we will never have a finite answer. In other words, the poem provides its own negative response. There can be no constitution of an "I" based on the elements of the past; neither language nor memory provides any firm constitution of identity. There is no "I am" available, only an "Am I?" with an abyss for an answer. But it is an abyss, an *Abgrund,* that can be explored in language—in the "llaves secretas y arduas álgebras de lo que no sabremos nunca."

The relation to the past as a collection or enumeration of objects and memories that do not add up to any particular identity, either a past or present identity, is common to many of the poems. In "El sur," for example, the remembered parts of a house are compared to the disperse stars, which the poet in his ignorance "has not learned to name or order into constellations" (23). In "Cercanías," the not-so-close "cercanía" ("closeness") of old houses is recited piece by piece (patios, windows, bedrooms) until what can be named is declared to be only the "scattering" of affect: "he nombrado los sitios / donde se desparrama la ternura" ("I have named sites / where tenderness is scattered," 52). At the end of this poem, as though anticipating the question at the end of "Líneas que pude haber escrito y perdido hacia 1922," the poet declares that he is "alone and with myself" ("estoy solo y conmigo"). Rather than a "yo soy," the poet "está": he is with himself like he is with the memories and objects that he enumerates. There is no naming of essential being ("ser"), only an enumeration that functions like the "arduas álgebras" that never lead to an essence. This is stated explicitly in a passage from *Inquisiciones:*

> El ser no es sino la cópula que une el sujeto con el predicado. Es decir, el ser no es categoría . . . sino gramatical. Dicho sea con palabras de lingüística: el depuradísimo verbo ser, tan servicial que lo mismo sirve para ser hombre que para ser perro, es un morfema, signo conjuntivo de relación; no un semantema, signo de representación. (cited in Pezzoni, *Texto* 73)

> The verb "to be" is nothing but the copula that connects the subject with the predicate. That is to say, being is not a category . . . but a grammatical effect. Put in linguistic terms: the bleached-out verb "to be," so servile that the same word serves to be a man as to be a dog, is a morpheme, a conjunctive sign of relation; not a semanteme, sign of representation.

We can read, then, Borges's statement-question at the end of "Líneas que pude haber escrito y perdido hacia 1922" as saying, I am not ("no soy") those things, but I am *with* that not-being, that is, I am in language—arduous algebras and secret keys to something we will never know. Language is the only connection we have to the past, but it is one that will never bring the past fully into the present, nor does it provide a basis for present identity.

In the poem "La Vuelta" ("The Return"), the poet describes returning to his childhood house after "years of exile" (OP 41). He acknowledges that the only return, however, can be a poetic one, which is never fully a return: "he repetido antiguos caminos / como si recobrara un verso olvidado" ("I have repeated ancient paths / as though I were recovering a forgotten verse"). Can a forgotten verse be recuperated? The poem does not say that it is, the subjunctive form conveying that it is only as though such a thing were possible. The question remains whether forgotten or lost language can be recuperated or whether it can recuperate anything of the past. Borges suggests that it can be recuperated enough so that, in the words of "Final de año," it can "keep looking." The arduous algebras of language will never recuperate anything ("lo que no sabremos nunca"), but it can and should be employed to think both life and loss.

A poem in *Luna de enfrente,* "Manuscrito hallado en un libro de Joseph Conrad" ("Manuscript Found in a Book by Joseph Conrad"), claims to be a recuperated verse; and as such, is the opposite of "Líneas que pude haber escrito y perdido hacia 1922." Yet as might be expected, the poem is precisely about the impossibility of recuperation or "finding" in language. The first stanza describes the blinding nature of daylight, perhaps too of linear time, the daylight observed as a straight white line in a blind ("In the tremulous lands that exhale the summer, / the day is invisible as pure whiteness. The day / is a cruel slit in a window blind," 74). The second stanza describes the night:

> . . . la antigua noche es honda como un jarro
> de agua cóncava. El agua se abre a infinitas huellas,
> y en ociosas canoas, de cara a las estrellas,
> el hombre mide el vago tiempo con el cigarro.
>
> . . . the ancient night is deep like a jar
> of concave water. The water opens to infinite traces,
> and in leisurely canoes, facing the stars,
> man measures vague time with his cigar.

Unlike the straight white line of the day, the water-darkness "opens to infinite traces." "El hombre" (a man or "man"), alone but afloat upon numerous canoes, perhaps following a number of the "infinitas huellas" and creating others, looks into the depth of the night at the stars.[15] The concave water of the night's time and space allows that which is distant, the stars, to be close, while at the same time always remaining distant, spelled out in the deep sky of the auratic night. Benjamin describes the constellation as an auratic form of representation par excellence, which contrasts with the "sun of revelation."[16] Stars, he says, "do not shine their light into the day of history, but only work within it invisibly. They shine their light only into the night of nature" (Cadava 30).

The third stanza describes the loss of an auratic relationship with the universe.

> El humo desdibuja gris las constelaciones
> remotas. Lo inmediato pierde prehistoria y nombre.
> El mundo es unas cuantas tiernas imprecisiones.
> El río, el primer río. El hombre, el primer hombre.
>
> The smoke blurs gray the remote
> constellations. The immediate loses prehistory and name.
> The world is a few tender imprecisions.
> The river, the first river. The man, the first man.

The clarity of the stargazing is obscured. The gray smoke from the man's cigar, which he uses to measure time, "blurs gray the remote constellations." The smokiness of time wafts into representation, the constellations are blurred or "undrawn," and "the immediate loses prehistory and name." Like the poems that list things the poet does not know how to "name or order in constellations," the world is left as "unas cuantas tiernas imprecisiones," unnamed reflections on the water's surface. Prehistory and name lost, the man becomes the first man and finds himself in the first river; that is to say, he is a creature of fundamentally temporal existence. What is "found" in the poem is temporal existence itself, including the temporal nature of language: a language that "undraws" or blurs its own representative capacity, and leaves us with no name, no constellations, but only "a few tender imprecisions." This imprecise language is like the arduous algebras that may never tell us what we want to know, an allegorical language that indicates its own blank spaces, the cracks and gaps in its representations. The name and prehistory, or access to a world before history and before "fallen" language, are shown in this poem the reflection of their impossibility. There is no reflection of who "I am" in the pool of language; there is only the reflection of "el hombre" as being always ("originally," as *Urmensch*) in the river of time.

In the face of the impossibility of ordering the fragments of the universe with names or constellations, our only recourse is to "be with" the pieces and represent the impossibility of coherence, the sites where the "tender imprecisions" of memory and representation are scattered. The de-constellation that remains, a collection that never coheres into a whole, is the only alternative to a sense of identity that incorporates these pieces into a single entity, a "yo soy" or a life concept, a "Begriff des Erlebnisse." Far from establishing his "sense of belonging to a city and to a lineage," as Sarlo suggests, Borges allows how he finds himself alone with these scatterings, a startled *Grübler* with fragments in his hands. He writes in one of the "desdibujadas" versions of the poems, "La ciudad está en mí como un poema / que no he logrado detener en palabras" ("The city is in me like a poem / that I have not managed to detain in words," *Obra poética: 1923–1964* 32). His poems are evidence of the impossibility of appropriation of either the city or himself, a failed life concept that leaves him "alone and with himself" and with the pieces that can never add up to a whole.

Borges boasts of how well he takes this condition. In "Jactancia de quietud" ("Boast of Tranquility") he proclaims the inevitability of temporal existence: "El tiempo está viviéndome" ("Time is living me," OP 72). But he does not try to escape it, nor order it into a progressive or accumulative narrative. In this he is different from the "ambiciosos," those "merecedores del mañana" ("ambitious ones," those "deserving of tomorrow") who try to cash in on a tomorrow in the name of "homeland" or "humanity"—a tomorrow that leaves the past in its wake. Crossing the "rush of their frenzied greed" ("cruzo el tropel de su levantada codicia"), Borges quietly picks up the pieces: "Hablan de patria. / Mi patria es un latido de guitarra, unos retratos y una vieja espada" ("They speak of homeland. My homeland is the beat of a guitar, some portraits and an old sword"). As elsewhere, these fragments do not add up to any coherent sense of identity, but remain as mere collections, scattered representations that contrast with concepts such as "homeland" and "humanity." The poet's passage through time is not in the name of anything, not even himself: "Mi nombre es alguien y cualquiera. / Paso con lentitud, como quien viene de tan lejos que no espera llegar" ("My name is someone and anyone. / I walk slowly, like one who comes from so far he doesn't hope to arrive"). Against the progressive and accumulative rush ("tropel," which comes from the same root as "tropa" or troop, suggesting a military advance) of modernization, the poet without a name passes through time as though he had no origin and no destination.

Throughout the poems, the past is figured as fragments and collections of fragments, but they are not collector's items that stay docilely in place. In "Casi juicio final" ("Almost Final Judgment"), the poet states confidently that his affairs are in order. He is in full possession of his faculties and the world is his oyster:

> Mi callejero *no hacer nada* vive y se suelta por la variedad de
> la noche.
> La noche es una fiesta larga y sola.
> En mi secreto corazón yo me justifico y ensalzo.
> He atestiguado el mundo; he confesado la rareza del mundo.
> He cantado lo eterno . . . (78)

> My streetwalking idleness lives and releases into the diversity
> of the night.
> The night is a long and lonely party.
> In my secret heart I justify and praise myself.
> I have testified to the world; I have confessed the strangeness
> of the world.
> I have sung the eternal . . .

The poet's belief in the solidity of language and the past—"A los antepasados de mi sangre y a los antepasados de mis sueños / he exaltado y cantado . . . He trabado en firmes palabras mi sentimiento" ("I have exalted and sung to the ancestors of my blood and dreams . . . I have fixed my sentiment in firm words")—is disrupted, however, by a memory that will not stay put: "El recuerdo de una antigua vileza vuelve a mi corazón. / Como el caballo muerto que la marea inflige a la playa, vuelve a mi corazón" ("The memory of an old atrocity returns to my heart. / Like the dead horse that the tide inflicts on the beach, it returns to my heart.") Like one of the imaginary repetitions of "La Recoleta," this memory disturbs the confident autonomy asserted in the previous lines. The past does not remain neatly in the past as passive material for the poet's labor. It does not allow itself to be fixed in firm words, but rather afflicts the poet's heart in a messy and endlessly changing repetition, like a corpse returned by the tide. The confident tone of the beginning of the poem is left behind, and the poet humbly submits that "Aún están a mi lado, sin embargo, las calles y la luna" ("The streets and the moon, however, are still by my side," 79). His eagerness to exalt, testify, and contain the world in words is disrupted by this memory that he cannot control, which infames the subjective autonomy that serves as the basis for his poetic glory.[17]

A similar disturbance of an interiorized present appears in a pair of poems, "Sala vacía" and "Rosas"—or rather, it occurs in one and is shown not to occur in the other. Both poems concern interiors, the living rooms of private homes, and at least in the final edition of *Fervor de Buenos Aires,* they are placed side by side. "Sala vacía" begins with the objects in a deserted living room chatting among themselves. The daguerrotypes join in on the furniture "tertulia":

> Los daguerrotipos
> mienten su falsa cercanía
> de tiempo detenido en un espejo
> y ante nuestro examen se pierden
> como fechas inútiles
> de borrosos aniversarios. (32)

> The daguerrotypes
> misrepresent their false closeness
> of time detained in a mirror
> and before our examination they are lost
> like useless dates
> of blurry anniversaries.

Like the sepulchral inscriptions in "La Recoleta," the pictures of the past serve only to mark the absence of any real containment or detention of the past within their frames. The image of containment dissolves beneath our gaze, and what we perceive in its stead are "anguished voices" that have "sought us for many years" (voices that "desde hace largo tiempo . . . nos buscan"). However, the search of these anguished voices goes unfulfilled. Their "flat voice" ("voz lacia") is lost in the light of day and the tumult of the present that enters from the street.

Voices of the past find a little more success in the next poem.[18] The title "Rosas" refers to the nineteenth-century dictator Juan Manuel Rosas, whose tyranny Borges denounced throughout his life (and who is most likely the referent of the "antigua vileza" in "Casi juicio final"). This poem also begins in a "sala tranquila," marked only by watch time:

En la sala tranquila
cuyo reloj austero derrama
un tiempo ya sin aventuras ni asombro
sobre la decente blancura
que amortaja la pasión roja de la caoba,
alguien, como reproche cariñoso,
pronunció el nombre familiar y temido. (33)

In the quiet room
whose austere clock spills
a time now lacking in adventures or surprises
onto the decent whiteness
that shrouds the red passion of the mahogany,
someone, as though in kind reproach
spoke the familiar and feared name.

The interior of the room, marked by a time lacking in surprises, is enclosed by white walls that "shroud" a passion latent in the red wood of the furniture. The shrouded present is soon disturbed, however, by an "asombro" not admitted by the ticking of clock time. The past bursts in upon the scene at the mention of the dictator's name:

La imagen del tirano abarrotó el instante,
no clara como un mármol en la tarde
sino grande y umbría
como la sombra de una montaña remota
y conjeturas y memorias
sucedieron a la mención eventual
como un eco insondable. (33)

The tyrant's image fills the moment,
not clear like marble in the evening,
but big and ominous
like the shadow of a distant mountain
and conjectures and memories
followed the casual mention
like an unfathomable echo.

Unlike the flat voice of the daguerrotyped ancestors, the past breaks through to the empty time of the present, the present instant suddenly full, packed ("abarrotado"), as with explosives. This is not the name as it appears in the sepulchers of the Recoleta, but the explosion of that kind of name, which reveals that the past is not safely and "clearly" ("clara") tucked away in marble boxes.[19] The explosion of the name brings an image that rolls in like shadows and an unfathomable echo, the opposite of a contained image of the past. In the second half of the poem, the blood of the past is said to be absorbed by the "open wound" of Time, although the first part of the poem would seem to indicate that the return of the past (like the dead horse, a repeated return) is part of Time's enigma as well. The blood of the past may be absorbed by time's passing, but something lives on latent in the shrouded present, like the "pasión roja" of the mahogany furniture in the white space of the tranquil home.

An endnote to the poem (which begins with Borges's acknowledgment that he shares a remote ancestry with Rosas) warns us to resist the human form of historical reabsorption, that of revisionism: "Este pasatiempo consiste en 'revisar' la historia argentina, no para indagar la verdad sino para arribar a una conclusión de antemano resuelta: la justificación de Rosas o de cualquier otro déspota disponible" ("This pastime consists in 'revising' Argentine history, not in order to find out the truth, but to arrive at a previously determined conclusion: the justification of Rosas or any other available despot," 60). Time and God can forget or absorb the past ("Dios lo habrá olvidado," 34), but that forgetting has its own life and its own means of return. Voluntary revisionism, on the other hand, shrouds the past in a kind of forgetting that the past cannot explode, and that the present forgets it has forgotten, placing all of history into the calm interior of a "tiempo . . . sin aventuras ni asombro."

The allegorist is one who refuses to let the past be tidily boxed up. Both past and present are revealed to consist of fragments that cannot be interiorized into a figure of progressive history. The apparent containment of the past by the present is exploded by the irruptive force of certain memories or returns of the dead. This is the opposite of an onomastic index where present identity is securely established on lines drawn from the past. Allegory ruptures the concept of an autonomous self-identity, revealing that there can only be a "being with" the fragments of existence, past and present. We have moved, then, from the "lentas filas de panteones" in "La Recoleta," where the engraved names and dates order the world into precise distinctions, to a poetics in which such distinctions do not seem to hold up: where the past intrudes on the sepulchers of the present, where the name explodes into echoes, and where the nameless poet walks slowly but endlessly through time with no apparent origin or end.

The *Orillas*

One of the places where the ideal of containment meets its limit is at what Borges calls the *orillas,* literally "edges," referring to the limits of the city but also of the present. As I mentioned earlier, Sarlo considers this figure to be a symbolic ground for Borges, as one of the sites where he founds his double origins as *criollo* and European. If at the city's necropolitan center he finds his name and past firmly inscribed, at the edges of the city he creates a topos in which the past and the pampa enter to resist and ground the changing city. The present is emptied out and replaced with remnants of a past that is exclusively *criollo:* "The imaginary space of the orillas appears little affected by immigration, by cultural and linguistic mix. At issue is, as always, the question of 'Argentineness' [*argentinidad*], a nature that permits and legitimates mixes: foundation of value and condition of valid (cultural) crossings" (*Modernidad* 43).

At first glance, Sarlo's description seems convincing. But if we examine the poems and essays where the *orillas* are mentioned, we see that they do not serve to represent a firm foundation of identity. Borges describes the *orillas* as an uncertain region where the city borders on the unknown. One poem describes them thus: "las orillas, palabra que en la tierra pone el azar del agua" ("the *orillas,* word which puts the randomness of water into the earth," OP 82). In *Evaristo Carriego,* he writes, "El término las orillas cuadra con sobrenatural precisión a esas puntas ralas, en que la tierra asume lo indeterminado del mar y parece digna de comentar la insinuación de Shakespeare: 'La tierra tiene burbujas, como las tiene el agua'" ("The term *las orillas* illustrates with supernatural precision those sparse points in which the earth assumes the indeterminacy of the sea and seems worthy of citing the insinuation made by Shakespeare: 'The earth has bubbles, just like water,'" 25). The line from Shakespeare comes from *Macbeth,* when the witches come out to taunt Macbeth and then disappear when Macbeth commands them to speak. Banquo exclaims, "The earth hath bubbles, as the water has, / And these are of them. Whither are they vanished?" (1.3.79–80).

These watery limits that put the "azar" of water or air into the apparent solidity of land do not constitute a site of identity, the solid limit of the poet's sense of what he or the city is, but rather describe an unstable limit where he experiences contact with what he is not.[20] The "puntas ralas" of the *orillas* are also referred to as "baldíos" or wastelands, which, rather than preserving a distinct rural past in the developing areas of the city, are sites of "shadow" filled only with the "vaivén de recuerdos" ("coming and going of memories," OP 93), empty spaces that keep the city from closing in on itself like the "historical" markers that Benjamin described in Baudelaire. In the prologue to *Cuaderno San Martín,* Borges says that as opposed to the false claim to eternity that European cities are capable of, what Buenos Aires has in the form of monumentalization is precisely these blank spaces ("huecos y callejones de tierra," 89) around which the city has sprung up. As in "La Recoleta," the city has spaces of dust as a historical index.

The *orillas* are also the last place in the city where it is still possible to see the horizon, and with it the sunset. But this does not mean, as Sarlo suggests, that they are the index of a simpler life, a site in which there is an unmediated relationship with the horizon (*Borges* 21).[21] Nor is it a site of mourning for a lost world. The sunsets—and with them, the ubiquitous figure of the "atardecer" or evening—burn, disturb, and wound the city landscape. A street at sunset is called a "herida abierta en el cielo" ("open wound in the sky," OP 81). Elsewhere the sun lingers, refusing to "cicatrizar" ("form a scar," 57). In "La Plaza San Martín," the evening collects in the plaza, weakening the rigidity of the "impossible" statue of the national hero (26).

The evening is the *orilla* of the day, and represents for Borges a place where the familiarity or even the knowability of the day is lost. In an essay that he described as an "abbreviation" of his early poems (cited in Lagmanovich 89), he writes that the evening

> es la dramática altercación y el conflicto de la visualidad y de la sombra, es como un retorcerse y salir de quicio de las cosas visibles. Nos desmadeja, nos carcome y nos manosea, pero en su ahínco recobran su sentir humano las calles, su trágico sentir de volición que logra perdurar en el tiempo, cuya entraña misma es el cambio. La tarde es la inquietud de la jornada, y por eso se acuerda con nosotros que también somos nosotros inquietud . . . Es a fuerza de tardes que la ciudad va entrando en nosotros. (I 88)

> is the dramatic altercation and conflict between shadows and the visible, it's like a twisting and a coming undone of visible things. It exhausts us, consumes us, and gropes us, but in its determination, the streets recover their human feeling, their tragic sense of volition that manages to endure in time, whose core is change. The evening is the disquietude of the day, and that is why it affects us, because we too are disquietude . . . It is because of evenings that the city comes to enter into us.

The evening takes things out of their senses ("fuera de quicio"), and brings us into contact with an unfamiliar aspect of the world, an unfamiliarity that is also within us. The evening is the time when we cannot avoid this unfamiliarity, and it is the time that the city, perhaps the most unfamiliar thing of all, enters us. It is an unfamiliarity that Borges calls in a later essay "el revés de lo conocido, su espalda" ("the reverse of the known, its back," OI 179).[22]

The strangeness that is revealed by the evening light is the subject of "Calle desconocida" in *Fervor de Buenos Aires*. The poet describes how walking one day at dusk he came upon an unknown street. Its apparent familiarity moves him, and he begins an enumeration of its familiar attributes:

> abierta en noble anchura de terraza,
> cuyas cornisas y paredes mostraban
> colores tenues como el mismo cielo
> que conmovía el fondo.
> Todo—la medianía de las casas,
> las modestas balaustradas y llamadores,
> tal vez una esperanza de niña en los balcones—
> entró en mi vano corazón
> con limpidez de lágrima. (OP 24)

> open in a noble expanse of terraces
> whose cornices and walls reflected
> tenuous colors like the sky
> that moved the background.
> Everything—the medium size of the houses,
> the modest balustrades and doorknockers,
> perhaps the hope of a girl in the balconies—
> entered my vain heart
> with the limpidity of a tear.

The poet muses that this scene is perhaps ("quizá") "as real as" the recuperation of a forgotten verse, a theme we have seen as a recurrent one throughout the poems. Then he realizes that he is fooling himself in his attempt to reconstruct a familiar past through the enumeration of fragments (for example, balustrades and doorknockers), and that there is no recuperation possible, but only the fragments themselves that go from seeming as familiar as a recuperated verse to appearing strange and alien ("ajeno"). It is the evening that brings on this sense of *enajenamiento:* at the hour at which the lights in the houses are lit, the space of the familiar interiors suddenly becomes strange, and the houses seem like candelabra in which the "lives of men burn" like isolated candles (25). This picture of mortality is concluded with the reflection "que todo inmediato paso nuestro camina sobre Gólgotas" ("every one of our immediate steps passes over Golgotha"). Golgotha comes from the Hebrew word meaning "skull" (like Calvary in Latin). Even without the etymological ghosting of the name, Golgotha unquestionably refers to mortality, as the site of death of the supposed son of God. The isolated houses "donde las vidas de los hombres arden" come to resemble skulls, the underlying mortality of every human being. Where the poet only recently saw visions of wholeness, with little girls waiting in the balconies, he now sees fragmentation and the ultimate limit of human existence.

Yet the recognition of this "desconocimiento," the other side of the known or knowable, does not represent an end. The poem's beginning announces the fall of evening as an "initiation," mistakenly called "shadow of the dove" after a Hebrew expression that is corrected in a note (it appears that in the expression the dove refers to the morning, while the evening is characterized by a crow, 60). Mistake or not (one never knows with Borges), the evening is characterized in the poem as a hopeful beginning, characterized by a dove rather than the more typical owl or crow. The poem describes it as the hour at which the "la venida de la noche se advierte como una música esperada y antigua" ("the coming of the night is announced like an ancient and long-awaited music," 24). The end of the day does not signify an end, but a beginning, a "coming" of something at once hoped for ("esperada") and ancient. This coming, which brings the unknown or unfamiliar to bear on the familiar world of day, not only destroys the structures of interiorization that the poet constructs in a moment of dreamy nostalgia and reminds him of death, but also invokes a different relationship to both the past and the future. This time or coming is like music, a form of representation that never arrives, or is always both "hoped for and ancient," existing outside of the discursive structures of internalization and progress.

Acts of Life

In the preceding pages I have tried to show how Borges has his ear out for this kind of music in his early poems. Even if he dreams of a return to a comforting sense of the past, or an integral form of identity based on that past, his poetry repeatedly acknowledges that the pieces of the past do not fit into a coherent whole. This allegorical fragmentation, however, does not allow the past to be safely buried in the past. Although Borges realizes that he cannot return to the past, the past has its own forms of return that exceed voluntary recall, but can and perhaps should be allowed into the present whenever possible. The past in this way becomes more than the past: it is the index of a historicity that interrupts an integral sense of identity that relies on the present and on a linear structure of history that disregards the past and views the future as an extension of itself. Borges's early poems waver between a quasi-religious fervor for poetic salvation and a melancholy acknowledgment of the nature of temporal being. His poems represent him wandering through liminal spaces such as cemeteries and the *orillas* of Buenos Aires, perhaps in the hope that he will see the possibility of a return to wholeness, or the past as property, but he is repeatedly foiled, and his fervor seems to change to that of representing the impossibility of such a return. These edges or *orillas* do not only suggest that no return to a solid sense of the past is possible, but they also indicate that a solid sense of the present is not possible either, if only because of the inescapable fact of mortality, which he represents as being a fundamental part of the city, and consequently of any identity that would be based on the city. We have seen how throughout his early poems he repeatedly passes over what he calls "el lugar de mi ceniza," as well as the ash or dust of the city's history. It is not surprising, then, that the last book of the early poems, *Cuaderno San Martín,* includes several poems about death, including a pair of poems about the principal cemeteries of Buenos Aires: Recoleta and Chacarita.[23] I will end with these two poems, as a complement to the poem "La Recoleta" with which we began.

Borges begins the poems entitled "Muertes de Buenos Aires" with a poem about the Chacarita, cemetery of the working and underprivileged classes. The second poem is dedicated to the Recoleta, cemetery of the privileged class, to which Borges, as we know, belonged. Here he begins with the cemetery that is situated on the *orillas,* and which historically received the deaths of those who did not fit properly into the city: "los conventillos hondos del Sur / mandaron muerte sobre la cara de Buenos Aires / . . . Buenos Aires no pudo mirar esa muerte" ("the deep tenements of the South / sent death onto the face of Buenos Aires / . . . Buenos Aires couldn't look at that death," OP 102). This death that does not have a place in the city fits well into the *orillas,* where loss is familiar and forms a subject of its music. The poet recites a song that he hears there, not dissimilar to the "música esperada y antigua" described in "Calle desconocida":

La muerte es vida vivida
la vida es muerte que viene
la vida no es otra cosa
que muerte que anda luciendo. (103)

Death is lived life
life is death that comes
life is nothing else
than death that walks around shining.

This song, which he says he hears as much in the *orillero*'s guitar as in the words, opposes the rhetoric of death represented in the structure of the cemetery. Here, different from the Recoleta's marble nobility, the Chacarita attempts to contain death in colorless plaques, cheaper versions of the same kind of rhetoric:

> En tu disciplinado recinto
> la muerte es incolora, hueca, numérica;
> se disminuye a fechas y a nombres,
> muertes de la palabra. (104)
>
> In your disciplined enclave
> death is colorless, hollow, numerical;
> it is reduced to dates and names,
> deaths of the word.

In the poem "La Recoleta" that follows "La Chacarita," we are returned to the ceremony and grandeur that was present in the first poem on the Recoleta. Yet the marble of privilege does no better than the Chacarita's hollow attempts to discipline death. Beneath the Recoleta's marble columns, "crece en disolución . . . la nación irrepresentable de muertos" ("the unrepresentable nation of the dead grows in dissolution," 105).

As in the first Recoleta poem, the two poems of "Muertes de Buenos Aires" concern the limit of representation that death represents, as well as its unrepresentable centrality to life in the city. Chacarita, the cemetery of the *orillas,* which in a way are the city's own cemetery, is particularly important in this regard. "Chacarita," the poem concludes,

> barrio que sobrevives a los otros, que sobremueres,
> . . . he oído tu palabra de caducidad y no creo en ella,
> porque tu misma convicción de angustia es acto de vida. (104)
>
> neighborhood that survives the others, that overdies,
> . . . I have heard your word of decrepitude and I don't believe
> in it,
> because your very conviction of anguish is an act of life.

The cemetery's rhetoric of death—its "colorless, hollow, and numerical" dates and names, its "palabra de caducidad"—represents what Borges calls the "deaths of the word." He is not, to use the phrase from the first "La Recoleta," convinced of this "caducidad." He does not believe the death of the word represented for him in the cemeteries' words of death, but observes in the cemetery's anguish an "act" of life.

This act concerns a concept of life that, as the first Recoleta poem suggests, bears a different relationship to death than the cemetery's attempt to contain it. Death, the unstable *orilla* of life, cannot be contained, ordered, disciplined, or even classified according to class. Any attempt to do so will result in the death of the word itself, the death of language's potential to point beyond itself, and therefore also the death of a historicity that lies outside of the dates and names that try to fix life into comprehensible structures. The Chacarita, situated as it is on the *orillas,* in the blank spaces of the city's history, belies its own words with its "act" of anguish, which is also an act of life. It cannot exclude or contain death: death's uncontainable anguish spills out of the dates and names and "lives on," or in the poem's neologism, "dies on," "sobremuere." Even when death is boxed up and labeled, it lives on, interrupting any attempt to keep it neatly distinguished from a forward-moving conception of life that has no time to contemplate the absent presence of the past.

The poetics of these volumes are based on an attempt to listen for a historicity that lives and dies beyond the death of the word. It is represented in the poems as an anteriority or repetition that returns from the past but also lies in the future, which the poet finds as he sifts among the remnants of the city's past and his own memories. While the city and the nation were pressing forward, eager to leave behind their undeveloped pasts represented by the sites and hollows of dust that in 1929 still dotted the outskirts of Buenos Aires, Borges wandered the city streets digging them back up. He breaks the city's historical structures into pieces and broodingly turns the pieces over in his hands. The anguish that his melancholic mind perceives in these pieces of the past is not a sense of grief that the past cannot be recuperated, or at least it is not just that. It is also, as he says, an "act of life," an acceptance of a temporal existence that does not fit neatly into names, numbers, and a progressivist concept of life. The allegorical strategy of these poems is to point to the limits of these figures of containment where autonomous identity and linear history break down, and life is allowed to live—and die—on.

Chapter 2

Bios-Graphus

Evaristo Carriego and the Limits of the Written Subject

Vida y muerte le han faltado a mi vida.

—Borges, *Discusión*

The activity connected with the centenary of Borges's birth seemed to produce fatigue and irritation among his critics. This reaction is evident in titles such as *AntiBorges,* "Cómo salir de Borges," and "Borges como problema," among others. Josefina Ludmer describes the glut of Borges-related paraphernalia during the centenary as resembling the invasion of editions, summaries, and translations of the "Great Work of Men" in Borges's story "Tlön, Uqbar, Orbis Tertius." She writes, "I ran into Borges in the street, on television, on the radio, in galleries, Sunday supplements, and even elementary schoolchildren [were] constructing labyrinths in his memory" ("Cómo" 289). This kind of biographical monumentalization was already evident at the beginning of the 1990s with the inauguration of the Centro Cultural Borges in an upscale shopping mall in downtown Buenos Aires, where shoppers can stop in to see blown-up reproductions of photographs and manuscripts superimposed with citations from Borges's texts.

Juan José Saer suggests that Borges himself encouraged the transformation of his image into a cult object. Saer describes how from the 1960s on, undoubtedly due to his increasing blindness, Borges began to favor oral presentations, giving countless interviews, lectures, and public appearances of all kinds, a turn that remains evident today in the vast quantity of oral transcriptions that occupy library shelves ("Borges" 80). The interviews, along with an astounding number of books dedicated to documenting his life—his neighborhoods, the cafés he used to frequent, his daily itinerary from the Biblioteca Nacional to his house—had the effect of turning Borges into a figure that everyone feels he knows, even if he wishes he didn't. Nicolás Rosa calls the equation "texto + personaje + autor + persona" the primary error of Borges criticism, in which Borges's oeuvre becomes a kind of "inverted narcissistic object, where the critic can only confirm his own specularity" (187).

It is ironic that "el texto Borges" tends to be read in light of his person and his life, because throughout his writings the question of subjectivity, and especially the relationship between subject and text, is understood to be extremely complex. This tension is the subject of the well-known parable "Borges y yo" ("Borges and I"). In this parable, the narrator "yo" reflects on the unstable relation between his proper name and the first-person experiential narrative, between "Borges" and "yo." "Borges" is identified with a public life of letters, a figure that receives correspondence from people he does not know, and whose name is inscribed in a university department and in biographical dictionaries. "Yo" is associated with a private side of life, personal preferences, daily existence in the city, and a sense of misrecognition with respect to the public figure that his name generates. Yet it is not a simple matter of separating out a sense of personal self, a private existence that "yo" can call his own. "Yo" is inextricable from "Borges": their respective autonomy dissolves and they turn into each other, to the point that the narrator is no longer certain which of the two has written the parable. The parable concerns, among other things, the slippery nature of any distinction between a biographical and an autobiographical subject, as well as the inevitability of mediation in any consideration of the self.[1]

A text such as "Borges y yo" demands that we read the figure "Borges" with a degree of caution. Readers should guard against the temptation to view a kind of immediate autobiographical confession in the oral interviews, as opposed to the more mediate nature of his written texts. Although I do not propose to explore this here, Borges seems to have been well aware of the tension produced between his oral and written productions, and could even be said to have fostered a misperception with regard to the different forms of his self-presentation. The interview form leads to a sense of intimate familiarity (or knowing: "conocimiento"), which Borges at once welcomed and revealed to be impossible, his interviews returning time and again to slippery reminiscence and the untotalizable complexity of the narrating subject.

In spite of the fact that Borges may have contributed to the construction of his life as a living monument, his writings question both the representability of life and its representational quality; that is, the sense in which an individual life can serve to represent something else such as a nation, region, or era. It is ironic that Borges's texts have come to be associated so much with his person and Argentine national culture—to the extent that schoolchildren construct labyrinths in his honor—because his writings frequently parody such associations. It is also ironic that the recent positions "against Borges" tend to conflate Borges's writings and the icon he has become without considering their inherent incompatibility.

The Fallible God of the "I"

The last chapter examined the suggestion that Borges attempted to found his representations of Buenos Aires in his early poetry on a conception of the past, including a solid and continuous sense of his familial roots. We saw how in these poems, where he is allegedly most "obsessed" with his origins, the past is represented as neither linear nor solid, and does not give any ground for the lyric "I" to stand on. Rather than presenting a city that serves as a kind of self-legitimation, the unknowable nature of time and the strangeness of the past disrupt the integrity and self-knowledge of the lyric subject and the city at every turn.

In 1930, at the end of the decade in which he wrote his first three books of poetry, Borges published *Evaristo Carriego*. The title would seem to suggest that the book is a biography of the turn-of-the-century poet, although in reality it is a series of essays collected under Carriego's name, some of them addressing his life and works, and others addressing different emblems of Argentine-*criollo* culture such as the card game truco, knife fights, the milonga, and a history of the tango. This chapter addresses what function the figure of life serves in this context: why, after a decade of writing poems on the undefinability of life in the city, Borges dedicated himself to a biography of a poet who, like Borges, wrote about Buenos Aires. Was he celebrating Carriego as someone who had done what Borges hoped to do? Was he designating himself a rightful heir to an inherently Argentine tradition, extending his "obsession with origins" to the realm of literary history, and founding his literary authority (his literary "I") on the biographical shoulders of his predecessor?

In an essay on autobiographical themes in Borges's early writings, Enrique Pezzoni describes how the "fervor" that Borges proclaimed in the title of his first book of poems was at once a quasi-religious yearning to merge self and city into an absolute, *and* a fervent renunciation of such a possibility. Even when he was ostensibly attempting to found a sense of identity through an ideal of ethno-regionalism represented in the figure of the city, Pezzoni suggests that Borges's fervor was radically ambivalent: "it is a fervor *for* and *against*" the "fallible God of the 'I'"

(*Texto* 68, 75). Pezzoni suggests that in his early years, Borges "anticipated, perhaps without a clear consciousness of what he was doing, the future, fervent resignation of the simulacrum of an 'I' that in its very inexistence finds its contradictory raison d'être" (72).

In his later writings, of course, Borges's ambivalent relation to the "simulacrum of an 'I'" is well-known.[2] Yet as we saw in the last chapter, Borges was actively questioning the possibility of a "*yo de conjunto,*" an integral or total "I," in the 1920s. In "La nadería de la personalidad" (1922), he writes that against the psychologism of the nineteenth century, he proposes to apply to literature the "explosive consequences" of the idea that the "yo de conjunto" is a "dream . . . without metaphysical foundations or internal [*entrañal,* literally "intestinal"] reality" (Inquisiciones 93). He explains, "I am not denying that consciousness of being, nor that immediate security of 'I am here' [el *aquí estoy yo*] . . . What I am denying is that all other convictions should correspond to the aforementioned antithesis between the 'I' and the 'not-I,' and that that antithesis be constant" (96). The oppositions inherent in language do not fix a stable self against a stable other. Rather our sense of identity, of both self and other, is based on nothing more than a set of grammatical relations.

> Being, unconditioned being (this Schopenhauer also foresaw) is nothing but the copula that connects the subject with the predicate. That is to say, being is not a poetic or metaphysical category, it is a grammatical one. Let us put it in linguistic terms: that most refined verb *to be,* so servile that the same word is used for being a man or being a dog, is a morpheme, a conjunctive sign of relation; not a semanteme, sign of representation. (cited in Pezzoni, *Texto* 73).

Our sense of identity necessarily takes shape through language, but the grammatical sense of self has no metaphysical foundations. Language both affirms identity and, through its very "servility," denies the absolute nature of its affirmations.

Life and Death

The relationship between language and the self is particularly relevant in writing about life, as in biography and autobiography. In another early essay Borges writes, "Todos viven en su autobiografía, todos creen en su personalidad, esa mezcolanza de percepciones entreveradas de salpicaduras de citas, de admiraciones provocadas y de puntiaguda lirastenia" ("Everyone lives in his or her autobiography; everyone believes in his or her personality, that mix of perceptions intermingled with sprinklings of citations, provoked admirations, and sharp lyrical weakness," cited in Pezzoni, *Texto* 73).[3] To live in one's autobiography, to take the subject pronoun "I" at face value, is an error. The "mix of perceptions intermingled with sprinklings of citations" is not reducible to a single subjective figure or image. Borges describes the fantastic figure of an individual "que se introduce en el cristal y que persiste en su ilusorio país . . . y que siente el bochorno de no ser más que un simulacro que obliteran las noches y que las vislumbres permiten" ("who introduces himself into a mirror and persists in his illusory country . . . and who feels the embarrassment [also 'suffocation'] of being nothing more than a simulacrum that the nights obliterate and glimpses allow," cited in Pezzoni 72). The representation of a self in language or images is declared to be an impossibility. To live in representation would mean essentially death; hence, Borges's well-known distrust of mirrors and mimetic language. And yet, Borges says several years later, "Toda literatura es autobiográfica, finalmente" ("All literature is ultimately autobiographical," cited in Pezzoni 74). How are we to understand this simultaneous impossibility and inevitability of autobiography?

In his essay "Autobiography as De-Facement," Paul de Man makes some similarly paradoxical claims. He writes that autobiography is a "figure of reading or of understanding that occurs, to some degree, in all texts" (70). This figure involves the specular presentation of a self or selves through writing, which of course is most explicit when the author presents himself as the subject of the text, as in autobiography, but is present to some extent "whenever a text is stated to be *by* someone and assumed to be understandable to the extent that this is the case. Which amounts to saying that any book with a readable title page is, to some extent, autobiographical." Nonetheless, at the same time that a text presents its specular self, it also presents *language* and language's inability to represent a whole and coherent life. De Man explains that

> just as we seem to assert that all texts are autobiographical, we should say that, by the same token, none of them is or can be. The difficulties of generic definition that affect the study of autobiography repeat an inherent instability that undoes the model as soon as it is established. Genette's metaphor of the revolving door helps us understand why this is the case: it aptly connotes the turning motion of tropes and confirms that the specular moment is not primarily a situation or an event that can be located in a history, but that it is the manifestation, on the level of the referent, of a linguistic structure. (70–71)

Writing refers to a self, whether represented in the text or implied by the figure of the author, but it also undoes the very notion of a self, or at least its totalizing, "metaphysical" nature. It posits a figure or trope that does not stop turning. Trope is related to the word "turn," and concerns language's turning from any coherent image of a self toward something like Borges's "mezcolanza" traversed by "sprinklings of citations": citations of language's impossibility of closure and totalization. Language, writing, and literature always imply a "yo de conjunto," and at the same time demonstrate its impossibility, its inadequacy to represent "life," a category that underlies all writing, not only the biographical variety. At the end of his essay, de Man defines *life* as a figure or structure of understanding that lends coherence to the incoherencies of life and world.[4] The limits of such a contained and coherent figure come to be called *death*. Death, de Man writes, "is a displaced name for a linguistic predicament" (81): that of indicating the impossible "conjunto" of life, rather than a determinate, biological end.

Given Borges's acknowledgment from the 1920s onward of the impossibility of representing a coherent life in language, it is interesting that at the end of the decade he undertook a biography of Carriego. The book purports to present a "life of Carriego," and also in some sense the "life" of a region. The chapter titled "Una vida de Evaristo Carriego" ("A Life of Evaristo Carriego") is the second chapter of the book, while the first chapter is about the Buenos Aires neighborhood Palermo. To the extent that the book is about the life of a man who wrote poetry about Buenos Aires, it also appears to be about Borges's own life, or a life that he might be trying to mimic. However, the book does not try to establish the coherence of Carriego's life, secure in an "illusory country" of representation, but rather addresses the incoherencies and contingencies of the biographical as well as the autobiographical subject.

Critics of *Evaristo Carriego* acknowledge that the book "critically questions the very idea of biography" (Sarlo, *Borges* 24). Sylvia Molloy writes that it is an error to assume "that 'A Life of Evaristo Carriego' is necessarily the central chapter, the real biographical core of a text that should make unequivocal sense of someone's life" (*Signs* 12). In the vein of "La nadería de la personalidad," she writes, Borges "insists on fragmenting Carriego as a character, presenting him (and presenting himself) *en abîme,* defined by his very displacement: 'a mode of truth, not of truth coherent and central, but angular and splintered,' reads the epigraph from De Quincey that questions the very unity of self" (13). Nevertheless, she suggests, the book ultimately rejects the "enclosure" of such ambiguity, and reaches out for a biographical "pre-text" that provides a sense of coherence for Borges and his ambitions as a writer: "The narrator of *Evaristo Carriego* makes a pact with a mediocre poet, Carriego, in order to write himself into a biography that serves him as a pre-text" (13).

Beatriz Sarlo develops the idea that Carriego served as a "pre-text" for Borges's literary projects (*Modernidad* 46). She argues that *Evaristo Carriego* demonstrates a "need for biographical construction in the early Borges," suggesting that Carriego serves as a literary "origin" from which Borges can found a new tradition of Argentine letters, much as his family origins entitled him to write about Argentina in the first place. Although in her later book on Borges, Sarlo acknowledges that *Evaristo Carriego* "critically questions the very idea of biography," she suggests that this "critical questioning" consists only of an appropriative cannibalism of the other author's life, and does not really question the structure of biography at all. She calls the book "an imaginary autobiography that has changed subjects: from Carriego to Borges / from Borges to Carriego" (*Borges* 24; *Modernidad* 46). She suggests that Borges chose Carriego because Carriego, having lived at the turn of the century, would have experienced a side of the city that Borges could only dream or read about, or glimpse through the garden gate of his childhood (the "verja con lanzas" that he describes in the prologue). While Borges looked out behind the garden gate and his books, Carriego was free to walk the streets where "Palermo del cuchillo y de la guitarra andaba (me aseguran) por las esquinas" ("Palermo of knives and guitars passed [they assure me] by the street corners," EC 9). Because of his proximity to a more authentic Buenos Aires, Carriego could be seen as someone who knew, lived, and could speak for the city, as a kind of voice of the barrio. Yet one might wonder, if Borges insists in other writings that there can be no "yo de conjunto," what kind of "conjunto" could Carriego represent, either for Borges or for Buenos Aires. What kind of "biographical construction," if one can really call it that, Borges does attempt with this book? Was it a pre-text intended to give "life" and legitimacy to Borges's representations of Buenos Aires, or was it in some sense a "post-text" intended to give "death" to the very idea of a legitimizing biographical narrative?[5]

The Other American Poet

In an essay titled "El otro Whitman," written the year before *Evaristo Carriego* was published, Borges considers the possible relations between an individual poet, and a region, era, or people; that is, the question of whether an individual life can represent a "conjunto" of lives. He describes Walt Whitman as a poet who attempted to fill the role of

"American poet" ("el poeta digno de América"), an endeavor in which he was enthusiastically received (D 52). By way of illustrating the greatness of Whitman's name, Borges recounts an anecdote of an anonymous compiler of the ancient *Zohar,* who, when ordered to give the attributes of his indistinct god, "divinidad tan pura que ni siquiera el atributo *ser* puede sin blasfemia aplicársele" ("a divinity so pure that not even the attribute *being* can be applied to it without blasphemy"), discovered "un modo prodigioso de hacerlo. Escribió que su cara era trescientas setenta veces más ancha que diez mil mundos; entendió que lo gigantesco puede ser una forma de lo invisible y aun del abstracto" ("a prodigious way of doing it. He wrote that [the divinity's] face was three hundred seventy times wider than ten thousand worlds; he understood that the gigantic can be a form of the invisible and even of the abstract," 51). Borges suggests that Whitman's name functions similarly, as a kind of gigantic face that represents the greatness not only of his poetic word, but also of the country that he represents, the United States. Whitman's name resounds with force and greatness, and we forget about what it does not show: "Así es el caso de Whitman. Su fuerza es tan avasalladora y tan evidente que sólo percibimos que es fuerte" ("Thus is the case with Whitman. His force is so tremendous and so evident that we only perceive that he is strong").

Borges proposes to read an "other" Whitman through three of his poems, poems that deny the personal and regional coherence that Whitman's name would seem to represent. The poems are cited in whole in the text, translated by Borges. The first poem, "Once I Passed Through a Populous City," describes a city that makes an impression on the poet that he tries to file away for future use. He finds, however, that the city is only accessible through his slippery recollections of an amorous affair:

> Pasé una vez por una populosa ciudad, estampando para
> futuro empleo en la mente sus espectáculos, su arquitectura, sus costumbres, sus tradiciones.
> Pero ahora de toda esa ciudad me acuerdo sólo de una mujer
> que encontré casualmente, que me demoró por amor.
> Día tras día y noche estuvimos juntos—todo lo demás hace
> tiempo que lo he olvidado.
> Recuerdo, afirmo, sólo esa mujer que apasionadamente se
> apegó a mí.
> Vagamos otra vez, nos queremos, nos separamos otra vez.
> Otra vez me tiene de la mano, yo no debo irme,
> Yo la veo cerca a mi lado con silenciosos labios, dolida y
> trémula. (53)

Once I pass'd through a populous city imprinting my brain
for future use with its shows, architecture, customs,
traditions,
Yet now of all that city I remember only a woman I casually
met there who detain'd me for love of me,
Day by day and night by night we were together—all else has
long been forgotten by me,
I remember only that woman who passionately clung to me,
Again we wander, we love, we separate again,
Again she holds me by the hand, I must not go,
I see her close beside me with silent lips sad and tremulous.
(Whitman 158–59)

The memories of this romance have a dissolving effect (that is, "nadería") on the poet and on the progressive movement of the city that imprints his brain for future use. Rather than the future and utilitarianism, the poet's mind wanders to a past image that does not stay in the past: "Again we wander, we love, we separate again." This unsettling effect of the woman's memory disturbs the poet's ability to affirm his present sense of self, and Borges's translation underscores this: "Recuerdo, afirmo, sólo esa mujer que apasionadamente se apegó a mí."

The second poem, "When I Read the Book," directly addresses biography and the limits of biographical or autobiographical representation:

Cuando leí el libro, la biografía famosa,
Y esto es entonces (dije yo) lo que el escritor llama la vida de
un hombre,
¿Y así piensa escribir alguno de mí cuando yo esté muerto?
(Como si alguien pudiera saber algo sobre mi vida;
Yo mismo suelo pensar que sé poco o nada sobre mi vida real.
Sólo unas cuantas señas, unas cuantas borrosas claves e
indicaciones
Intento, para mi propia información, resolver aquí.) (D 53)

When I read the book, the biography famous,
And this is then (said I) what the author calls a man's life?
And so will some one when I am dead and gone write my life?
(As if any man really knew aught of my life,
Why even I myself I often think know little or nothing of my
real life,
Only a few hints, a few diffused clews and indirections
I seek for my own use to trace out here.) (Whitman 80)

In line with the dissolution of a present sense of self in the first poem, and bearing a striking resemblance to Borges's own reflections on the incoherence of the "I" in other texts, this poem concerns the instability of the poet's sense of personal identity and perhaps of all individual histories. It is almost as though Whitman in this poem were looking in a mirror at his "face," fantastically engorged by fame, and does not recognize himself. Although rather than in a reflection, he does not recognize himself in a particular use of language or naming: "what the writer calls the life of a man." Biography, a written life, which can only be written in some sense when life is over ("And so will some one when I am dead and gone write my life?"), is like the gigantic face described in the essay's beginning. "Life" is a name that writers give to designate something so disperse and so extensive "that not even the attribute *'ser'* can be applied to it."[6]

In the poem an "I" in parentheses breaks up the deixis: "this is then (said I) what the author calls a man's life." This parenthetical remark is not meant to suggest that the first-person pronoun is more true to life than the third-person "man's life." Rather, it is the interruption of what at the end of the poem the poet says is the only thing he has to try to understand his life: linguistic marks, "unas cuantas señas, unas cuantas borrosas claves e indicaciones." Language is not something that can metaphysically contain life or being, but serves only as a vague means of approximation. Like the "llaves secretas y arduas álgebras" that appear at the end of *Fervor de Buenos Aires,* the "borrosas claves" seem to function less as keys to a secret interiority than as interruptions ("clave" coming from the root "clavar," to cleave, like the parenthetical "I"), as grammatical "keys" or "signs" that break up the naturalized copula of the verb *ser*. The completion implied by the use of the preterit at the beginning of the poem ("When I read the book, the biography famous")—that is, the idea that the life of a man is already enclosed in this book—is broken off after the third line when the rest of the poem, bracketed by parentheses, addresses the unknowability of life, even one's own, except through the inexact tools of language. The poem ends with a grammatical awkwardness that is itself difficult to "resolver." The resolution is purely formal, represented only by the final parenthetical mark, which marks the poem's inability to represent completion.

The final poem indicates in more general terms what Borges is trying to achieve with his translations of the three poems. It describes how the poet rejects the different sums, proofs, and maps presented to him by the academy and ends up contemplating the stars in silence.

Cuando oí al docto astrónomo,
Cuando me presentaron en columnas las pruebas, los guarismos,
Cuando me señalaron los mapas y los diagramas, para medir,
  para dividir y sumar,
Cuando desde mi asiento oí al docto astrónomo que disertaba
con mucho aplauso en la cátedra,
Qué pronto me sentí inexplicablemente aturdido y hastiado,
Hasta que escurriéndome afuera me alejé solo
En el húmedo místico aire de la noche, y de tiempo en tiempo,
Miré en silencio perfecto las estrellas. (D 54)

When I heard the learn'd astronomer,
When the proofs, the figures, were ranged in columns before me,
When I was shown the charts and diagrams, to add, divide,
  and measure them,
When I sitting heard the astronomer where he lectured with
  much applause in the lecture-room,
How soon unaccountable I became tired and sick,
Till rising and gliding out I wander'd off by myself,
In the mystical moist night-air, and from time to time,
Look'd up in perfect silence at the stars. (Whitman 279–80)

In the final part of the essay, Borges describes the three poems as "confessions" that concern the "negación de los esquemas intelectuales" and the "inconocibilidad y pudor de nuestro vivir" ("negation of intellectual schemes" and the "unknowability and shame of our life," D 54). The poems address the unknowability that lies behind some of the different proofs, figures, or "faces" that we use to understand the world: the city, the biographical self, and various academic schemes and classifications that we use to map our lives or the universe. The poet who runs out of the astronomy lesson and looks in silence at the stars—from time to time, or *in* time, as Borges's translation puts it—is the opposite of the compiler of the *Zohar*. Rather than thinking up a face to explain the inconceivability of his god, he contemplates it without any face or abstraction to give it coherence.

Borges suggests that in these poems, Whitman confesses to the impossibility of being a giant: a "poet . . . of America" whose name, like the enormous face of the Zohar, signifies immensity and force. Neither his face nor his name can lend coherence to the scattered pieces of America ("las diversas Américas," 51).[7] Borges suggests that the very failure of coherence could function as "an abbreviated symbol of [America]" (54).

Like the city, the self, and the universe, "America" too reveals its limits, pieces that will always challenge attempts to turn it into a single, abstract figure: "Una vez hubo una selva tan infinita que nadie recordó que era de árboles; . . . hay una nación de hombres tan fuerte que nadie suele recordar que es de hombres" ("Once there was a forest so infinite that no one remembered that it was made up of trees; . . . there is a nation of men so strong that no one tends to remember that it is made up of men"). Borges calls these components of the imperialistic nation a "human condition." The United States is made up of nothing more than "men, men of human condition."

The Paradoxes of Biography

Given his reflections about Whitman and America in "El otro Whitman," it seems strange that in the following year Borges would publish what appears to be a biographical text about a poet who is considered to represent Buenos Aires. As Sarlo says, however, the idea of biography is critically questioned throughout the book (*Borges* 24). For example, at the beginning of the chapter "Una vida de Evaristo Carriego," Borges proposes that biography is based on several paradoxes. He writes, "Que un individuo quiera despertar en otro individuo recuerdos que no pertenecieron más que a un tercero, es una paradoja evidente. Ejecutar con despreocupación esa paradoja, es la inocente voluntad de toda biografía ("That an individual would want to awaken in another individual memories that belong only to a third is an evident paradox. To execute with a clear conscience that paradox is the innocent wish of all biography," EC 35).

Biography or the biographical "will" ("voluntad") is the "innocent" attempt to carry out, cover up, or literally kill ("ejecutar") the paradox upon which it is based: the paradox that the past, which is hard enough to grasp even when it is one's own, is even more inaccessible for another, and is certainly impossible to represent in any stable way to a third. Borges explains that the fact that he knew Carriego does not make the attempt to represent him any easier. He "possesses" memories of Carriego, but what he possesses are "recuerdos de recuerdos de otros recuerdos, cuyas mínimas desviaciones originales habrán oscuramente crecido, en cada nuevo ensayo" ("memories of memories of other memories, whose original minimal deviations will have obscurely grown in each new attempt [to remember]"). Memory is a slippery possession at best, and in its infinite changes and deviations, it is hard to set down in a form of representation that could resist change. As Whitman's poem "When I Read the Book" suggests, the project of biography implies completion, a book that can be read in its entirety and that can be written only when life is completed; that is, when life is death. But Carriego is not dead for Borges. His memories change with every new effort to remember, with every new "ensayo." Although the word "ensayo"—effort or attempt—does not necessarily imply a mode of writing, there is no reason to exclude the secondary meaning of a written essay, particularly in evident contrast to the notion of a completable biography or "book." Here the sense of memory's attempts to recover a past, or "memories of another," would admit its paradoxical nature, and rather than gathering together a single and comprehensive life story, would represent a series of attempts or "ensayos" in "essay" form. From the beginning of *Evaristo Carriego,* then, Borges acknowledges that a proper life-writing is ultimately impossible, although the book will attempt—essay—a series of attempts to represent a life, while at the same time acknowledging the paradoxical nature of such an endeavor.

There is another paradox that underlies the desire to write a biography of Carriego: "hay otra paradoja" (EC 36). Insomuch as one might want to take Carriego as a representative poet of his generation, as the "voice of the suburbs" (like Whitman was the poet of America), no such embodiment is possible. Borges notes that in his memories of Carriego, physical aspects—that "idiosyncratic flavor that allows us to identify a face in a crowd," "the tone of his voice, the habits of his gait and uneasiness, the use of his eyes"—make up a "light mnemonic archive" that is the least communicable aspect of anything he could say about him (35–36). To name these characteristics, Borges avers, serves only to transmit the word "Carriego," which demands "la mutua posesión de la propia imagen que deseo comunicar" ("the mutual possession of the same image that I wish to communicate"). The mention of Carriego's name calls up an image, but only one that is already possessed by the listener or reader. Or rather, Borges adds dryly, any naming or description of Carriego will serve to call up an image only when it does not interfere with the image that the listener already possesses: "A las relaciones de Evaristo Carriego les basta la mención de su nombre para imaginárselo; añado que toda descripción puede satisfacerlos, solo con no desmentir crasamente la ya formada representación que prevén" ("For Evaristo Carriego's relatives, the mere mention of his name is enough for them to imagine him; I would add that any description will satisfy them, as long as it doesn't crassly refute the image they already have of him").

De Man describes this as a fundamental paradox of biography and autobiography. In his "Autobiography" essay, he explains that (auto)biography seeks to base itself on a particular idea of referentiality.[8] It "seems to depend on actual and potentially verifiable events in a less ambivalent way than fiction does. It seems to belong to a simpler mode of referentiality, of representation, and of diegesis . . . It may contain lots of phantasms and dreams, but these deviations from reality remain rooted in a single subject whose identity is defined by the uncontested readability of the proper name" (68). Biography and autobiography assume an empirical ground for their descriptive projects, which they guarantee by means of the proper name, which by virtue of its ostensible properness, appears to confirm the coherence and autonomy of the biographical subject. De Man explains that in this sense, (auto)biography functions as an instance of prosopopeia or personification, which he describes as a "giving and taking away of faces" based on the root word *prosopon-poeien,* which means to give a face (76). If there is a perceived need to give a face, the very act of giving also *takes away* the presumed naturalness of the face, which is what de Man calls the "defacement" of (auto)biography. The acknowledgement that there is a need to give a face implies that "the original face can be missing or nonexistent," or that there may have been no face to begin with (*Resistance* 44).

We have already seen the double-edged nature of face-giving in "El otro Whitman," when the face of the Zohar's god and the face or name of Whitman serve only to represent the impossibility of representing something vast and unknowable. Borges says that Carriego has a name and a "face that permits us to identify him in a crowd," but they refer tautologically to the same name and face that are used to identify him. Any invocation of his name or description of his person serves only insomuch as it does not interrupt the image previously held of him. Against such a preformed image of Carriego, Borges suggests that there is a certain disembodied nature to Carriego's memory.

In the following chapter on Carriego's writing, Borges describes the "ingenuous physical concept of art" that all writers tend to hold: the idea that a book is considered to be not "una expresión o una concatenación de expresiones, sino literalmente un *volumen,* un prisma de seis caras rectangulares hecho de finas láminas de papel que deben presentar una carátula, una falsa carátula, un epígrafe en bastardilla, un prefacio en una cursiva mayor" ("an expression or a concatenation of expressions, but literally a *volume,* a prism of six rectangular faces made of fine sheets of paper that should present a title page, a false title page, an epigraph in italics, a preface in cursive," EC 57). The corporeal figuration of books or works of art is not unlike the mnemonic archive of Carriego himself, which preserves an image of his body (gait, tone of voice, face, and so on) against the deviations of memory and writing. Such an "ingenuous" conception resembles the "innocent will of . . . biography": the attempt to preserve a life by embodying it in an archive that would protect against precisely such deviations. Borges's description of the corporeal conception of books indicates the unnatural and many-layered nature of such an archival embodiment. The book has numerous faces that peel away prismatically to reveal ever more faces: false faces, pre-faces, epi-graphs written in "bastardilla."[9]

In any case, the project of writing "a life of Evaristo Carriego" is revealed to be no easy task, as the faces that Carriego's name evokes proliferate and refract in the prismatic media of memory and language. Furthermore, his own face appears to indicate death more than, or as much as, life. Borges quotes a description of the poet from the magazine *Nosotros:* "magro poeta de ojitos hurgadores, siempre trajeado de negro, que vivía en el arrebal" ("lean poet of furtive little eyes, always dressed in black, who lived in the suburb," 36). He adds,

> La indicación de muerte, presente en lo de *trajeado siempre de negro* y en el adjetivo, no faltaba en el vivacísimo rostro, que traslucía sin mayor divergencia las líneas de la calavera interior. La vida, la más urgente vida, estaba en los ojos. También los recordó con justicia el discurso fúnebre de Marcelo de Mazo. "Esa acentuación única de sus ojos, con tan poca luz y tan riquísimo gesto," escribió.
>
> The indication of death, present in the description *always dressed in black* and in the adjective ["lean"], was not lacking in his vivacious face, which showed without much divergence the lines of the interior skull. Life, the most urgent life, was in his eyes. This was remembered also in the funeral speech of Marcelo de Mazo. "That unique accentuation of his eyes, with so little light and such rich gesture," he wrote.

Not only his face, but his life itself seemed dedicated to death. He died young, at the age of twenty-nine—the age, incidentally, of Borges when he was writing this book—apparently of tuberculosis, although his family denied this cause of death. But, Borges says, it was evident to everyone, since his very life burned ("arder") as though in a feverish state (48–49). Borges describes him as a near-megalomaniac who "se sabía dedicado a la muerte" ("knew that he was dedicated to death"), who wrote his poems motivated by a "premonition of incessant death," and who was driven by an inner ardor that Borges suggests acidly was an ardor for his own fame, more than for any excellence of poetic creation (49–50).

In addition to calling biographical writing a kind of prosopopeia, de Man describes it as epitaphic, in the sense that it presents the subject in monumental form, giving form and figure to what has no form or figure: "the fiction of the voice from beyond the grave" ("Autobiography" 77). The biographical presentation of "life" is always mounted against an opposite "death," but in presenting a face or facade that designates "life," we are made aware that it is precisely a facade, behind which can be found death as well as life. De Man explains that such "epitaphic inscriptions" of life and death are not really about life or death, living and breathing, but are figures that concern

> the shape and the sense of a world accessible only in the privative way of understanding. Death is a displaced name for a linguistic predicament, and the restoration of mortality by autobiography (the prosopopeia of the voice and the name) deprives and disfigures to the precise extent that it restores. Autobiography veils a defacement of the mind of which it is itself the cause. (81)

Biography, precisely by trying to represent a stable image of life, brings us face to face with death, or the possibility that "life" as such—an identifiable life, the determinate object signified by a face and a name—does not exist. The epitaphic deixis of biography ("here lies so-and-so," or the similar "this is the life of so-and-so") runs the risk of confronting an empty tomb or the abyssal possibility that no life can be told as such. Carriego, the biographical subject of the book that bears his name, but also, it appears, the (auto)biographical subject of his own life—spurred to write like Scheherezade, threatened by death and as a means of prolonging life—ran dangerously close to that abyss. Even in life, Carriego's face showed the silhouette of death: what he was not and what no one can "be," death nonetheless shone through his "vivacísimo" features, as well as his gestures, his conversation, and his writing.

Carriego Is (Not) Carriego

Perpetually threatened by death, life was not a simple matter for Carriego. In a later chapter, Borges describes how he considered "life" to be something that occurred only in France or in past centuries, and that he, Carriego, was in a perpetual state of exile from that privileged state of existence: "se creía desterrado de la vida" ("he believed himself exiled from life," EC 152). Then suddenly while he was reading one day, which was his only means of contact with the inaccessible concept of life, "something happened" ("algo sucedió"):

> Un rasguido de laboriosa guitarra, la despareja hilera de casas bajas vistas por la ventana, Juan Muraña tocándose el chambergo para contestar a un saludo (Juan Muraña que anteanoche *marcó* a Suárez el Chileno), la luna en el cuadrado del patio, un hombre viejo con un gallo de riña, algo, cualquier cosa. (152–53)

> A strum of a laborious guitar, the uneven line of low houses seen from the window, Juan Muraña touching his coat by way of responding to a greeting (Juan Muraña who the night before last *marked* Suárez the Chilean), the moon in the square of the patio, an old man with a fighting cock, something, anything.

Something interrupted him: "something that we cannot recuperate, and whose sense ("sentido") we will know but not its form, something quotidian and trivial and not perceived until then," shook Carriego out of his reading and made him realize that "el universo (que se da entero en cada instante, en cualquier lugar . . .) también estaba ahí, en el mero presente, en Palermo, en 1904" (the universe [which gives itself fully in every instant, in any place . . .] was also there, in the mere present, in Palermo, in 1904"). Life, or the universe, did not exist only in France in the nineteenth century, but also in Argentina and in "cada instante, cualquier lugar." This "imprecisable revelación" came to him in his reading from a sound or scrape, a gesture, a chance image, all of which are curiously graphic images, and which have in common the figure of a mark or scrape: the "rasguido," the line of houses, the mark that Juan Muraña made on Suárez el Chileno, the fighting cock. Or, the list concludes, something, anything, "cualquier cosa."

What are these things or anythings that jolt Carriego out of his lifeless, "exiled" reading? They are "something" but also anything; something that we cannot (literally, "will not be able to") recuperate, something "whose sense we will know but not its form," something "quotidian and trivial and not perceived until then". These indefinite somethings lead us back to the end of the chapter "Una vida de Evaristo Carriego," where it is described how Carriego's daily life revolved around a series of repeated motifs: the big cherrywood cup at the store on the corner of Charcas and Malabia streets, visits to the neighborhood bar at the corner of Venezuela and Perú, a house with a pink vestibule, the customs and love of the night (51–52). Of these somethings—habits, customs, "frequencies" ("frecuencias," vaguely suggestive of a radio metaphor, which helps in what follows), Borges says that he sees in them something more than the private customs of a man. He says that he sees in them "un sentido de inclusión y de círculo en su misma trivialidad" ("a sense of inclusion and circularity in their very triviality") and calls them, surprisingly enough, "actos comunísticos" ("communistic acts"), in the sense that they are something "compartido entre todos" ("shared among everyone").

> Esas frecuencias que enuncié de Carriego, yo sé que nos lo acercan. Lo repiten infinitamente en nosotros, como si Carriego perdurara disperso en nuestros destinos, como si cada uno de nosotros fuera por unos segundos Carriego. Creo que literalmente así es, y que esas momentáneas identidades (¡no repeticiones!) que aniquilan el supuesto correr de tiempo, prueban la eternidad. (52)
>
> I know that these frequencies that I described of Carriego take us closer to him. They repeat him infinitely in us, as though Carriego remained dispersed in our destinies, as though each one of us were for a few seconds Carriego. I think that it is literally that way, and that those momentary identities (not repetitions!) that annihilate the supposed flow of time prove [the existence of] eternity.

The repeated motifs that Carriego enacts in his daily life are also repeated in his poetry, which potentially serves to bring "us" together even more. Borges cites some of these motifs with a good dose of Carriegan kitsch: "el patio que es ocasión de serenidad, rosa para los días, el fuego humilde de San Juan, revolcándose como un perro en mitad de la calle, . . . la mampara de fierro del conventillo, los hombres de la esquina rosada" ("the patio which is the occasion for serenity, pink for daytime, the humble fire of San Juan, rolling around like a dog in the middle of the street, . . . the iron screen of the tenement building, the men of the rose-colored corner," 52–53).

The community or "sharing" to which these images and acts contribute does not congeal into a single, stable "we." The "nosotros" in this passage, which we can take to be a specifically Argentine "we" in spite of the fact that no nationality is mentioned (and, on the contrary, "todos" can very well mean a boundaryless "everyone"), is a very complex construction, not what we tend to think of as national or collective identity, or perhaps not as identity at all. The turn to "eternity" in the context of national identity is slightly disturbing; that is, the idea that there would be elements that unite a given group of people, and that those elements function as indices of eternity, "allegorical" in the traditional sense of the word, individual items that refer to a larger abstraction. An eternal, essential "we" would mean a never-ending "life," a perpetual distance from the unknown and unfigurable that we tend to designate, as de Man suggests, as "death." It would imply that we *can* know who or what "we" are, which we learn and confirm through our reading of Carriego's poetry and life.

But eternity does not appear as absolute transcendence, whether in national or divine form. It is something that is proven or shown ("probar")—or, in the other senses of the word "probar," tested or attempted (like "ensayar")—by infinite recurrences that are nonetheless not repetitions: recurrences of "momentary identities" that are not only fleeting (not what we usually think of when we think of identities), but which are continually dispersing, dissolving into other identities or individualities.[10] Like the images that Borges imagines interrupted Carriego's reading of his self-exile from life, they disrupt the sense of a restrictive, privative identity. Every single conception of who we are is constantly shifting, disrupted by the infinite repetitions of Carriego in us, us in Carriego, and any number of other "frequencies" that push us out of our sense of ourselves, while at the same time showing us who and what we are. In a radical sense of the term *communism,* nobody is anything, and any particular thing ("algo") can be anything ("cualquier cosa").

The infinite repetitions that are not repetitions recall a number of figures in the Western intellectual tradition, including Nietzsche's eternal recurrence of the same (or as Deleuze rephrases it, of the not-same); Freud's notion of the motif;[11] and Benjamin's reading of memory motifs in Baudelaire and Proust: especially that of a "vie antérièure," a "life" that has always already preceded present existence and that interrupts it with fragments, memories that are not memories because they were never possessed as part of one's own "lived experience" of the present (I 180–82). Benjamin calls this part of a "nonplatonic" conception of eternity in Proust, in which memory's repetitions open onto the infinite "convolutions" of time: time as it is infinitely convoluted in the objects, images, and sensations in the world around us.[12] The infinite repetitions, connections, and correspondences of memory or "anterior lives" do not synthesize in transcendence, but continue infinitely, "eternally" interrupting the concept of a knowable, autonomous present. Like the images that interrupt Carriego from his reading, the recurrences in his life and poetry interrupt the sense of an autonomous present, permeated as it is with repetitions and memories that do not belong to him or to anyone. Neither his life, nor the life or identity of a collective "we," is safe from the eternity of what he or we or anyone is not, which is infinitely moving, revolving, convoluting in the world about us.

This is how the chapter "Una vida de Evaristo Carriego" ends: with death, or as de Man suggests, death as a cipher for what cannot be known as life. Borges notes that Carriego "would have liked to live" in the momentary identities that repeated infinitely in his life ("En ellas hubiera querido vivir"); but he could not, and he instead remained "porous for death" (EC 52–53). Borges writes, "yo imagino que el hombre es poroso para la muerte y que su inmediación lo suele vetear de hastíos y de luz, de vigilancias milagrosas y previsions" ("I imagine that man is porous for death and that his immediate surroundings tend to streak him with tedium and light, with miraculous vigilances and predictions," 53). A person's life is not an autonomous entity, easily defined in the present, but is porous, open to an alterity that includes a peculiar sense of community, an omnitemporal "eternity," a universe that exists "entirely" in every instant and every place. In other words, it is *life,* but life that cannot be known completely, and thus appears as death. This death–life permeates the figure of individual life with both light and tedium ("hastíos," also surfeit, heaviness, excess), and brings to bear on it the past and also the future. "Man" is porous to repetitions as well as "previsiones," glimpses of a future promised by endless recurrence that never recurs exactly the same.[13]

A similar image appears later in the book. After Carriego is interrupted from his reading of a life that was not his and experiences a momentary recognition that the universe also exists in "el mero presente, en Palermo, en 1904," his sense of self-identity is forever changed. Borges writes, "Yo he sospechado alguna vez que cualquier vida humana, por intricada y populosa que sea, consta en realidad de un momento: el momento en que el hombre sabe para siempre quién es. Desde la imprecisable revelación que he tratado de intuir, Carriego es Carriego" ("I have suspected on occasion that any human life, however intricate and populous it may be, consists in reality of one moment: a moment in which the man knows forever who he is. From this indeterminable revelation that I have tried to intuit, Carriego is Carriego," 153). This tautology is altered slightly by the fact that it is a near-repetition of an earlier sentence in the chapter: "Carriego es (como el guapo, la costurerita y el gringo) un personaje de Carriego" ("Carriego is [like the tough, the seamstress, and the gringo] a character of Carriego," 151). This repetition modifies the identity logic of the statement "Carriego es Carriego," and even suggests that the copula of the "is" is a grammatical fiction, or that predication serves only to indicate fictional personae. "Personaje" comes from the same root as person, which has the peculiar quality of referring to both an identifiable human being and to a mask or adopted identity, in the sense of the English "persona." Here it would appear that any sense of self-identity is always a personification, what de Man describes as a giving of faces, which is also always a defacement, a denaturalizing of the figure or persona.

It is perhaps not surprising, then, that the supposed proof that "Carriego es Carriego," or the logical conclusion that he would always be who he once saw himself to be, is demonstrated by a poem that concerns a disfigured face. Borges enigmatically proposes that the fact that Carriego was always already Carriego can be seen in the following lines:

> Le cruzan el rostro, de estigmas violentos,
> hondas cicatrices, y tal vez le halaga
> llevar imborrables adornos sangrientos:
> caprichos de hembra que tuvo la daga. (153–54)
>
> Crossing his face, as violent stigmas,
> are deep scars, and perhaps it flatters him
> to wear indelible bloody adornments:
> feminine whims that the dagger had.

The chapter ends with a citation from a medieval German poem that describes a similar wound or betrayal by a weapon: "In die Friesen trug er sein Schwert Hilfnot, / das hat ihn heute betrogen" ("In the friezes he betrays his own desperate sword, which today had betrayed him").

Carriego's self-invention, Borges suggests, his invention of the "personaje" Carriego, is demonstrated by the figure of a face that is itself "porous for death." The face, conceived as that which presents life or a knowable entity that we identify as life, is streaked through with death. Like the description of Carriego's own face, in which the lines of his skull shone through his "vivacísimo" face, this face shows through to its other, the facelessness of death. Life and face, as figures of identity, are crossed with disfigurement and death: "As violent stigmas, deep scars cross his face, and perhaps it flatters him to wear indelible, bloody adornments." The "adornos sangrientos" do not signify death, but are worn in the face as "deep scars," as a porosity for death. A stigma—a betraying mark—indicates that the limits of determinable, identifiable "life" are not always as far off as they may appear to be. The life of Carriego as it is biographically displayed in these chapters is crossed with various marks, scars, and adornments that restore a sense of mortality to the project of life-writing as a metaphysical determination of identity. Death represents here not the deprivation of life, but the limits of what de Man calls "the shape and sense of a world accessible only in the privative way of understanding" ("Autobiography" 81).

What weapon betrays the man with the wounded face, the wounded identity, Carriego who is not quite Carriego? It is the man's own weapon that has made these stigmas of mortality. At least on one level, we can read the weapon as Carriego's writing: a use of language that does not seamlessly complete the personification of Carriego as Carriego, (auto)biography that "deprives and disfigures to the precise extent that it restores" (de Man 81). Language's figuration (particularly the figure of the self as the central figure of literature, if we agree with de Man and Borges that all literature is autobiographical) is betrayed by the fact that it is made up of language: that is, marks, scratches, *rasguidos* that cross all "faces" and all "lives." Like the scrape of a guitar that interrupts Carriego's contemplation of a distant "life," language is revealed to interrupt the figuration that its marks and scratches also create.

One last point remains to be considered in the poem that closes the section of the book dedicated to Carriego, which is the femininity that betrays the masculine face ("el rostro"): the womanly caprice of the dagger as it turns against the man, leaving him marked for death. In a discussion that followed Jacques Derrida's lecture "Otobiography," Claude Lévesque quotes a passage that Derrida had written about Antigone: "Human law, the law of the rational community which is instituted over against the private law of the family, always represses femininity, rises up against her, binds her, presses in upon her, and restrains her. But masculine potency has a limit—an essential and eternal one: the weapon, doubtless an impotent one, the all-powerful weapon of the impotent, the inalienable stroke of the woman is irony. Woman, 'internal enemy of the community,' can always burst out laughing at the last moment. She knows, in sorrow and in death, how to pervert the power that represses her" (Derrida, *Ear of the Other* 75). Regarding this passage, Lévesque asks: "If, on the one hand, man's substantial, effective life is in the State, in science but also in war and in work . . . and, on the other hand, if woman, with her irony, her veils, and her lies, is allied with the singularity of the unconscious, . . . can one say that autobiography . . . can be produced only as the autobiography of the woman, in both senses of that genitive? In autobiography, only femininity would . . . lead one to hear and understand the singular secret that constitutes it. Only a feminine writing . . . can (even as it cannot) tell its story as the unrelenting quest of that terrible thing which opens language to its own beyond" (76).

Here a feminine element of writing—which does not necessarily have anything to do with women, but is an aspect of writing—underlies and undermines a masculine, specular, legalistic form of representation based on the positive affirmation of identity, the identity logic of "I = I" or "Carriego es Carriego." Lévesque suggests that the repression of the unknown in the legalistic assertion of the known comes up against a limit that functions as a weapon against it: the impotent weapon of language's resistance to the comprehension of an object. Irony and veils—associated here with the feminine—work to show that every face is itself a veil. They work to mark tears in the veil that is the "face" of legalistic, identity-affirming language. Lévesque cites Derrida's assertion (repeated on more than one occasion, his response to Lévesque in the pages that follow notwithstanding), that only a "feminine" form of writing that emphasizes the limits of such a language can write (oto)biography.[14] Only a form of writing that interrupts identity and self-presence can write about life and death in a nonprivative way.

Violence, Life, and Law

In a provocative study discussed by both de Man and Derrida, the critic Philippe Lejeune demonstrates the relationship of autobiography to law, arguing that the project of autobiography works not only to represent a subject, but also to confirm it contractually through speech acts. The proper name in this sense becomes a signature, not an indication of a subject already known, but the contractual affirmation that the text will make it known to the reader.[15] Derrida notes that this kind of legal confirmation of identity becomes necessary when "the authority of law comes to take turns with . . . its own supplement, the impossible gathering of Being" (*Memoires* 24). That is, when society begins to require that identity be a fixed and permanent thing, that same requirement reveals that it is not naturally that way, thereby creating the necessity for identity to be defined by an external force, which is law.

There is an important subtext in *Evaristo Carriego* that concerns law. Borges tells us that Carriego died in 1912, and notes a few pages later that this was the same year of the implementation of the Sáenz Peña law, which was the law that instated obligatory suffrage for adult male citizens of Argentina (46).[16] The changes associated with this year—the implementation of a different kind of law, and its effect on the concept of life—are addressed throughout the book. Although the figure of the outlaw (a figure that would fascinate Borges throughout his life) is a central theme of the book, the relationship of outlaws to the law is not a simple opposition. The era preceding 1912 was not, of course, lawless. It merely had a different kind of law. Borges describes how "la votación se dirimía entonces a hachazos" ("voting was resolved in those days by ax blows"), and how rough gangs enforced the "independent vote" of the landowning caudillos (46). The 1912 law disbanded those militias and replaced them with another kind of law and perhaps another kind of violence, or at any rate, a different relationship to life and representation. His characterization of a society suddenly "more interested in the gymnasium than death" (80) may not only be a complaint of the exchange of outlaw heroes for buff businessmen, but (particularly in 1930, with the cult of the body beautiful sweeping Europe, and with it the nefarious category of biological identity as a political force) of a conservation and fetishization of "life" in its most biological sense.

Borges tells the story of these changes in law and representation in the penultimate section of the book, titled "Historia del tango" ("History of the Tango"). Like the category of life in "Una vida de Evaristo Carriego," Borges underscores the complexity that the tango presents for history, and discusses some of the facile ways in which its history has tended to be told. He begins with academic studies of the tango, and he says with false piety that he has no problem subscribing to all the conclusions their authors make "y aun a cualquier otra" ("and even to any other," 157). He then turns to the version that is periodically produced in the cinema, which, owing to its "photographic virtues," sets the tango's origins in the picturesque neighborhood of La Boca and tells in the style of a Bildungsroman how the tango made it to Paris and only later was accepted in its own country. This sentimental version, Borges says, does not hold up to his own memory or to the oral accounts with which he is familiar. He proceeds to tell the results of some informal oral research he conducted in which he asked a variety of people where the tango originated and he received a different response from each source. The only point on which they all seemed to be in agreement was that the tango originated in houses of prostitution.

From its origins in the sites of illegitimacy to its outlaw themes, the tango resists the laws of life history. It cannot be told like a life, in the style of a Bildungsroman. It also concerns a particular relationship *to* life. To begin with, its overt sexual nature defies the norms of social reproduction, which monitor the clear definition of origins required to legislate identity. The tango was engendered in districts of prostitution, its lyrics and figures were lascivious, and its erotic steps were often enacted between men: "porque las mujeres del pueblo no querían participar en un baile de perdularias" ("because the women of the town did not want to participate in a dance of profligates," 159). Even in the neighborhoods that lay on the limits of the law and the city center,[17] there was a self-imposed law of sexual normativity ("decencia") that tried to contain the "orgiástica diablura" that the tango represented.

Together with its sexual disposition was a certain bellicose nature, and the two aspects formed "part of a single impulse." Borges notes that the Latin word *virtus* contains the root word "vir" or "man," and in addition to its meanings of strength, force, or anger ("coraje"), suggests a peculiarly generative force. He cites a line from Rudyard Kipling's *Kim* in which an Afghan declares that he killed a man and begot a man in the same moment, "as though the two acts were, essentially, one": "When I was fifteen, I had shot a man and begot a man" (161). Borges proposes that in the tango, violence has a procreative force that is also connected to celebration and play: "Hablar de tango pendenciero no basta; yo diría que el tango y que las milongas, expresan directamente algo que los poetas, muchas veces, han querido decir con palabras: la convicción de que pelear puede ser una fiesta" ("To speak of the violence of tango is not enough; I would say that the tango and the milonga express directly something that poets have often wanted to say with words: the conviction that fighting can be a party," 161–62).

This peculiar conception of violence involves a procreative or generative force that is not connected to the production and reproduction of life. Like George Bataille's economy of excess, also linked to play and orgiastic energy, it rebels against any closed economy.[18] It also recalls Benjamin's distinction between the Latin terms *potesta* or power, which involves control and repression, and *vis* or *violentia,* implying a vital destructive force, a violence or force that is part of life itself.[19] Benjamin describes "a violence that is not related as a means to a preconceived end . . . not a means but a manifestation" (R 294). Beatrice Hanssen associates this noninstrumental violence with Hannah Arendt's description of a power conceived as a pure end (*Zeil*), which would resist the figure of either individuals or the state as ends (*Critique* 25). Such a conception of violence does not justify killing others, which is almost always instrumental in nature, but it does alter a relationship to life and death based on self-protection and regulation.

The strange notion of a procreative violence resonates with a phrase that appears a number of times in Borges's writings: the idea that "paternity and mirrors are abominable."[20] In light of the description of procreative violence, this idea seems to condemn the concepts of reproduction and representation as mere reproduction. Borges discusses the question of representational violence in the passage that follows the association of violence and procreation in *Evaristo Carriego,* where he explains that a certain kind of figurative language—"estructuras de palabras, formas hechas de símbolos" ("structures of words, forms made of symbols")—is the "original sin of literariness," because it invites us to unite two disparate representations ("nos invita a unir dos representaciones dispares," 163). Contrasting with this is music, which does not try to submit anything to an identity or representation that would try to unite two unequal things, but operates outside the law and order of figuration—in the disorder, rather, of war, sex, and play. Music is "will and passion," and the tango in particular "suele . . . transmitir esa belicosa alegría cuya expresión verbal ensayaron, en edades remotas, rapsodas griegos y germánicos" ("tends . . . to transmit that bellicose joy whose verbal expression was attempted, in remote ages, by Greek and Germanic rhapsodies," 163–64).[21]

Borges calls the tango a "long civic poem" ("un largo poema civil"), but he says that it represents the *civis* not in epic form or at least not in what tends to be thought of as epic, but rather, as the *Iliad* itself is reported to have been before being transformed into an epic, as a series of "songs and rhapsodies" (170). Citing another classical example, he explains that the songs and rhapsodies of the tango attempted to represent the dynamism of the city, the "quid quit agunt homines" of Juvenal's satires: "todo lo que mueve a los hombres—el deseo, el temor, la ira, el goce carnal, las intrigas, la felicidad . . . Todo el trajín de la ciudad fue entrando en el tango" ("all that moves men—desire, fear, anger, carnal pleasure, intrigues, happiness . . . All the traffic of the city entered into the tango," 169–70). This movement or force represents a disruptive potential within the order and law of the city, which is the political and social site par excellence of the kind of representational violence that is based on the uniting of two different entities. Borges says that the tango's lyrics are capable of transmitting this dynamism, but he stresses that it is the tango's quality as music that makes it a dynamic and potentially disruptive force.

The daily movements of the city represented through the rhapsodic nature of song are opposed to official law. Borges cites Andrew Fletcher to say "Si me dejan escribir todas las baladas de una nación, no me importan quién escriba las leyes" ("If they let me write all the ballads of a nation, I don't care who writes the laws," 169). This preference does not make music into a kind of law or model. If that was the intention of the sentence in its original enunciation, it is not the case with the tango. Borges notes that to the extent that the tango is a model, it is a model "maléfico" which corrupts and inspires vice rather than normalization.

In a section titled "Un misterio parcial," Borges poses the question as to why, given the fact that Argentina contributed greatly to Latin American independence from Spanish colonial rule, Argentines do not identify with the military past connected to that event and the liberal state that was set up in its wake: "Nuestro pasado militar es copioso, pero lo indiscutible es que el argentino, no se identifica con él (pese a la preferencia que en las escuelas se da al sentido de la historia) . . . El argentino, a diferencia de los americanos del Norte y de casi todos los europeos, no se identifica con el Estado" ("Our military past is abundant, but it is indisputable that the Argentine does not identify with it (in spite of the preference that they give to the sense of history in the schools) . . . In contrast to the North

Americans and to almost all Europeans, the Argentine does not identify with the State," 165–66). Rather than the official history of the State, he says, Argentines tend to prefer figures such as the gaucho and the compadre, figures "imaginados como rebeldes" ("imagined as rebels"). Both traditions are based on violence and "coraje," but violence in the name of the state is different from outlaw or rebel violence because the latter "no está al servicio de una causa y es puro" ("is not in the service of a cause, and it is pure"). Outlaw violence, not directed toward an end, is fundamentally different from violence that establishes states, such as the wars of independence or the civilizing "campaigns" that lay the ground for the construction of modern Argentina by killing off the indigenous populations,[22] or the ongoing violence of governmentality, which involves among other things a representational violence that involves the continuous linking of the individual to an abstract idea. "The State," Borges asserts, "es una inconcebible abstracción" ("is an inconceivable abstraction"), and the idea, postulated by Hegel, that it can contain the moral actions of the individuals that it represents, is taken by Argentines to be a "sinister joke." "El argentino," Borges insists, "es un individuo, no un ciudadano" ("The Argentine is an individual, not a citizen").

Borges suggests that the linking of an individual to an abstraction or of individuals to the State is something that must be resisted. Hollywood tales of individuals who enter into friendship with a criminal only to later turn them over to the police are incomprehensible to Argentines: "The Argentine, for whom friendship is a passion and the police a mafia, feels that this 'hero' is an incomprehensible swine" (165). It is not just that the police force in Argentina is assumed to be corrupt, but the very idea of an abstract state having control over individual freedoms is itself considered to be criminal. Borges cites don Quijote on this: "allá se lo haya cada uno con su pecado," and "no es bien que los hombres honrados sean verdugos de los otros hombres, no yéndoles nada en ello" ("let everyone go on with his own sin," and "it is not good that honest men be executioners of other men, not having anything against them").

I have already mentioned how Borges describes a certain kind of language—"structures of words, forms made of symbols"—as the "original sin of the literary" because it tries to unite two diverse representations. As I mention in my introduction, in the essay "De las alegorías a las novelas" Borges calls such linking "allegory" and contrasts it with the attention to individuality in the novel (OI 153–56). He calls the "allegorical" linking of individuals an "aesthetic error." Especially in light of the discussion in *Evaristo Carriego* of individuals and the state, it seems to imply an ethical error as well, since the subjection of individuals to the ideal of the state is described as a violation of freedom. Appropriately, such a violation is denounced by none other than the first novelistic figure, don Quixote. However, as Borges suggests in "De las alegorías a las novelas," the novelistic focus on individuality does not save it from an "allegorical"—or in *Evaristo Carriego,* "symbolic"—form of abstraction. Even novelistic representations or individual heroes tend to be linked with some sort of abstraction, even if it is only the idealization of individuality itself. The Hollywood hypostatization of individuality exemplifies this: the heroes are depicted as working for an unquestioned sense of self, which is unproblematically linked to a side of good represented by the state.

How to conceive of a noninstrumental defense of freedom that would not be idealized into a figure such as the individual or the state? Clearly the rough days of the compadres would not be entirely free of such an idealization. It is not even possible to talk about them without falling into idealization. But for Borges the compadres and gauchos represent not heroes on which the value of a nation (or an ethno-regional identity such as *criollismo*) can be based, but a kind of violence that interrupts just such idealization. Theirs, he says, is a "pure" violence, because it does not work in the service of a cause, perhaps not even their own names, that end toward which Hollywood rebels endlessly labor.

"Generous" Duels

To demonstrate the nature of noninstrumental violence, Borges recounts a pair of legends of duels from the compadre past. The duel in the Borgesian topography tends to represent an extreme limit between individuals, and between life and death. The first story concerns Juan Muraña, the tough who is also mentioned in the passage on the interruption of Carriego's contemplation of life.

> Un hombre de los Corrales o de Barracas, sabedor de la fama de Juan Muraña (a quien no ha visto nunca), viene a pelearlo desde su suburbio del Sur; lo provoca en un almacén, los dos salen a pelear a la calle; se hieren, Muraña, al fin, lo *marca* y le dice: "Te dejo con vida para que volvás a buscarme." (EC 174)

> A man from Corrales or from Barracas, knowing of the fame of Juan Muraña (whom he has never seen), comes to fight him from a suburb in the South; he provokes him in a bar, the two go out to the street to fight; they wound one another, Muraña, in the end, *marks* him and tells him, "I leave you with life so that you can come back and look for me."

The other tale concerns Wenceslao Suárez ("el chileno"), a man in his forties or fifties who is reported to be courageous and who takes care of his mother (175). One day Suárez, who does not know how to read, receives a letter from someone who, it is surmised, does not know how to write. This missive is interpreted and exchanged through the local storekeeper (mercenaries being the only ones who had recourse to written language), who deciphers the letter as a greeting from an anonymous stranger, and a desire to meet. Suárez responds through the storekeeper, and one day the stranger appears at his ranch and Suárez invites him to drink and dine. After the meal, the stranger challenges Suárez to a duel. Suárez, while regretting that he ate and drank so much, accepts, and the two men begin to fight. The stranger, who is young and strong, seems to have the upper hand, when Suárez allows the contestant to wound his hand that holds the poncho, cape and dagger-style: "El cuchillo entra la muñeca, la mano queda como muerta, colgando" ("The knife enters the wrist, the hand remains as though dead, hanging," 177). Suárez then "da un gran salto, recula, pone la mano ensangrentada en el suelo, la pisa con la bota, la arranca, amaga un golpe al pecho del forastero y le abre el vientre de una puñalada" ("gives a great leap, falls back, puts his bloody hand on the ground, steps on it with his boot, pulls it off, fakes a blow to the chest of the stranger and opens his abdomen in one stab"). From here Borges says that there are two versions of the tale, one that tells of the stranger's probable death, the other of his return to his province after Suárez "le hace la primera cura con la caña del almuerzo" ("performs first aid with the wine from lunch," 178).

These two stories illustrate what Borges means by pure violence, a force that is not exercised in the name of an abstraction such as the state or the individual. It also concerns a form of representation that does not try, like literary or symbolic language, to unite two distinct things in a single figure: individuality with the state, or life (*vir, virtus, vis*) with a single, defendable individuality. The provocateurs in the stories want to make a name for themselves by killing the hero with the name. But their projects fail. In the first story, Muraña marks the face of his opponent, as though to show the "hondas cicatrices," to use Carriego's words, of individual identity—the gaps in the face or figure of what the provoker wanted to establish as the appropriable end of his bravery. What Muraña shows him, and what is even more distinct in the second story, is that bravery (force, strength, "coraje") is not about promoting or even protecting the figure of the individual. Suárez allows himself to be marked and even disfigured before he makes his mark on the other. In both cases, the men leave a gash in their opponents as though to open up the figure of the individual name-seeker, to open his idealized individuality to a vital force that goes beyond any individual end.

Such a "marking" bears a special relationship to representation. The exchange of letters between the two men who are unable to write, exchanged through the merchant shopkeeper, who is the only one in this rural world who works with exchange value—the identification, in terms of value, of two disparate things—demonstrates that the compadres operate with a different kind of representation. Writing for them is done with knives: the emphasis on the verb "marcar," italicized in different parts in the book, suggests that Muraña's marking of his opponent's face functions as a kind of writing. It is a kind of writing, however, that does not form figures, but that interrupts figure: that disfigures or defaces, to use de Man's terms. Like music, which does not try to unite two separate figures, and like the "rasguido" of the guitar that appears next to Muraña's mark in the list of interruptions that may have startled Carriego out of his contemplation of the alien concept of life, this kind of writing works to interrupt all figuration that is taken to be complete, or all abstraction taken as an end. When individuality becomes legislated and the possibility of "pure violence" is increasingly contained by social regulations (for example, to mark another's face is to also mark the state, and will consequently land you in jail), the only place that such an interruptive violence remains is in writing itself: a writing that marks the faces of life and identity, that writes "hondas cicatrices" into all faces of abstraction. The scratch in the face of abstraction could be thought of as an allegory of allegory: an allegorization, in the sense of an other-writing or allography,[23] of allegory's abstractions.

Borges explains that the tango, itself a kind of other-writing, declined at a certain point. This decline is not due to the Italian immigrants, as Borges admits he once believed, but is the cause of the "entire republic" (171).[24] In fact, it lost its dynamic and disruptive force precisely when it became representative of the entire republic, when it became, like Borges himself is today, a national symbol. Based on the various examples of defaced or disfigured faces that appear throughout this book, one could argue that Borges's project in *Evaristo Carriego* was to conceive a kind of allegory of allegory, an interruption of abstraction that does not try to replace abstraction with the novelistic abstraction of individuality, but which tries to show the limits of individuality or of the concept of an autonomous "life."

Language perhaps inevitably lends itself to figuration and abstraction. It is, after all, constituted by copula that appear to unite disparate things, the object-world with signs, and so forth. But it is also made up of marks and scratches on paper that do not, to use Borges's favored figure of the mirror, reflect anything at all. We could say that

Borges's allegorical biography shows us that when we look into the (non)mirror of language, we see marks where our faces should be. We are confronted with the "hondas cicatrices" in our conceptions of identity, the limits of the "shape and sense of a world accessible only in the privative way of understanding." This allows us to begin to ask, as we will do in the next chapter, what is *not* said in language's saying, and how the faces of history are used to maintain the violence of social exclusion and oppression.

Chapter 3

Allegory, Ideology, Infamy

Allegories of History in *Historia Universal de la Infamia*

> Se movió mudo el silencio
> y dijo algo.
> No dijo nada.
>
> —Rafael Alberti, "El ángel de la ira"

Allegory is one of those peculiar terms that lives on through a series of afterlives, with an ongoing discomfort with regard to its own past. Doris Sommer, in her "Allegory and Dialectics," describes the repeated attempts to redeem and appropriate the term as examples of a kind of repressive hypothesis. It is a term that is invoked nearly apologetically, with the idea on the one hand that it has been so stretched out as to be nearly unusable (Northrop Frye suggested that allegory describes all acts of commentary), and on the other hand that it bears certain inferences or traces that make the term untranslatable out of a certain historical specificity. Does a given reference to allegory suppose a medieval, baroque, or postmodern, a Benjaminian, de Manian or Jamesonian conception of the term? Fredric Jameson's 1986 essay, "World Literature in an Age of Multinational Capitalism," in which he introduces the idea of a "national allegory," includes a brief nod to Walter Benjamin's conception of allegory, but for the most part ignores the history of the term, adding to its general confusion. Nevertheless, the figure of "national allegory" has received an inordinate amount of attention in studies concerning peripheral world regions such as Latin America. Sommer, in her adaptation of Jameson's work to the Latin American context, attempts to map out the differences among some of the different theories of allegory, but in doing so, she commits what she admits is a willful misreading of Benjamin. This misreading is instructive, in that it allows us to see a fundamental distinction between two kinds of allegory, a difference that I will suggest Benjamin himself makes in his *The Origin of German Tragic Drama*. What the different theories of allegory have in common is an understanding of that trope as a form of writing history; they differ in what they understand history and writing to be. In *Historia universal de la infamia* (*Universal History of Infamy*), Borges addresses this very question. The *Historia universal* is, I argue, a book about history itself, which employs both kinds of allegory discussed by Benjamin. The stories take up something that we might call national allegory and allegorize it, parodically and paradoxically telling a history that by its very nature cannot be told, that is *infame*.

"National" Allegory

Jameson introduces the term "national allegory" in his essay "World Literature in an Age of Multinational Capitalism," in which he famously attributes a political level of significance to all third world texts. Although his use of the term "allegory" is clearly inflected by a number of different thinkers, he does not so much theorize the term as mark its place (and that of literature in general) in the age of multinational capitalism. What allegory boils down to for him is a representation of the seemingly inextricable relationships between private and political narratives within third world literature. In a statement that has been roundly criticized for its generalization, he writes, "the story of the private individual destiny is always an allegory of the embattled situation of the public third-world culture and society" (69).

Doris Sommer takes up the idea of the national allegory in her work on nineteenth-century Latin American fiction. Although she criticizes what she regards as Jameson's freehanded approach to the "third world," she stresses the importance of what she calls the dialectical aspect of allegory in understanding Latin American foundational fictions. She interprets the dialectical nature of allegory as the indication of a specific relationship between the individual and the sociopolitical realm, which she supports with a quote from Benjamin's *The Origin of German Tragic Drama:* "'The baroque apotheosis is a dialectical one' because its subject could not stop at the individual but had to include a politico-religious dimension" ("Allegory and Dialectics" 64). Sommer explains this to mean that the individual is enmeshed in the "worldly . . . breadth" of history in such a way that he or she has as much a chance of making her mark on it as it has on her. In her application of this idea to nineteenth-century

Latin American narrative, Sommer connects the dialectical nature of allegory to romance, describing what she sees as a romantic/erotic relationship between the personal and the political in both private and national narratives. She describes how in these texts individual passions are linked, in an interlocking and not parallel relationship (74), to constructions of post-independence national imaginaries, the individual's love story tipping over into national procreation as a matter of course.

Both Sommer and Jameson indicate a fundamental discontinuity in the modern allegorical tracing of the relationship between the private and the political. Jameson writes that as opposed to a traditional conception of allegory, in which "an elaborate set of figures and personifications . . . [are] read against some one-to-one table of equivalences," we are presented with the "alarming notion that such equivalences are themselves in constant change and transformation at each perpetual present of the text" ("World Literature" 146–47). For Jameson, it seems that the very instability of the public and the private spheres opens a potential space for theorizing that relationship, the different levels of allegory bearing a direct relation on the different levels of the social. For Sommer, it is more specifically a question of the act of writing, the way the instability of the two terms is represented in the romances "as a dialectical structure in which one page of the narrative is a trace of the other, in fact, where each helps to write the other" ("Allegory and Dialectics" 74).

In both cases, the concept of allegory is understood as what Borges calls a "mapa del universo" (OI 99), which would function as a way of locating—and perhaps thereby dislocating—the individual with respect to his or her sociopolitical circumstances. Jameson is well-known for his belief in the emancipatory potential of mapping. He calls allegory a new kind of mapping process based on "breaks and heterogeneities" which opens a space within national or multinational imaginaries for a new kind of agency and potential for change ("World Literature" 146). The virtues of a "situational consciousness" that in 1986 he attributed to a third world perspective he later expanded to represent the only hope for both first and third worlds—both "master" and "slave"—to "grasp our positioning" within the confusing and contradictory landscapes of multinational capitalism, and establish ourselves with respect to "collective pasts" and futures of "social totality" (157–58; *Postmodernism* 54).

In his article "Pastiche Identity, and Allegory of Allegory," Alberto Moreiras considers Jameson's model of national allegory in relation to the Antillean writer Edouard Glissant's theory of a national or regional literature. For Glissant, national literature has both a "'desacralizing function,' which is demystifying and deconstructive, *and* a 'sacralizing function,' which reassembles the community around its myths, its beliefs, its imaginary, and its ideology" (221). National literature, even that which is written from peripheral regions or the "third world," serves to create a homogeneous representation of what is an essentially heterogeneous area, forming part of a more general "system of exclusion or misrepresentation of that which resists being homogenized" (223). Collective pasts and social totalities are always formed at the expense of a heterogeneity not reducible to community definition. The common assumption that since third world identities are heterogeneous to metropolitan centers they are less guilty of a violence of exclusion is erroneous. The foundational myth of "difference" as distinct from "identity" conceals the fact that the former is merely the underside of the latter (205). Yet within the sacralizing function of national literatures lie destabilizing forces that can potentially disturb or undo the pretended coherence of any stable identity. In certain cases a national literature self-consciously destroys the ground of its own identity: "community definition poses itself as its own undermining" (222). But even within a sense of identity based on self-questioning and rewriting, the heterogeneity released by such a gesture is reorganized around a sense of identity. In such cases, which Moreiras likens to Jameson's conception of allegory, the dialectical relationship between the poles of stability and instability, sacralization and desacralization, never allows for a stable sense of identity but neither does it allow for its undoing.

Ideology

The idea that a national literature or a national allegory necessarily has a desacralizing function because it is based on discontinuities is a dangerous one, because as Ernesto Laclau tells us, ideology itself is based on a constitutive discontinuity. He explains ideology's primary function as a representation of the impossible fullness of the community, "the presence of an absence," which is based on "an insurmountable split which is strictly constitutive" ("Death" 302–3). The ideological operation is based on a dialectical relationship between the ideal of wholeness and the particular bodies that inhabit the community, between the "incarnation" of the absent fullness in the particular bodies of individuals, and a "deformation" in the representation of that particular body in an equivalential chain (304). Yet the relationship between the particular and the abstract is not, as Jameson says of traditional allegory, a static model based on one-to-one equivalences, but rather is a representative model based precisely on the impossibility of such equivalence. The equivalential chain involves a process that is based on heterogeneity and an unstable relationality.

> [R]epresenting the fullness of the community cannot do entirely away with the particularity of the content through which the incarnation takes place, for in the case that such a doing away was complete we would arrive at a situation in which incarnated meaning and incarnating body would be entirely commensurable with each other—which is the possibility that we are denying *ex hypothesi*. We see here what it is that makes possible the visibility of the distortive operation: the fact that neither of the two movements in which it is based can logically reach its *ad quem* term. (304)

Particular and abstract, individual and community are never matched up in perfect romance, but evade closure even as their uneven engagement paradoxically represents a certain union. This is the relation on which national allegory is based: the map that, holding its constituent parts apart, also holds them together.

In ideology, the impossibility of wholeness is constitutive, that is to say necessary and acknowledged as such, and necessarily disavowed: "(mis)represented" or misrecognized.[1] Laclau illustrates this contradiction with the example of mysticism, the "extreme limit (of) the logic of equivalence" (311). God is the impossible fullness commensurable with no mundane entity: "For the great monotheistic religions there is an unsurpassable abyss between the creator and the *ens creatum*." The paradox of mysticism, Laclau quotes Gershom Scholem as saying, is that it "does not deny or overlook the abyss; on the contrary, it begins by realizing its existence, but from there it proceeds to a quest for the secret that will close it in, the hidden path that will span it" (311). In this sense, I want to suggest, the desacralizing gesture of national allegory may be nothing more than a function of a sacralizing effect already at work in ideology itself.

Sommer goes much further than Jameson in her theorization of allegory in her attempt to discuss the predominantly romantic form of nineteenth-century national allegories in terms of Benjamin's discussion of allegory in German Baroque drama.[2] She explains that she turns to Benjamin because he conceives of allegory as a "vehicle for time and dialectics" ("Allegory and Dialectics" 42), but what she understands by dialectics in Benjamin's text is a form of history essentially coincidental with the progressive time of nineteenth-century liberal ideology. It is on this ground that she rejects Paul de Man's understanding of allegory, which she describes as being mired in a "Romantic enchantment of timelessness," and eventually Benjamin's as well, because, she claims, he "never made his dialectic count for anything constructive. It moves only downward and backward into an infinite regression" (44). She admits to a "willful misreading" of Benjamin's conception of time in the structure of allegory (70), but I believe that her reading is based on what is perhaps a not so willful mistake. Benjamin's allegory does not represent regressive time any more than it describes progressive time, but rather concerns the possibility of a nonlinear conception of history, and implies a very different conception of dialectics than that described by Sommer. While she wants to read Benjamin's notion of allegory as a near mirror image (distorted, perhaps, as Laclau says of ideology itself) of the teleological, progressive history of Baroque theological politics and nineteenth-century developmental schemas, Benjamin's conception of allegory represents a radical alternative to the false dilemma of progression and regression.

Two Moments of Allegory

In *The Origin of German Tragic Drama,* Benjamin begins his explanation of allegory with the figure of origins, which he distinguishes from genesis or beginning (*Entstehung*). The term "origin" (*Ursprung*) "is not intended to describe the process by which the existent came into being, but rather to describe that which emerges from the process of becoming and disappearance. Origin is an eddy in the stream of becoming, and in its current it swallows the material involved in the process of genesis" (45). The origin is not something that comes from a stable place, a beginning as such (the root in *Entstehung* meaning standing, to stand), but is always already in history—a history that is rooted in temporality, rather than constituting a discrete and stable entity.[3] There is no beginning as such, there are only relationships between phenomena and history, and what Benjamin calls *Ursprung* is the initial "leap" (*Sprung*) into, or in, this dizzying existence. The *Ursprung* thus understood is inherently dialectical, not in the sense in which Sommer uses the term, but in the sense that it describes a relationship that each phenomenon has with the stream of becoming in which it finds itself, with what it is not but might be: "That which is original is never revealed in the naked and manifest existence of the factual; its rhythm is apparent only to a dual insight. On the one hand it needs to be recognized as a process of restoration and reestablishment, but, on the other hand, and precisely because of this, as something imperfect and incomplete" (45).

Whereas the traditional, metaphysical concept of dialectics that Sommer employs relates the individual to an abstract totality without remainder (nation or history), Benjamin's dialectic, perhaps best understood as a dialectic of dialectics or a negative dialectic, places a central importance on what remains external to both individual and abstraction.[4] He explains his notion of dialectical historicity in terms of language, both in the Epistemo-Critical prologue to *The Origin of German Tragic Drama* and also in the "The Task of the Translator," which is referred to in a footnote in the passage I just quoted. In the translation essay, Benjamin proposes that history is best considered in a form other than human or organic life, for which we have too many preconceived ideas concerning linearity, descent, and completion. Instead, he turns to the "life" and "afterlife" (*Nachleben*) of works of literature as they are represented in their translations. A translation does not derive from the original work in a relation of dependence to its claim to truth, but continues and develops (in the sense of unfolding) its "life" in succeeding generations, "the more encompassing life of history" (I 71). The original work's relationship to history is present in what he calls its "translatability": not a translatability without excess, but rather one whose excess is present in the original and is brought to light by the necessarily incomplete act of translation. Perhaps better conceived as the work's *un*translatability, Beatrice Hanssen describes this translative potential always already present in any original work as a "temporal kernel" that translation opens up to a specifically inorganic (in spite of his use of the term "life") concept of history (*Walter Benjamin* 32). Unlike a traditional concept of dialectics, the history that translation reveals refers to neither an anthropocentric "consciousness" nor a transcendent closure. Rather, like the *Ursprung* to the stream of becoming, translation opens the original work to "the remotest extremes and apparent excesses" of historical possibility represented by language itself: what a work is not, but might be (OGD 47).

In the translation essay, the extension of these extremes and excesses is conveyed by the term "pure language" (*reine Sprache*), which in spite of its theological overtones does not refer to metaphysical completion. Pure language is described as the "central reciprocal relationship between languages," the dialectical flux of possibility represented by language itself (I 72). The translation of a work refers not to the uniqueness of the original, but to the "foreignness" of all languages, including the language of the original (75). Tom Cohen describes "pure language" as the "purely material order of effects shared by the work of the trace in all tongues, all languages. What aims to be true to an original for purposes of translation, and thus seems to return or fold back as such, must pass through this site common to the intersections of all linguistic entities" (*Ideology* 13–14). As opposed to ideology, which invokes heterogeneity only to have it subsumed under an equivalential chain, translation tells us its relation to all that it itself is not. It is a form of representing what Scholem called the abyss with a path that does not promise to span it, a secret that does not hope to close it up. The path that translation traces "cannot possibly reveal or establish this hidden relationship in itself (that is, the confrontation with the abyss), but it can represent it in embryonic or intensive form" (I 72).

Translation in this sense is a form of "telling history," as is allegory and what Benjamin calls in the Epistemo-Critical prologue the "idea." All three are essentially "ideal" or virtual perceptions of history in (as he says of the idea) a "gathering or redemption" of different moments, of "the remotest extremes and apparent excesses" of a given historical entity (OGD 46–47). I will return to the question of redemption shortly. What is important here is that these three forms represent ways of representing history that are fundamentally different from what Sommer calls "dialectical stories" that we tell ourselves to avoid the incomprehensibility of being ("Allegory and Dialectics" 69).

The Baroque was a time radically shaken by its confrontation with the possibility that divine containment or total knowledge might not exist, that there might not be any escape from temporal existence. It not only looked this possibility in the face, but, Benjamin avers, attempted to represent it. The result was the Baroque form of allegory, in which a new sense of mortality—not an eschatology, but a sense of existence in the fall, with neither ascension nor descension—was linked to language's own mortality or historicity, represented in the Baroque figure par excellence of the skull. This is the point of a well-known passage.

> In allegory the observer is confronted with the facies hippocratica of history as a petrified, primordial landscape. Everything about history that, from the very beginning, has been untimely, sorrowful, unsuccessful, is expressed in a face—or rather in a death's head . . . This is the allegorical way of seeing, of the baroque, secular explanation of history as the Passion of the world; its importance resides solely in the stations of its decline. The greater the significance, the greater the subjection to death, because death digs most deeply the jagged line of demarcation between physical nature and significance. (OGD 166)

Allegory, which is "in the world of thoughts what ruins are in the world of things" (178), does not just thematize death, but endeavors to represent death or a fall from transcendence in and as language. The Baroque contemplated a temporal existence without a divine end, and represented the lack of transcendence in a form of representation that represented its own "mortal" limits. Although the figure of death appears to contrast with the figure of life in the translation essay, they indicate much the same thing: a conception of temporality not limited to an individual or to a transcendent end.[5] Language, freed from pretensions to transcendent meaning, represents this nonfinite history mournfully but insistently, as though language itself becomes a way of passing through the stations of the secular Passion of history (the "decline" describes only its fallen state, not a decline *to* something). The obsession with death that marked allegory was paradoxically a point of hope for Benjamin, in that it represented the possibility of a new kind of historical understanding outside of the paradigm—the "dialectical story"—of Judeo-Christian teleology.

This is the hope that Benjamin holds out for Baroque allegory, but at the end of the book he explains that the Baroque's look into the face of death was only a look, and a look away. He describes how the Baroque performed an *Umschwung*—an about-turn or turnaround—from its nonredemptive consideration of the fall, into salvation and resurrection. Here the Baroque allegory parts ways with the "idea" as described in the book's prologue: the *Umschwung* marks "the limit set upon the allegorical contemplation, rather than its ideal quality" (232). Returning to a Christian cosmogony, the transitory nature of life is read as its opposite, not "allegorically represented, so much as, in its own significance, displayed as allegory": "Yea, when the Highest comes to reap the harvest from the graveyard, then I, a death's head, will be an angel's countenance." In the end Baroque allegory

> clears away the final phantasmagoria of the objective and, left entirely to its own devices, re-discovers itself, not playfully in the world of things, but seriously under the eyes of heaven. And this is the essence of the melancholic immersion: that its ultimate objects (*Gegenstände*), in which it believes it can most fully secure for itself that which is vile, turn into allegories, and that these allegories fill out and deny the void in which they are represented, just as, ultimately, the intention does not faithfully rest in the contemplation of bones, but faithlessly leaps forward to the idea of resurrection (*zur Auferstehung treulos überspringt*). (OGD 232–33; GS 1.1.406)

The *Umschwung* leads to an *Übersprung,* a leaping not only forward but over, an "overspringing to."[6] Here allegory has turned into a Jacob's ladder, in which the objects of this world serve as steps out if it into resurrection. This *Übersprung* is an entrance or reentrance into the ideology of a teleological history, but with a difference. It is more truly ideological because the abyss of temporality has been contemplated and denied, sutured in spite of "the impossibility of any ultimate suture" (Laclau, *New Reflections* 92). To paraphrase Žižek, it is not that they know not what they do, but that they know it and do it anyway (32–33).

"'Weeping we scattered the seed on fallow ground and sadly went away.' Allegory goes away empty handed" (OGD 233). Benjamin's book began with the *Ursprung,* the dialectical beginning of a nonteleological history, and ends with an *Übersprung,* a leaping over this possibility, right back into the ontoteleological structure of a Christian history of resurrection. This *Übersprung* marks the beginning of the modern state: having glimpsed the precarious nature of the world, power learns to assert itself in new ways, taking that precarious nature into account. The metaphor of monarchy is no longer sufficient; the prince himself becomes an allegorist of the sadistic kind, writing his stories into the bodies of his subjects (184). This is due in part to what Benjamin calls the Baroque's "theological essence of the subjective." In spite of its conception of a nonhuman history that leaves skulls in its wake, Baroque allegory reveals itself in the end "to be a subjective phenomenon," in which the "subjective perspective is entirely absorbed in the economy of the whole" (233).[7] Benjamin's examples illustrate the bizarre extent to which such a subjective perspective was taken. He tells of the pillars of a Baroque balcony that were "in reality arrayed exactly the way in which, in a regular construction, they would appear from below," and of Santa Teresa's response to a confessor who did not see the roses she claimed to see: "Our Lady brought them to *me*" (234). In the end, modern constructions of power would rely on more than hallucinations and trompes d'oeil to govern their constituents, but the fiction of the subject's centrality would maintain a critical importance.

"Allegory goes away empty-handed": Benjamin ends his book here. But I want to argue that allegory does not end here, with the *Übersprung* of the modern state, but rather ends in the beginning, in his discussion of the *Ursprung.* If there is any hope in the face of the modern state, it is in the beginning of a different conception of history, a different relationship to time and being. Baroque allegory fails in the end to remain open to such a difference: it closes off what it began in a faithless leap into the figure of Christian redemption. But the Epistemo-Critical prologue presents another conception of redemption, in which history is "redeemed or gathered" into the idea. Benjamin has come under frequent attack for the notion of redemption that appears in much of his work, fueled particularly by the description of redemption that appears at the end of this book.[8] But the kind of redemption offered by the idea in the prologue is fundamentally different from the subject-centered and transcendent redemption that appears in the final chapter.

Throughout his works, Benjamin used different words for what tends to be translated into English as "redemption." In his "Theses on the Concept of History," for example, he uses the most common word for theological redemption, *Erlösung*. Benjamin avoided that word in the Baroque book, and used instead *Rettung* and *Heil,* the latter only at the end of the book, in the context of Baroque allegory's failure. He describes the redemption that occurs in the idea as "Rettung oder Einsammlung," redemption or collection or gathering (OGD 47; GS 227). While *Erlösung, Heil,* and *Rettung* all mean redemption or salvation in the ecclesiastical sense, *Rettung* means a kind of salvation that is also a salvage, escape, or recovery, as though of a shipwreck. The "redemption or gathering" of the idea, or of allegory in the ideal sense, is one that does not "überspringt" the *Ursprung* and try to force it into a teleological narrative, but which, like translation, gathers together pieces of the nonsequential, nonteleological historicity that Benjamin describes, to represent it "in embryonic form."

In his book *Ideology and Inscription,* Tom Cohen describes allegory or "allography" (of which translation and the Epistemo-Critical prologue's "idea" are versions) as a "*techne* of historial intervention" (7–8). He contrasts it with ideological modes of representation based on mimetic, anthropocentric forms of historicism, in which human history, based on a belief in the autonomy of the subject and the coherence of collective identity, is deemed fully representable through mimetic-descriptive language. Both ideology itself and many forms of ideology critique tend to rely on such forms of representation, disavowing the "constitutive distortion" that Laclau locates at the center of ideological representation in order to assert the fullness (the "social totality," in Jameson's words) of community and historical continuity (Cohen, *Ideology* 18–19). Allegory signifies the possibility of representing history without the idealization of a redemptive wholeness characteristic of ideology. It would intervene in such historical representations by opening them up to their constitutive distortion, to what they tend to exclude. The redemptive nature of the allegorical operation is based on what Cohen, following de Man, calls an act of inscription or incision into ideological forms of representation. Allegory "would suspend naturalized genres on behalf of a pragmatic cut—opening alternative itineraries to those of fixed inherited narratives legislated by . . . historicist regimes" (12). Rather than destabilizing representations of identity only to suture them back into ideal "futures of social totality," allegory would trace paths of a history not reducible to such ideals, opening the ideological concept of history to its unrecognized exclusions.

Infamy

I now turn to Borges's *Historia universal de la infamia,* which, read in allegorical terms, is a "historia" of history itself. The stories in the volume have frequently been read as allegorical in the traditional sense of the word, that is, that the stories say something other than what they appear to say on the surface (allegory of course comes from *allos-agorein,* speaking other than publicly). What they parabolically refer to, however, is the telling of history itself, and above all, history that cannot be reduced to its telling. The title of the book announces a contradiction. The word "infamy" comes from the Greek *pheme,* an utterance or report, so that which is infamous would seem to be that which is absent from history by definition, that which cannot be told.[9] I want to suggest that in this *historia universal* there are two kinds of allegory going on, two forms of telling history. On the one hand, there is a parodying of something that could be called national allegory, and on the other hand, there is an allegorization or other-writing ("allography") of that kind of allegory, an allegory that tells a history which by its very nature is *infame.*[10] This second kind of allegory is related to what historian Dipesh Chakrabarty describes as the project of a subaltern history, namely, "a history that will attempt the impossible: to look towards its own death by tracing that which resists and escapes the best human effort at translation across cultural and other semiotic systems" (quoted in Moreiras, *Tercer espacio* 290). Allegory, as a form of subaltern history, is a mode of writing history that shows the ruins, the *naufragios,* of the translations it proposes.

The "historias" revolve around the twin themes of recognition and death. Nearly all the stories include some element of recognition or misrecognition of the individual within his or her sociopolitical dimension. "El tintorero enmascarado Hákim de Merv" ("Hakim, the Masked Dyer of Merv") and "El impostor inverosímil Tom Castro" ("The Improbable Impostor Tom Castro") are the most obvious examples, in which a political or social construction depends on the recognition or misrecognition of the faces of the eponymous characters. Hakim's governance of the province of Jorasán is conditional on the mask that covers his disfigured features. Tom Castro receives a handsome salary for allowing himself to be misrecognized as the military son of a wealthy English family.[11] The fact that both figures are illegitimate pretenders to the positions that gain them wealth and power is incidental. The play of recognition and misrecognition that the stories describe is merely an exaggerated example of the subsumption of the individual to an equivalential chain. The relationship of Tom Castro and Lady Tichborne who sees in Tom the face of her lost son is similar to that of every social or political construct that endeavors to link individual existences to its destiny.

While not always as evident as in the cases of these two stories, the themes of recognition and misrecognition occur throughout the book, paired in importance if not always in direct relation to the theme of death, the ultimate limit of all recognition. A notable example is that of "El incivil maestro de ceremonías Kotsuké no Suké" ("The Uncivil Master of Ceremonies Kôtsuké no Suké"), in which the central misrecognition hinges on the trappings of status and allegiance rather than the physical features of an individual, and which ends in an impressive series of hara-kiri. In other stories the theme of recognition revolves around the figure of *infamia* in the traditional sense, in which bad guys and pirates represent a limit to the social wholes that exclude them. Their deaths, or the ends of their reigns, represent the consummation of the equivalential chain. This is evident in the story of the widow-pirate Ching, when she surrenders to the history that is performed for her in the sky with kites and her legendary rule is followed by a return to commerce and development. Yet death in other instances is less fortuitous. If Sommer's national allegories end in fruitful unions between individuals and the social wholes that contain them, Borges's stories end in deaths that render such romance impossible. The characters are either killed in the name of "national" (or ethnic or regional) history, or are completely unassimilable to it.[12] In a sense, the stories represent a series of deaths that repeat the "jagged line of demarcation" that limits all attempts to write universal history.

The stories, as I have said, resemble national allegories. They all refer in one way or another to the constitution of national, regional, or ethnic imaginaries. The narratives revolve around emblematic figures who represent different historico-geographical myths. The most obvious of these, or at least the most well-known, is "Hombre de la esquina rosada" ("Man on the Pink Corner"), a story about compadres from the suburbs of Buenos Aires, which is written in a regionally inflected dialect, a dialect Borges admits in the prologue is not quite right. He says that compadres are individuals, and as such do not talk like the Compadre, which is a Platonic figure (HI 10). In a sense, this is true for all the protagonists in the volume. They bear resemblance to an ideal or emblematic figure, but then the abstraction is broken, the affiliation between the individual character and the larger fiction it is supposed to represent is unraveled. Besides "El hombre de la esquina rosada," there are three stories about the United States, which focus on three of its most mythic areas: Brooklyn, the Wild West, and the slave South. There is a story about commerce between the antipodes and Europe, a story about China, one about Japan, and one about the Middle East. In this way, Borges constitutes his own parodic "mapa del universo," not exactly in national allegories, since what are represented are not individual nationalities, but rather different sites in the Western global imaginary. Although Borges says there is a "buena falta de orientalismo" ("good lack of orientalism," 74) in the book, the stories are in fact based on pure orientalism and other mythic-isms that outline a specifically Eurocentric or Western "universal history."

The *infamia* of history, the unsaid or unsayable, does not lie only in the ends of the stories, in their fatal conclusions, but runs throughout the book. In the prologue to the 1954 edition, Borges explains that beneath the tumult of the book's *barroquismos,* "no hay nada":

> Los doctores del Gran Vehículo enseñan que lo esencial del universo es la vacuidad. Tienen plena razón en lo referente a esa mínima parte del universo que es mi libro. Patíbulos y piratas . . . pueblan (el libro) y la palabra infamia aturde en el título, pero bajo los tumultos no hay nada. (10)
>
> The doctors of the Great Vehicle teach that vacuity is the essential element of the universe. They are completely right in terms of that small part of the universe that is my book. Gallows and pirates . . . populate (the book) and the word "infamy" rattles in the title, but there is nothing beneath all the tumult.[13]

Contrary to appearances, Borges is not dismissing his book. The undercurrent of this nothing is the *infame* itself, not only that which is figured as infamous characters playing famous roles in foundational myths, but that which cannot be told as such, which can only *aturdir*. The nature of this "nada," and its telling and retelling throughout the book, reveals the undersides of the histories that are told, and thereby the nature of exclusion on which the *historias universales* are constructed. Universal histories, or histories that purport to define a certain universe, be it national, regional, or truly cosmic (as in the case of Hakim), are based on the exclusion of things that were they to "speak" would dissolve the history's pretension to represent a whole. Yet these things never go away completely, but remain there unspeaking, *infame,* potentially disruptive to the history that does not give them space.[14] The *infamia* or "nothing" that runs beneath the *historiar* of the book represents in fact the possibility of another kind of history. Through a peculiar form of parody, Borges endeavors to write "otherly"—that is, allographically—about history, thereby indicating the closure represented by "universal" versions of history and opening up the act of *historiar* in such a way as to point beyond such closure.

One of the figures most representative of the Western form of history appears in "El asesino desinteresado Bill Harrigan" ("The Disinterested Assassin Bill Harrigan"): the cowboy, fulfilling the mandate of the manifest destiny in the deserts of the southwestern United States. The story begins with the space on which this history is to be written and rewritten into its own mythic image: "La imagen de las tierras de Arizona, antes que ninguna otra imagen" ("The image of Arizona's lands, before any other image," 65). The opening paragraph describes these lands as a page (or screen—the cinematic allusion is clear throughout the stories) to be written, and Billy the Kid arrives on cue, an "emissary" who will write a story well-known to all with his "magic" bullets. Like the numerous cinematic cowboys who have traced this story before him, Billy moves from a "larval state" (indissociable, perhaps, from the larval beginnings of the nation) to the wide expanses of the West, following the "symbols and letters of his destiny," the Scripture-like destiny of a history already written (67).

The land itself calls, and history begins to rumble across the West: "Detrás de los ponientes estaba . . . la tierra fundamental cuya cercanía apresura el latir de los corazones como la cercanía del mar. El Oeste llamaba. Un continuo rumor acompasado pobló esos años: el de millares de hombres americanos ocupando el Oeste" ("Behind the sunsets was . . . the fundamental land whose proximity made the heart race just like the proximity of the sea. The West was calling. A continuous rhythmic rumbling filled those years: that of thousands of American men populating the West," 67–68). People move across the continent in waves, following the rhythmic march of their own desires. From this "rumor acompasado," the indistinguishable sounds of thousands of "hombres americanos" making their way across a land that is already theirs, we are taken to an individual story. The allegorical figure of *La Historia* herself begins to direct the scene, like a "certain movie director" (undoubtedly Josef Von Sternberg, mentioned in the prologue). The scene takes place in a bar situated in a desert, complete with cow skull, coyote howls, and, inside, "quienes hablan un idioma con muchas eses, que ha de ser español, puesto que quienes lo hablan son despreciados" ("people[15] who speak a language with many s's, which must be Spanish, since those who speak it are held in contempt," 69).

Billy, "rojiza rata de conventillo" ("a ruddy tenement rat"), is among the drinkers. The mention of his origins and his complexion remind us of the peculiar privilege he has possessed since birth, when his red hair and freckles contrasted with the hair of the African Americans among whom he grew up: "En ese caos de catinga y de motas, gozó el primado que conceden las pecas y una crencha rojiza. Practicaba el orgullo de ser blanco" ("In that chaos of odors and nappy hair, he enjoyed the privilege granted to those with freckles and red hair. He practiced the pride of being white," 66). After fourteen years of practicing this privilege, he finds himself in a New Mexican bar, surrounded by men who "overwhelm him" (69). Against this background falls "un silencio total," ignored only by the off-key singing of a drunk. A big Mexican man with the face of an old Indian woman ("un mejicano más que fornido, con cara de india vieja") has entered the bar. "En duro inglés" he wishes all the sons of bitches at the bar a good evening. Nobody responds. Billy asks who the man is; they whisper fearfully that he is Belisario Villagrán, from Chihuahua.

> Una detonación retumba en seguida. Parapetado por aquel cordón de hombres altos, Bill ha disparado sobre el intruso. La copa cae del puño de Villagrán, después el hombre entero. El hombre no precisa otra bala. Sin dignarse mirar al muerto lujoso, Bill reanuda la plática. "¿De veras?", dice."* "Pues yo soy Billy Harrigan, de New York." El borracho sigue cantando, insignificante. (69–70) (*Is that so? he drawled.)

> All of a sudden a shot rang out . Protected by the ring of tall men, Bill has shot the intruder. Villagrán's cup falls from his fist, and the man himself follows. He doesn't require a second bullet. Without deigning to look at the impressive corpse, Bill turns back to the conversation. "Is that so?" he says.* "Well I'm Billy Harrigan, from New York." The drunk continues his singing, insignificant. (*Is that so? he drawled.)

Against the murmur of the bar, a murmur that is different from the *rumor* that is rhythmically sweeping across the country—this one is filled with strange "s's" and doesn't seem to go anywhere nor permit any movement (Billy finds it "anonadante")[16]—Billy the Kid makes his first mark. The passage is full of references to sound: everything is indistinct until his shot rings out. The fearful whisper of the first half of the "plática" (and Villagrán's own harsh English) is then followed by a sentence as distinct as the shot: "Is that so? Well I'm Billy Harrigan, from New York," with the translation from the English provided at the bottom of the page as though to reinforce the clarity, against a text full of "s's," of Bill's self-assertion. History is thus written against this indistinct sound, which thereby becomes what we could call *infamia,* the unsaid that rumbles beneath the dominant form of history. Billy's white privilege allows him to speak—to drawl, no less—over the heads of, but protected by ("parapetado por"), the men that surround him in this desolate bar. His speech-shot (literally a *detonación*) effectively silences the formidable figure of Villagrán, who, feminized and linguistically at a disadvantage (with his "cara de india vieja" and his "duro inglés"), was in spite of the fear he produced in his compadres already excluded from the scene of phallogocentric history.[17]

In this land of like heroes, the outcome is predictable: "ya se adivina el apoteosis" (70). Everyone cheers, and someone observes that there are no marks on Billy's revolver and offers to carve one in to "significar" the death of Villagrán. Bill, now Billy the Kid, responds, "no vale la pena anotar mejicanos" ("it's not worth making marks for Mexicans"). Here the *infamia* of history is made explicit: Mexicans—along with Indians, blacks, and women, one presumes—are not worth "being noted down" ("anotados"), not worth being counted or told (at the end of his life Billy would boast that he had killed around twenty-one men, "sin contar mejicanos," 71). History is written without them, their voices stay back, in the indistinct murmur of the West, signified only perhaps by the drunk who continues to sing throughout this scene, "insignificante."

In the end Billy is betrayed by the history he helped write. In the "civilized" West that is erected thanks to figures like him, being white is no longer enough. A different kind of signification begins to reign. It is no longer the white hats against the dark ones, the sound of one gun against the other, but the commercial success of the frontier town against the wilderness of which the cowboy is now a part. Ironically, Billy dies *infame*. He wrote his own legend against the silence of others, and ends up sharing their silence: "puso en los mejicanos el odio que antes le inspiraban los negros, pero las últimas palabras que dijo fueron (malas) palabras en español" ("he placed in the Mexicans the hate that the blacks had earlier inspired in him, but the last words that he said were [bad] words in Spanish," 71). In his last moments, he represents the infamy of that history he earlier helped write, a history that leaves out the murmur of everything that is not (or is no longer) useful to it. The success of this history is staged by the townspeople, who dress up Billy's dead body and place it in the window of the best store in town, on the third day having to apply makeup (72).

From the cinematic image of the Southwest and the heroic figure of the cowboy to the phantasmatic grimace of Billy's face at the end, we see the jubilant march of history gone awry. What lies beneath film director History's direction is not the triumphant gleam promised by the silver screen, but a fundamental discontinuity: "La Historia, que a semejanza de cierto director cinematográfico, procede por imágenes discontinuas"

("History, who in resemblance to a certain film director, proceeds by discontinuous images," 68). Here we see the double tendency of cinema toward suture, on the one hand, and an acknowledgment of suture's own incompleteness, on the other, which is also the double possibility of allegory.[18] The story perfectly constructs a national allegory, moving back and forth between the individual and the national destinies with a deliberateness that can only be said to "linda[r] con su propia caricatura" ("border on its own caricature," 9). Yet the future of "social totality" (Jameson, "World Literature" 158) toward which this unstable union moves is represented in such a way as to reveal its own relationship to death. Bracketed between the cow-skull prop that History uses to decorate her desert scene and the made-up figure of Billy's dead body, Borges's *historia* represents, as Benjamin's description puts it, "the *facies hippocratica* of history as a petrified, primordial landscape. Everything about history that, from the very beginning, has been untimely, sorrowful, unsuccessful, is expressed in a face—or rather in a death's head." Clearly different from the image of death in the Baroque, however, Billy's death head represents a new kind of death for the West: one that is not, as the story's title puts it, disinterested, but which is geared precisely toward generating a particular kind of interest in the West. The rough years of expansion and lawlessness having ended, what remains is for the merchants and speculators to spur the interest of history by turning the Wild West into a tourist attraction. The grotesque death head of the process of commodification represents the silent face of history that can only look mournfully out from the shop window where it is placed on display.

The first story in the collection examines the pursuit of history's "interest" in another time and place. "El espantoso redentor Lazarus Morell" ("The Horrible Redeemer Lazarus Morell") concerns the slave South of the United States in the early years of the nineteenth century. The story begins, however, with a retrospective reflection on the beginnings of the history of the Americas, beginning with Carlos V and Bartolomé de las Casas. The "remote cause" of the events of the story is traced back to the imperial monarch and the perverse piety of the Catholic father who proposed to import African slaves to relieve the sufferings of the Indians forced to toil in the Antillean mines. To this curious version of philanthropy, the narration tells us, we owe a lengthy list of results:

> los *blues* de Handy, el éxito logrado en Paris por el pintor doctor oriental D. Pedro Figari, la buena prosa cimarrona del también oriental D. Vicente Rossi, el tamaño mitológico de Abraham Lincoln, los quinientos mil muertos de la Guerra de Secesión, los tres mil trescientos millones gastados en pen-

> siones militares, la estatua del imaginario Falucho, la admisión del verbo *linchar* en la décimatercera edición del Diccionario de la Academia, . . . la gracia de la señorita de Tal, el moreno que asesinó Martín Fierro, la deplorable rumba *El Manisero,* el napoleonismo arrestado y encalaborazado de Toussaint Louverture, la cruz y la serpiente en Haití, . . . la habanera madre del tango, el candombe. (17–18)

> Hardy's blues, the success achieved by the Uruguayan painter Dr. Pedro Figari, the good runaway prose of the also Uruguayan Dr. Vicente Rossi, the mythological stature of Abraham Lincoln, the five hundred thousand dead in the War of Secession, the three hundred thousand millions spent on military pensions, the statue of the imaginary Falucho, the admission of the verb "to lynch" into the thirteenth edition of the Academic Dictionary, . . . the grace of so-and-so's wife, the black man who killed Martín Fierro, the deplorable rumba *El Manisero,* the stunted and imprisoned Napoleonism of Toussaint L'Ouverture, the cross and the serpent in Haiti, . . . the habanera, mother of the tango, the candombe.

The origins of this story can be traced back to a beginning in the "laborious infernos of the Antillean mines," which was followed by a motley series of events, including the invention of musical genres; the wild or runaway ("cimarrona") prose of Uruguayan Vicente Rossi and his compatriot who achieved success in Paris; Abraham Lincoln's mythic dimensions, but also the thousands who died in the War of Secession, as well as the thousands of dollars spent on military pensions; the addition of new words such as *linchar* to the dictionary; so-and-so's grace; Martín Fierro's murderer; symbols of Haitian santeria; the habanera and the candombe. The items named include some of the most emblematic figures of American—North, South, and Caribbean—history: Martín Fierro and the tango, Abraham Lincoln and the blues, as well as the obscure mention of little-known painters, an unnamed lady's grace, a particular rumba. The list pieces together an "uneven enumeration" (7) of black experience throughout the Americas, a history that was begun by Las Casas and Carlos V. The list's excesses lead the critic Jorge Panesi to remark that "America itself is a Borgesean subject" (165). Perhaps the punctum of the list is the "statue of the imaginary Falucho." The epithet is in the inverse: the reference concerns a statue that no longer exists of a real historical figure, a black Argentine soldier who fought in the Argentine war of independence.[19] His statue used to stand near the statue of San Martín, a white hero of the same war, whose statue continues to be one of the most celebrated monuments of the nation. Such an "imaginary statue," like a phantom limb, indicates the presence of a "nothing" that can neither be allegorized into a discourse of black inter-American identity, nor completely erased from history. At the end of the list appears the story's protagonist, the apparent redeemer of these discordant elements of history: "la culpable y magnífica existencia del atroz redentor Lazarus Morell" ("the guilty and magnificent existence of the atrocious redeemer Lazarus Morell," HI 18).

The "theater" of this tale of atrocious redemption is the Mississippi River, "Father of all Waters" and "infinite and obscure sibling of the Paraná, Uruguay, Amazon, and Orinoco rivers." The story is a continental drama, involving events that could have taken place in any number of other places throughout the Americas, which are united, as the opening of the story reminds us, by their imperial beginnings. A parenthetical statement observes that Spanish imperialism formed a part of the development of North American history as a little-known crossover from South America: two Spanish conquistadores were the first to explore the waters of the North American river, one of whom—Hernando de Soto, who allegedly taught the last Incan monarch Atahualpa how to play chess during his months in prison—lies buried at its bottom. The Mississippi, the narration tells us, is a "río de aguas mulatas; más de cuatrocientos millones de toneladas de fango insultan anualmente el Golfo de Méjico, descargadas por él" ("river of mulatto waters; more than four hundred million tons of mud annually insult the Gulf of Mexico, discharged by it," 18–19). This description of a river of "aguas mulatas" with siblings throughout South America, underscores that the story does not just concern Southern blacks, but represents an example of something that has occurred in other parts of the hemisphere as well.

The "fango" expelled by the river flows between the two Americas, as though the sordid remainder of the shared history. The result is a swampland, evocative of Billy the Kid's and Monk Eastman's origins in the "pantanos" of New York: "Tanta basura venerable y antigua ha construido un delta, donde los gigantescos cipreses de los pantanos crecen de los despojos de un continente en perpetua disolución, y donde laberintos de barro, de pescados muertos y de juncos, dilatan las fronteras y la paz de su fétido imperio" ("So much old and venerable garbage has constructed a delta, where the gigantic cypresses of the swamps grow out of the ruins of a continent in perpetual dissolution, and where labyrinths of mud, dead fish, and reeds expand the borders of its fetid empire," 19). The "fetid empire" of the Father of all Waters, the river that runs through the heart of the United States, related to the central rivers of South America, transforms "old and venerable garbage" into "labyrinths of mud": the modern *despojos* of imperialist history, begun with Las Casas and Carlos V and merely grown more entrenched with time. Empire did not end with the conquest, remains of which lie buried ("sepultado") in the Mississippi's waters, but has followed its course through to the nineteenth century, where descendants of the African slaves that Las Casas brought to the Antilles were forced to toil under much the same conditions for a developing world economy. At the center of this economy was the massive figure of the United States, which, however, bore at its very center the seeds of its own destruction: the marshy lands around the Mississippi that represented "los despojos de un continente en perpetua disolución." The dissolution was not confined to the Southern states, but reached up into the North as well, along the Arkansas and Ohio rivers, where there dwelled an impoverished race of "squalid men" who possessed nothing more than sand, wood, and "turbid water" (19). The space of dissolution is "perpetual": it is not discharged with the "fango" into the Gulf of Mexico. The cypress, ancient symbol of mourning, grows to a gigantic size. It is the only thing that can thrive in this uncertain ground.

It is in here on the banks of the Mississippi where the descendants of Africans brought over by Las Casas and still living in slavery are forced to work "de sol a sol" ("from sun to sun"). There were no sunsets for the slaves like there were for the whites crossing the continent, writing the history of the West with their wagon wheels. In fact, there was no temporality at all, just a long, unending workday. Their only connection with history was through Scripture ("la Escritura"), and a metaphoric comparison between the Mississippi and the river Jordan, which they hoped would carry them away from their miserable conditions (20). Yet they possessed no "escritura" of their own. Their personal histories were "turbias" and hard to trace. They had names but no last names. Apart from mother–son relations, family connections were situational at best (19). "No sabían leer": like the men in the desert bar in "El asesino desinteresado Bill Harrigan," they lacked access to written language, either to read, write, or be written. And like the Mexicans' "idioma con muchas eses," the slaves' spoken language serves only to mark their absence from phallogocentric discourse. Theirs is an "inglés de lentas vocales" ("English of slow vowels"), in which they sing softly to themselves ("canturrear") in an "enternecida voz de falsete" ("tender falsetto voice"). This singing is not the "insignificant" singing of the drunk in the New Mexican bar. Though sung in falsetto, and each one to him or herself, they also sing "deep and in unison" ("hondos y en montón," 20), their song for freedom running deep beneath their bowed isolation. It was this singing that permitted them to invert the immobility prescribed in a scriptural history that was not theirs. In their song the Mississippi became the "magnificent image of the sordid Jordan," rather than the other way around, and the hope of redemption became a latent force ready to explode into a history that kept them chained beneath the interests of the white landowners.

The landowners were idle but avid figures who were intent on squeezing every possible penny out of both the land and their human property, the latter of which represented a bad but necessary investment (20). A good slave would cost a thousand dollars and then have the "ingratitude" to get sick and die. This is why they had to work from sunup to sundown to produce the annual harvest of cotton, tobacco, or sugar, exhausting not just the slaves but also the land, which began to turn into a muddy wasteland (a "desierto confuso y embarrado"). In the ruins of this ruinous land lived the "*poor whites,* la canalla blanca" (21). The poor whites were bottom-feeders from the very dregs of the social hierarchy, who would beg from the blacks pieces of food that had been stolen from the whites. But even in this abject position they maintained a sense of pride in being white, "sin un tizne" (without a stain). Lazarus Morell, the "atroz redentor," was one of these.

There are two Lazaruses in the Bible. One, the one Jesus raised from the dead, is the more well-known. There is another, however, whom Abraham specifically refused to raise from the dead (Luke 16:19–31). It is this tale that resonates with the story of Lazarus Morell. The parable tells of a rich man and a poor man named Lazarus, who lay at the rich man's gate and "desired to be fed with what fell from [his] table" (16:21). Both men die, and Lazarus is carried up to heaven and the rich man down to hell. The rich man calls up to heaven and asks Abraham to send Lazarus down to give him water, but Abraham refuses, first because the rich man didn't help Lazarus when he was alive, and secondly because "between us and you a great chasm has been fixed, in order that those who would pass from here to you may not be able, and none may cross from there to us" (16:26). The rich man then begs that Lazarus be allowed to go warn his five brothers who are still alive, but Abraham says that if they do not hear Moses and the prophets, "neither will they be convinced if some one should rise from the dead" (16:31). Lazarus Morell is in the peculiar position, thanks to the paradoxes of the slave South, of being able to play both sides of this story. He is, in a sense, both the poor man and the rich one. He was born at the bottom of the social order but, because of his whiteness, he can identify himself as an "old Southern gentleman" (HI 21). His white privilege enables him to cross the "great chasms" of Southern society—constituted by both race and class—preaching redemption and getting away with a pretty profit for himself.

Like the slaves, Morell "was no stranger to Scripture," but unlike them he was able to preach, "con singular convicción." A witness describes having heard him preach, with edifying ("edificantes") words and tears welling up in his eyes: "I knew he was an adulterer, a slave thief, and a murderer in the face of the Lord, but my eyes also cried" (22). Another account comes from Morell himself. He tells how one day finding himself in the pulpit, "Abrí al azar la Biblia, di con un conveniente versículo de San Pablo y prediqué una hora y veinte minutos. Tampoco malgastaron ese tiempo Crenshaw y los compañeros, porque se arrearon todos los caballos del auditorio. Los vendimos en el Estado de Arkansas" ("I opened the Bible at random, came across a convenient verse from St. Paul, and preached for an hour and twenty minutes. Crenshaw and the boys didn't waste that time either, because they rounded up all the horses from the audience. We sold them in the state of Arkansas"). In stark contrast to the language of slow vowels of the blacks, which wells up like a river but cannot, beneath the watchful eyes of the slave drivers, "build" anything, Morell's "edifying words" are capable of swindling an audience even when the audience knows perfectly well that he is a thief and a killer. The willing victims of his depredation lose their horses. The blacks are not so lucky: Morell's promises of redemption lead them straight to their deaths.

The original idea was not necessarily to kill anyone, but merely to capitalize on the slaves' hopes for freedom by offering to help them escape and then selling them again, with the idea that they would be helped to escape a second time and be given part of the proceeds from their own sale (23–24). There was only one problem: "el negro podía hablar; el negro, de puro agradecido o infeliz, era capaz de hablar" ("the black could speak; the black, out of pure gratitude or unhappiness, was capable of talking," 25). Morell had no real intention of really helping any slaves to freedom; he merely wanted to pocket the money from the sales to which the slaves willingly submitted themselves. He did not want to be confused with one of those anarchists from the North: "No era un yankee, era un hombre blanco del sur, hijo y nieto de blancos, y esperaba retirarse de los negocios y ser un caballero y tener sus leguas de algodonal y sus inclinadas filas de esclavos" ("He wasn't a Yankee, he was a white man from the South, son and grandson of whites, and he hoped to retire from his dealings and be a gentleman and have acres of cotton and inclined rows of slaves"). So in order to prevent the slaves from "spilling the secret" ("derramar el secreto"), the emancipation had to be complete: "los mulatos nebulosos de Lazarus Morell se transmitían una orden que podía no pasar de una seña y lo libraban [al negro] de la vista, del oído, del tacto, del día, de la infamia, del tiempo, de los bienhechores, de la misericordia, del aire, de los perros del universo, de la esperanza, del sudor y de él mismo" ("Lazarus Morell's nebulous mulattos would transmit an order that might be nothing more than a sign and they would liberate the black man from sight, from hearing, from touch, from the day, from infamy, from time, from his benefactors, from compassion, from the air, from the dogs of the universe, from hope, from sweat, and from himself," 25–26). A bullet, a knife, or a blow and the turtles and catfish of the Mississippi were the only receptors of the slave's "última información."

Lazarus, whose namesake in the Bible was presented with an unbreachable chasm, talks his way across the "great chasm" dividing the antebellum South, represented by the mulatto waters of the Mississippi. The river, which represented the hope of freedom to the slaves, so much so that just touching its waters and feeling oneself in movement brought a sense of liberation (24), represents to Lazarus a singular source of income. He knew from his humbug readings of the Bible that the promise of freedom or redemption it described was negotiable. With some fast talking, he was free to use the abyss as he wished: to maintain the great divide between the blacks and the whites, and merely situate himself more comfortably on one side of it, thus raising himself out of the abject social conditions that placed him, a white man, beneath the blacks.

Language, specifically the word of Scripture, serves as the medium by which he convinces the slaves to entrust themselves to the redemptive waters of the chasmic river. This has the effect of turning what might be the river of history—representing change and the hope for freedom—into an abyss: the same ahistorical abyss that Abraham points to from on high, and which Morell attempts to capitalize on from below. The illiterate slaves and the mulattos who speak in barely imperceptible signs can then be thrown into its muddy waters, fetid and filled with garbage after centuries of similar conditions. They are silenced, but it is hard to silence that which is already silent. The sinking of the unspoken or *infame*, the secrets the slaves were not allowed to spill, does not make them disappear entirely. It is the slaves' unsaid histories, including their sight, hearing, touch, infamy, time, and hope, among other things, that creates a latent, but also *perpetual* dissolution at the center of the North American continent. Like the "nothing" that rumbles ("aturde") beneath the text of the "Historia universal" itself, and the language of s's that whistles through the West in "El desinteresado asesino Bill Harrigan," the *infamia* of the slaves lies beneath the surface of history as it is told: unspoken, but speaking its silence. This unspoken history threatens to turn the ahistorical abyss represented by Abraham's chasm and Morell's secular appropriation of it, back into a river: the magnificent symbol of freedom that the slaves could voice only in song.

That the force of the "perpetual dissolution" did not quickly destroy individuals like Morell, nor an entire tradition of the brutal silencing of people based on the color of their skin, does not prove its inefficacy. As the beginning of the story tells us, the silenced secrets of the slaves had distant and irregular ("dispar") historical influences, largely, but not by any means exclusively, in musical form. Slavery at least was dissolved, though not until five hundred thousand lay dead. The forms of violence specifically reserved for blacks were eventually, like the word "linchar," acknowledged in written discourse. But, as the opening list of blacks' contributions to history tells us, music continued to be a favored form of expression of the descendants of those whose secrets could not be told, perhaps because it is a telling that does not, like the admission of the verb "linchar" to the Academic Dictionary, attempt to reduce the past to what can be known and incorporated into official history. Music is a form of expression that allows the unsaid to "aturdir" (bang, rattle, or disturb) what is said or sung in the form of rhythm and beat.[20] Furthermore, the dissolution that the story describes at the center of the continent and throughout the Americas constitutes a perpetual disturbance that lies at the center of all universal history. A relationship with this perpetual force represents the possibility of redemption, one that is not an interested swindle like Morell's, but which would, as in the slaves' songs, turn the mire of history into freedom.[21]

Ironically, in the remainder of the story Morell tries to tap into the power represented by the slaves he was accustomed to killing. The nephew of a white landowner who had lost a number of slaves turns him in to the authorities, the social chasm that Morell had tried to conquer proving ultimately insuperable. In revenge, Morell decides to turn things around and foment a major slave rebellion—"una sublevación total . . . una respuesta continental: una respuesta donde lo criminal se exaltaba hasta la redención y la historia" ("a total uprising . . . a continental response: a response in which criminality would be exalted all the way to redemption and history," 27). Yet it was not given to Morell to lead the continent to redemption. Unlike the cinematographer "La Historia" who directed the scenes of "El asesino desinteresado Bill Harrigan" with some degree of finesse, the lower-case "history of the Mississippi" neglects to take advantage of the "sumptuous opportunities" of scenes such as "Morell capiteando puebladas negras que soñaban ahorcarlo, Morell ahorcado por ejércitos que soñaba capitanear" ("Morell leading black groups that dreamed of hanging him, Morell hung by armies that he dreamt of leading," 29).

Juan José Saer notes Borges's propensity for the "dismantled" epic, in which an apparently epic quest ends prosaically with a death in a hospital bed (*Concepto* 285–87). Morell's story is "interrupted" (the final section is titled "La interrupción"), and the epic end he would have wished for himself, or which "la historia" lets slip by, fizzles into a distinctly unepic end. Against poetic "symmetry," Morell does not even end up at the bottom of the great river. Instead, he dies "infame" like Billy, although less spectacularly: he dies of pulmonary congestion, outside of the history he tried to create, nearly unnoticed under an assumed name in the common room of a hospital. In the days that followed, the slaves he had tried to organize attempt their rebellions ("quisieron sublevarse"), but they are put down, "sin mayor efusión de sangre" ("without much loss of blood"). In the end, his efforts at redemption prove useless at both ends at which he tried it. He was not able to rise in the social order, nor was he able to raise ("sublevar") the bottom of the social order to overturn it. He dies a failed redeemer forgotten by a history that nonchalantly refuses his offers of redemption.

Magical Endings Et Cetera

As though a commentary on the nature of endings in general, the final section of *Historia universal de la infamia* is titled "Etcétera," and is made up of what Borges says in the prologue to the book are translations and readings: "En cuanto a los ejemplos de magia que cierran el volumen, no tengo otro derecho sobre ellos que los de traductor y lector" ("As for the examples of magic that close the volume, I have no other right over them than that of translator and reader," 7). The title of the section itself is enough to suggest an ending that is neither finite, transcendent, nor epic, but one that leads to an ongoing alterity: "cetera" means "for the rest" or "otherwise." The fact that this "and otherwise" is constituted by translations and readings further suggests the form of an ending that is not definitive. Several of the parables show the only possibility of an epic or finite ending to be precisely a display of magic, a "(mis)representation" that its observers are all too willing to believe. In this section of endings, however, such illusions are dismantled and the ongoing nature of history—including both life and death—is shown to be the only real ending. Like the apparent closure and autonomy of a work of literature that is opened up by the act of translation and made to go on "otherwise" into a historical movement that reveals that it too was part of an "et cetera," the stories in this section reveal that life and death continue on regardless of all attempts to produce closure, whether in a sociopolitical constitution or divine transcendence. This unending "otherwise" is a continuation of the "nothing" that "aturde" beneath the stories of the *Historia universal,* and its perpetual potential to disturb all claims to a universal history or the equivalential chains of more local—that is, regionalist or nationalist—ones.

One of the stories in this section emblematically represents how the "nothing" on which political-historical constitution is based must be carefully guarded for that constitution to function. "La cámara de las estatuas" ("The Chamber of Statues") tells a tale of monocracy from *A Thousand and One Nights*. The story goes that in Andalucía there was a strong castle whose gate "no era para entrar ni aun para salir, sino para que la tuvieran cerrada" ("was not for entering nor leaving, but only to be kept closed," 113–14). Every time one king died and another inherited the throne, the new king would add a new lock to the gate. This went on for twenty-four years, until the twenty-fifth king (a usurper) was throned and, against the wishes of the court, instead of adding another lock to the gate, ordered that the twenty-four locks be removed and the gate opened. Inside the castle was a series of rooms that represented different elements of historical governance: warfare, cartography, science, genealogy, a mirror, a table, an elixir for converting currency. Yet the final room, which was so long that an archer could shoot an arrow as far as he could and still not touch the other side, was empty but for an inscription that said that any intruder to the castle would be overthrown within the year. This indeed came to pass, and the conquering nation, not to repeat the mistake of the usurper, entombed the contents of the castle in a pyramid.

The allegorical representation of the kingdom's elements of power opens onto a space of nothing: an empty room, empty except for an inscription that explains the consequences of having trespassed its empty space, the internal limit of all political constitution. The court is well aware of this nothing, and knows that it needs to keep it enclosed for the governing body to function. History is constructed through a generational transmittance of this knowledge and by the addition in every generation of another lock to keep it safe. The illegitimate twenty-fifth king did not know of the nothing, nor of the necessity to keep it enclosed, and rather than add a lock he opened those of his twenty-four predecessors. What he found was a fantastic representation of everything the kingdom already had, with the inexplicable addition of the empty room, the trespass of which signaled the end of the royal reign. History could no longer be constructed around a carefully guarded emptiness, but was opened up to an invading "otherwise," in this case a body of invaders who were interested in constructing their own claim to history, and who knew better than to leave the empty basis of their power unguarded.

This is not, it must be added, the only hope for the "nothing" that lies at the center of political constitution. The Arab invaders were not interested in acknowledging a self-constitutive otherness. Like the Christian defenders they wanted Andalucía for themselves, and the story switched sides several times until the Christians found the bigger lockbox in the form of the Inquisition. This is different from what the slaves in "El espantoso redentor Lazarus Morell" want. Their singing for a river of redemption represents a force that would break all possibility of enclosure or exclusion, and open the constitution of the social to a form of history that would not be represented by the addition of locks and increased immobility, but by the breaking of all such devices of enclosure.

Another story in the "Etcétera" section describes a visit to a similarly vaultlike space as that of the chamber in "La cámara de las estatuas." In "El brujo postergado" ("The Wizard Who Was Made to Wait") a Spanish dean visits a magician in Toledo to learn the art of magic. The magician responds to the dean's request with suspicion, suggesting that the dean would use whatever skills the magician taught him for his own power, and would soon forget the magician who had taught them to him. The dean assures him that this will not happen and that he will always be at the magician's orders. Apparently reassured, and after having ordered his servant to prepare some partridges for dinner, the magician leads the dean to an iron door in the floor, which they lift and proceed down a stone staircase for what seems like such a long way that the dean reflects they must be nearly underneath the nearby Tajo River. At the bottom of the staircase there is a library and a room of magical instruments. The two men are looking over the books when a succession of peculiar events begins to take place.

First, two men walk in with a letter for the dean from his uncle the bishop, telling him that he is very ill and that the dean should come at once. The dean is disturbed by the news, but decides that he wants to stay to continue with his studies, and sends a letter of regret back with the men. Three days later some men dressed in mourning arrive with a letter telling the dean that his uncle has died and that he is being considered as his successor. Ten days after that some more men arrive and kiss his hands, addressing him as bishop. The magician tells his student that he is very happy that such good news should make its way to his house, and asks the newly ordained bishop if he would consider giving the vacant deanship to one of his sons. The bishop responds that he had reserved that position for his own brother, but that he is determined the magician should be rewarded, and proposes that the two men travel together to Santiago de Compostela. Six months later, the bishop receives news that the Pope has offered him the archbishopric of Tolosa. Hearing this, the magician reminds him of his promise, and asks him to leave the bishopric to his son. The archbishop responds that he had reserved that position for his own uncle, but promises he will not forget the magician. And so it goes, until he is appointed Pope, at each step filling all the positions with his own family and denying the magician anything, until one day the magician asks for just a bit of food so that he might return home to Spain, and the Pope refuses this as well. At this point the passed-over magician ("el brujo postergado") says in a steady voice: "Then I guess I will have to eat the partridges that I ordered for tonight's dinner," and it is revealed that the entire ascent to power was merely a display meant to test the dean's intentions (123).

Like the curious king in "La cámara de estatuas," the dean yearns to discover the secrets of governance. He is led underground to a secret chamber that is so far from the iron door where they began that it seems like it must be beneath the river that crosses Spain and Portugal. There beneath the currents of the sociopolitical world the dean sees history unfold before his eyes and then disappear, his own glory and his family's power reduced to nothing. Like the previous story, the discovery of this nothing signifies mortality, although in this case it is only the mortality of hearing that it is dinnertime when one thinks one is the pope. The tomblike space, however, is common to both stories, and the desire to enter it is followed in both cases by a realization that its locked abyss is deleterious to the political aspirations of the two men. In the latter case, the question of representation is more clearly addressed. The magician actively misrepresents the nothing that underlies history so as to show the dean who has the greater power. The illusion he produces is along the lines of the nearly epic endings that conclude in frustration in hospital beds. In this sense, the story stages the "examples of magic" that Borges says end the *Historia universal:* the illusion of ending that in the end opens history up to its own inconclusive nature. Rather than a glorious ascent to the papacy, the dean finds himself stuck with the "*etcétera*" of life and death, in a dark cell beneath the Tajo River. The magician, to his credit, remains there as well, puttering with his books and revealing to church fathers their mortal shortcomings.

It is the opposite with the writer and theologian Melanchthon, who is the subject of the first story of the "*Etcétera*" section, "Un teólogo en la muerte" ("A Theologian in Death"). Like the dean who would be pope, and like Lazarus Morell, Melanchthon is a firm believer in the redemption of history, and particularly in the redemptive power of his own words. The story tells that when the scholar died, he was given a house "in the other world" that looked just like his house on earth (111). Everything in the house looked exactly the same, so that when Melanchthon woke up, "reanudó sus tareas literarias como si no fuera un cadáver" ("he resumed his literary tasks as though he were not a corpse"), and he wrote for several days on the justification of faith. After several weeks, the furniture in his house began to fade away, but Melanchthon continued writing. At a certain point he is placed in an underground chamber ("un taller subterráneo," 112) with other theologians like him. He has admirers, although some are without faces and others look like dead people, and at a certain point the words that he writes start to disappear. To convince his admirers that they are in heaven, he arranges with a magician to construct images of splendor and serenity, but these would disappear when the admirers went away, and sometimes before.

Unlike the passed-over magician of the previous tale, Melanchthon denies his mortal, earthly (or subterranean) existence, believing himself to be either in heaven or on the way to heaven in spite of all evidence to the contrary. He is an almost literal representation of the baroque dramatists who saw in the face of death an "angel's countenance," although in his case (as perhaps in the Baroque as well) the angels' countenances eventually begin to disappear and he has to hire a magician to create a spectacle of divine transcendence. What is perhaps most striking about this passage is the scene of his writing of redemption in the midst of unrecognized death: he continues to write "as though he were not a corpse." Language is a tool that he uses to ignore his condition of mortality, to misrecognize or misrepresent it, like the faces and furniture that represent transcendence or at least a sense of home, but which—like the faces and furniture as well—begins to write its own erasure. The story demonstrates an undying belief in language's transcendent qualities, but in the end language asserts its nontranscendent quality, disappearing and decomposing like the mortal bodies around him. In a sense, this story is like the final story of the "*Etcétera*" section, Borges's well-known parable about the imperial map that was designed to coincide exactly with the Empire's territories, and which began to decompose beneath the ravages of time and weather until only a few tattered shreds of the map remained, which were inhabited by animals and beggars (131–32). Here the "otherwise" of history manifests itself in the writing—theological or cartographical—that it was hoped would deny it, language proving itself to be, as Benjamin described, stations in the secular Passion of history, rather than the means of ascent to an ahistorical transcendence.

Time and again, the stories in the *Historia universal de la infamia* represent failed attempts to raise history to a final totality. Lazarus and Melanchthon, the two would-be redeemers, as well as Billy, the Spanish dean, and the Andalusian king, all find themselves in a fallen state in spite of their attempts to achieve the contrary. The representations of history that they hope to embody and produce are structures of equivalence that are based on a constitutive exclusion, a "nothing" that nonetheless disrupts the claims to wholeness of such representations, and in the case of our protagonists, reduces them to nothing as well. This repeated trope of a fall represents not a final closure, but a fall into historical existence, an unending historicity that cannot be contained in structures of identity and exclusion. Borges's stories represent the limits of such structures, allegorically or allographically inscribing into their aspirations to totality the irreducible alterity of history, a "nothing" that lies beneath their claims and interrupts and distorts their gloriously configured ends. The end of the book represents the never-ending nature of history as a series of translations and readings in which the magic of closure is revealed to be a spectacular ruse that begins to disappear even as it reaches its most conclusive representation. The final story of the volume emblematically represents the historical representation that is told throughout the stories as the allegorization of all ideological "mapa[s] del universo." The stories enact what Chakrabarty describes as a kind of history writing that attempts "to look towards its own death by tracing that which resists and escapes the best human effort at translation across cultural and other semiotic systems" (290). This death is not an end, but the possibility of a beginning, an *Ursprung,* of a mode of writing history that does not try to complete translations of national (or ethnic, regional, or social) identities at the expense of an untranslatable excess.

Chapter 4

Reading History's Secrets in Benjamin and Borges

> Buscad, buscadlos:
> en el insomnio de las cañerías olvidadas,
> en los cauces interrumpidos por el silencio de las basuras.
> No lejos de los charcos incapaces de guardar una nube . . .
> Porque yo los he visto:
> en esos escombros momentáneos que aparecen en las neblinas.
> Porque yo los he tocado:
> en el destierro de un ladrillo difunto
> venido a la nada desde una torre o un carro.
> Nunca más allá de las chimeneas que se derrumban
> ni de esas hojas tenaces que se estampan en los zapatos.
> En todo esto.
>
> —Rafael Alberti, "Los ángeles muertos"

The driving question behind the preceding chapters, and perhaps behind any reading of Borges, is, does Borges present the world as something that can be contained in words, concepts, or structures, or does he repeatedly disavow all possibility of containment? In the first two chapters we examined the idea, proposed by some of his most influential critics, that in his early writings Borges was intent on establishing a firm *criollista* identity for the cultural space of Buenos Aires: in the first case, by grounding his representations of the city with roots that extend back into his own familial past, and in the second, by creating a biographical frame that would give a finite structure to a regional form of identity. We also saw how Borges, while at times acknowledging a desire for such mythical foundations, repeatedly stages their impossibility. Rather than rejecting modernity in favor of a timeless past, his city poems and the biography of Evaristo Carriego are acutely attentive to a historicity that cannot be contained either in regressive constructions of identity, or linear and progressive narratives. In these works, Borges effectively critiques the notion of progress and a privative understanding of life that would deny anything that does not fit into representations of identity and linearity, including memory, mortality, and the complex nature of life itself. In chapter 3, we considered the potential consequences of a representation that does not acknowledge its own specters, or which keeps them locked up as a means of asserting its hegemony. What lies outside of representations of linearity and identity are often voiceless forces of history that do not have direct access to language, but which are nevertheless capable of shaking and disturbing dominant forms of representation in such a way that opens new possibilities for the future.

In this attention to a historicity that can never be fully represented, Borges demonstrates important similarities to Benjamin. Both writers are interested in the way life, history, and time manifest themselves through language and memory as an excess or alterity that interrupts naturalized narratives of history and identity that, as Benjamin puts it, tend to favor the "victors of history." Although Benjamin attributed a more explicitly political function to such epistemological interruption, Borges also understood the ethical and political implications of practices of thinking, reading, and writing that were attentive to the limits and contingencies of progressive representations of history and totalizing distinctions between self and other. Both thinkers stress the need to look for ways to represent life—past and present, individual and collective—that actively indicate an exteriority to representation and what they both call the "secrets of history."

Historical Idealism and the Materiality of Writing

Benjamin and Borges are both concerned with the distinction between what could be called an idealist and a materialist conception of history. This distinction corresponds to the clumsy distinction that Borges quotes Schopenhauer as making between the world "inside our heads" and the world "outside our heads" (OI 173). Generally speaking, idealism is the belief that the world is essentially "in our heads" or can be contained by our heads: by concepts, language, or other kinds of representation. Borges acknowledges that such a division is a suspect one, because as Berkeley and others have pointed out, the minute we consider something as being outside our heads, it is already in our heads. We cannot conceive of exteriority without internalizing it. The very notion of exteriority is an internalizing one. Berkeley fantastically concludes from this that there is nothing outside our heads: we cannot determine an autonomous existence to anything outside of our own consciousness. All materiality exists and all events in the world occur just because we think they do.

Exteriority thus contained and alterity denied, Berkeley makes an exception, which operates only on belief: that of the divine. Reality does not exist, a given object does not exist without one's own awareness of it, except for the fact that it is also in God's awareness, and since God is aware of everything all the time, we could say that things do have a kind of autonomous existence. But this "outside of the head" is not really an external or autonomous existence, since everything exists in God's head. That is to say, the world is ideally contained, either in our heads or in God's head, the latter of which contains the former, like the concentric spheres of the Ptolemaic universe.

Idealism, in this sense, can be understood as a doctrine that posits that there is nothing that is not or that cannot be comprehended by our minds, except perhaps the divine. This is not an incomprehensible divinity, but one that defines comprehension: it *is* absolute comprehension. Pascal was one of the first (although Borges points out that he was not really the first) to contemplate the possibility that the divine might not be something containable, but might in fact define the undefinable, a possibility that he found "terrifying." Yet even more frightening, Borges suggests, is the idea that there is nothing outside our heads except another head that contains us—this is the familiar Borgesean motif of the dream within the dream, or the god behind the god.[1]

The sense of containment professed by idealism reached particularly dangerous heights in the twentieth century. Borges suggests that the belief that the world can be contained, comprehended, or represented without remainder is the basis of totalitarian movements such as fascism and Stalinism. It is also the basis of what Benjamin calls historicism. Benjamin wrote his most urgent writings on history under increasing and ultimately fatal persecution from the Nazis, but he was adamant that it would not suffice to name the enemy "fascism." In "Theses on the Philosophy of History," written just months before his death on the occupied French border, he argues that part of fascism's success was due to the fact that those who want to fight it share some of its fundamental concepts, and are therefore unable to defeat it without also defeating themselves. One of the most important of these concepts is that of history. Historicism is the belief that what goes on in the world—the "outside the head"—can be contained "within the head" or within representation, and especially within a progressively oriented structure that subsumes both past and future under an ever-expanding present.

Borges similarly acknowledged that the threat represented by fascism was not limited to fascism alone, but was constituted by some of Western thinking's most basic principles. In *Otras inquisiciones,* written mostly during the 1940s, the question of history forms an important subtext, and includes various mentions of fascism's relative victories and defeats. In a review of a book by H. G. Wells on world revolution, Borges observes that "incredibly, Wells is not a Nazi" ("Dos libros," OI 126). This bizarre statement about the evidently left-wing Wells is explained in the next sentence: "Increíblemente, pues casi todos mis contemporáneos lo son, aunque lo nieguen o lo ignoren" ("Incredibly, because almost all my contemporaries are, even if they deny or ignore it"). This powerful accusation that the majority of Borges's contemporaries are Nazis, whether or not they know or admit to it, concerns the use of concepts that defined Nazism but which are commonly employed throughout the rest of the political spectrum. Borges gives the example of how even "vindicators of democracy, who believe themselves to be very different from Goebbels, urge their readers in the same dialect as the enemy" to follow the logics of nationalist and ethnic identity that form the basis of Nazism.

In the essay that follows, "Anotación del 23 de agosto de 1944," Borges ponders the perplexing fact that at the news of the Nazi defeat in Paris, Argentine supporters of fascism seemed to show signs of happiness and relief.[2] He explains this paradox as owing to the fact that Nazism is based on the same principles as nonfascist Western culture, which asserts that "there is an order—a single order—possible" in the world ("hay un orden—un solo orden—posible," 132). Nazism, which is based on the same belief in a singular order as the rest of the West, suddenly recognizes itself as an outsider—as "barbarism," "a gaucho, a redskin"—and desires its own destruction. Nazism carries out the logic of Western civilization to its extremes, which means on the one hand that almost everyone is a Nazi, and on the other hand that Nazism itself is an impossibility, since it tries to put a different name to something that is already universal. It is therefore unreal ("el nazismo adolece de irrealidad, como los infiernos de Erígena"), reality being defined as what is contained within the single order of the West, and it desires its own annihilation to the point that even "Hitler wants to be defeated."

It is clear that the world cannot be contained by a "single order." Taking into account the idealists' caveat that when we consider things that lie outside our comprehension we are in a sense comprehending them, how then do we think of an exterior to our comprehension, to the orders and concepts that we use to understand the world? This is one of the questions that Borges and Benjamin address in their writings on the representation of life, time, and history. They attempt to conceive of a form of representation that, rather than condemning to unreality what it does not comprehend, opens a closed sense of reality to what it does not contain.

Both thinkers can be said to engage in what Benjamin calls a "materialist historiography": a way of thinking and writing about history that represents in its writing (*graphy*) traces of a "materiality" that lies outside of the idealist ordering of things. De Man provides one of the most incisive interpretations of the Benjaminian relationship between history and materiality when he describes "the materiality of actual history" (*Rhetoric* 262).[3] In his reading of this phrase, Derrida cautions that de Man's term refers to a "materiality without matter" ("Typewriter Ribbon" 281). Benjamin's historiographical materialism is not concerned with a determinate analysis of the physical objects and institutions that make up everyday life. Although Benjamin was a collector of bits and pieces of the world around him, it was not the physical nature of these artifacts that defined the sense of their materiality for him. Materiality is not synonymous with "concrete." It describes something that exceeds conceptualization; it is the very name of the "outside our head," and as such, is intelligible only as traces on our experience.

None of these writers takes the phenomenological path that would seem to follow from such a description of materiality. Much as Benjamin says that an original text can be understood through its translations, de Man insists that history occurs (is enacted—"actual history") in representation and can be understood only through representation (*Resistance* 83). This does not mean that history is contained in representation or in our "heads." On the contrary, writing or translation (translation coming from the Latin *trans-latio,* changing from one side to another—from the "outside our heads," let's say, to the "inside our heads") breaks open the sense that we can contain the world inside our heads, and indicates that the concepts that we use to order the world are not capable of containing the infinite multiplicity of the universe. De Man and Derrida ascribe a sense of "mourning" to such an acknowledgment of incompletion. Derrida, discussing a passage in de Man, describes "the irreducibility of a certain history, a history with which all one can do is undertake 'true' mourning" (*Memoires* 53). He says that what de Man means by "true" mourning," which may not be "truly possible or possible at present," seems to dictate a tendency: "the tendency to accept incomprehension, to leave a place for it, and to enumerate coldly, almost like death itself, those modes of language which, in short, deny the whole rhetoricity of the true (the non-anthropomorphic, the non-elegaic, the non-poetic, etc.)" (31). Benjamin and Borges share this tendency. They both undertake, in different ways and with different urgencies, what can be called a mournful kind of writing—although it might also be called celebratory[4]—that leaves a place for what cannot be comprehended, and seeks to open the present to what they both call history's secrets, which includes among other things the absolute uncontainability of the future.

The Conquests of Time

Borges tends to be more associated with the question of time than with history per se. His fictions play with different notions of time, he mock refutes it in his "Nueva refutación del tiempo" ("New Refutation of Time"), and he considers its possible transcendence in *Historia de la eternidad* (*History of Eternity*), whose title is of course a paradox, since eternity is something that by definition should be beyond temporal-historical change. Although his interest in time may seem on the surface to be nothing more than conceptual games, it concerns the very serious issue of how we order our world. Beneath his playfulness, Borges is warning us that the structuring of time is an act that can have very real consequences.

In an essay from 1928, "La penúltima versión de la realidad" ("The Penultimate Version of Reality"), Borges considers the concept of a single and unifying time as a kind of imperialism. The essay begins with a consideration of a book by [Count] Korzybski, *The Manhood of Humanity,* based on a "passionate" review of it by Francisco Luis Bernárdez. The book describes three different dimensions of life: plant, animal, and human. This absurd concept of vital dimensionality, described respectively as "length, width, and depth," is related to how the respective forms of life occupy or take up the world around them (D 39). Plants, which supposedly live a two-dimensional life—hence, the designation "length"—do not have a notion of space. Animals do possess a notion of space, hence their occupation of a spatial width. Plants are said to "acopiar" (gather) only energy, while animals "amontonan" (accumulate) space. Humans, on the other hand, are unique in that they "acaparan" (hoard or monopolize) time:

> La diferencia substantiva entre la vida vegetal y la vida animal reside en una noción. La noción del espacio. Mientras las plantas la ignoran, los animales la poseen. Las unas, afirma Korzybski, viven acopiando energía, y los otros, amontonando espacio. Sobre ambas existencias, estática y errática, la existencia humana divulga su originalidad superior. ¿En qué existe esta suprema originalidad del hombre? En que, vecino al vegetal que acopia energía y al animal que amontona espacio, el hombre acapara tiempo. (40)

> The substantive difference between vegetable life and animal life resides in one notion. The notion of space. While plants are ignorant of it, animals possess it. The former, Korzybski affirms, live gathering energy, and the latter accumulate space. Against both existences, ecstatic and erratic, human existence divulges its original superiority. In what does the supreme originality of man consist? In that, neighbor to the vegetable that gathers energy and the animal that accumulates space, man hoards time.

Borges recounts how Rudolf Steiner presents a similar vision of the universe. According to Steiner, man is master of the plant, animal, and mineral kingdoms, and also has dominion over time, owing especially to the concept of "self": "Dueño de esas tres jerarquías es . . . el hombre, que además tiene el yo: vale decir, la memoria de lo pasado y la previsión del porvenir, vale decir, el tiempo" ("Master of these three hierarchies is man, who moreover has the 'I': that is to say, the memory of the past and the foresight of the future, that is to say, time," 41). Master of the universe, and armed with a solid sense of who he is, man is also master of time, a concept that he uses to order the world according to a structure based on "succession and duration." Borges observes that the association of time with human domination over the universe is a constant in the metaphysical tradition. He declares dryly, "Sea de Schopenhauer o de Mauthner o de la tradición teosófica o hasta Korzybski, lo cierto es que esa visión sucesiva y ordenadora conciencia humana frente al momentáneo universo, es efectivamente grandiosa" ("Whether it be from Schopenhauer or from Mauthner or from the theosophic tradition or even from Korzybski, what is certain is that that successive vision and ordering human consciousness in face of the momentary universe is effectively grandiose," 42). With evident Nietzschean overtones, Borges observes that man's capacity to order the world around his sense of who he is is truly staggering.

To dominate the plant, mineral, and animal realms, Steiner and Korzybski agree, is not enough. In man's eagerness to conquer the material side of the world, he forgets his primary task, which is to conquer time: "El materialismo dijo al hombre: Hazte rico de espacio. Y el hombre olvidó su propia tarea. Su noble tarea de acumulador de tiempo" ("Materialism said to man: Make yourself rich in space. And man forgot his proper task. His noble task as accumulator of time"). This is how the "sombra" of progress, imperialism, is born: "Quiero decir que el hombre se dió a la conquista de las cosas visibles. A la conquista de personas y de territorios. Así nació la falacia del progresismo. Y como una consecuencia brutal, nació la sombra del progresismo. Nació el imperialismo" ("I mean to say that man gave himself over to the conquest of visible things. To the conquest of peoples and territories. This is how the fallacy of progressivism was born. And as a brutal consequence, the shadow of progressivism was born. Imperialism was born"). Korzybski insists on the necessity of returning man to his true capacity of conquering time, instead of just space: "Que el hombre vuelva a capitalizar siglos en vez de capitalizar leguas" ("May man return to capitalizing centuries instead of capitalizing leagues").

Borges insists that he does not understand this distinction. Imperialism, he says, has always been a conquest of time as well as space. The conquest of space—territories, peoples—implies the conquest of time as well: "acumular espacio no es lo contrario de acumular tiempo: es uno de los modos de realizar esa para nosotros única operación" ("the accumulation of space is not the contrary of accumulating time: it is one of the modes of realizing what is for us the same operation" (43). He gives the example of the British colonization of India: "No acumularon solamente espacio, sino tiempo: es decir, experiencias, experiencias de noches, días, descampados, montes, ciudades, astucias, heroísmos, traiciones, dolores, destinos, muertes, pestes, fieras, felicidades, ritos, cosmogonías, dialectos, dioses, veneraciones" ("They did not accumulate only space, but also time: that is to say, experiences, experiences of nights, days, terrains, mountains, cities, cleverness, heroisms, betrayals, pains, destinies, deaths, diseases, beasts, happiness, rites, cosmogonies, dialects, gods, venerations").

Time in this sense is linked for Borges to a kind of domination or conquest: the grandiose imposition of a "sucesiva y ordenadora conciencia" on the momentary and ephemeral nature of the universe and its experiences. It is a conquest that is akin to, and indeed part of, the imperialist conquest of territories such as India but also, of course, Argentina and Latin America, as well as the global accumulation of capitalism. Korzybski's plea to return to a capitalization of centuries instead of a capitalization of leagues, far from being a shadow of progressivism, would seem to be its very essence. As Borges points out, it is inextricable from the imperialist tradition, and the English empire would seem to be the perfect example of the conquest or capitalization of a century. The English empire imposed its never-ending "day"—on which the proverbial sun was never to set—on the territories it occupied, thereby conquering not only the visible aspects of the land ("la conquista de las cosas visibles"), but also the "invisible" ones, including days as well as nights, pains, joys, mountains, rites, and cosmogonies.

History's Secrets

In "La penúltima versión de la realidad," Borges describes an imperialist concept of time that admits no shadow. In a later essay, "El pudor de la historia" ("The Shame of History"), he discusses the question of history's shadows, or literally its "shame." The essay begins with an anecdote about Goethe, who had accompanied the Duke of Weimar in a military campaign to Paris in 1792. The Prussian party, the first representatives of a European army to attempt a peaceful missive after the Revolution, were "inexplicably rejected," an event that prompted Goethe to declare to his companions, "En este lugar y el día de hoy, se abre una época en la historia del mundo y podemos decir que hemos asistido a su origen" ("In this place and on this day, an epoch in the history of the world is opened, and we can say that we were present at its origin," OI 166). Borges remarks, "Desde aquel día, han abundado las jornadas históricas y una de las tareas de los gobiernos (singularmente en Italia, Alemania y Rusia) ha sido fabricarlas o simularlas" ("Since that day historic days have abounded, and one of the tasks of governments [especially in Italy, Germany, and Russia], has been to fabricate or simulate them"). Since Goethe's observation of the rejection of the Weimar party in Paris, there have been many "historical days" or historical military excursions, the word "jornada" connoting both senses: days that are at the same time military jaunts, days that are conquered or fabricated as political property. Such days, Borges goes on to say, "tienen menos relación con la historia que con el periodismo: yo he sospechado que la historia, la verdadera historia, es más pudorosa y que sus fechas esenciales pueden ser, asimismo, durante largo tiempo, secretas" ("have less relation with history than with journalism: I have suspected that history, true history, is more bashful and that its essential dates can be, for a long time, secret"). History—not that fabricated by governments, journalists, or those whom Borges acidly calls "professionals of patriotism" (168)—is something secret, or perhaps something so strange we cannot see it, even when we think we see everything. He cites as an example the unicorn, which, "en razón misma de lo anómalo que es, ha de pasar inadvertido" ("for the very reason of its anomaly, tends to pass unobserved," 166).

This shy or bashful history that guards a secret concerns a kind of representation that, unlike journalistic representation, does not pretend to make everything visible, or that does not attempt to conquer the "invisible" as well as "visible things." It is like what Borges describes as writing itself, which he distinguishes from the common perception of translation as the direct imitation of a visible text (D 105). Against this naive conception of translation as a traffic between visibilities, Borges describes writing as "un olvido animado por la vanidad . . . el conato de mantener intacta y central una reserva incalculable de sombra" ("a forgetting animated by vanity . . . the attempt to maintain intact and central an incalculable reserve of shadow"). In full Benjaminian fashion a few years avant la lèttre, Borges argues that translation is not exempt from this "olvido" or "sombra": "Un parcial y precioso documento de las vicisitudes que sufre [a text] quedan en sus traducciones" ("A partial and precious document of the vicissitudes that a text suffers remains in its translations"). The "affliction" of translation occurs whether one changes languages or not: "No hay esencial necesidad de cambiar de idioma" ("there is no essential need to change languages"). Furthermore, Borges says, continuing to resonate with Benjamin's theory of translation, no text is really an original one: "Presuponer que toda recombinación de elementos es obligatoriamente inferior a su original, es presuponer que el borrador 9 es obligatoriamente inferior al borrador H—ya que no puede haber sino borradores. El concepto de *texto definitivo* no corresponde sino a la religión o al cansancio" ("To assume that any recombination of elements is necessarily inferior to its original is to assume that draft 9 is necessarily inferior to draft H—since there can be only drafts. The concept of a definitive text corresponds only to religion or fatigue" (105–6).

Possession or the "Weak Force" of Redemption

This writing that keeps its "sombra" in reserve, a shadow that is also a "labyrinth of preterit projects," resembles Benjamin's descriptions of a history writing that would differ from the kind of historical representation privileged by fascism. Benjamin expresses at one point his intention to devise concepts that would be "completely useless for the purposes of fascism" (I 218). In "Theses on the Philosophy of History," he specifies that one of these "useless" or inappropriable concepts must be the concept of history. Like Borges, Benjamin stresses that the concepts employed by fascists are frequently engaged by even the most stalwart enemies of fascism. No matter how good their intentions, politicians who oppose fascism but insist on using the same concepts of history and identity cannot help but betray their cause. Benjamin urges the need to develop a "conception of history that avoids any complicity with the thinking to which these politicians continue to adhere" (258).

One of the concepts that the left was reluctant to let go of was the concept of progress and the idea that the working class would bring about the redemption of future generations (260). The most insidious of the aspects of the concept of progress is the role that is given to time: the idea that time is an empty track, a long empty hallway waiting to be filled by the march of history. Benjamin writes in a well-known passage, "The concept of the historical progress of mankind cannot be sundered from the concept of its progression through a homogenous, empty time. A critique of the concept of such a progression must be the basis of any criticism of the concept of progress itself" (261). The conception of time as empty space is like Korzybski's description of temporal colonization in which time is regarded as a passive object waiting for someone to come along and take possession of it. Like language that grasps its object as though it were a piece of bourgeois merchandise, such a conception implies a false sense of possession. Benjamin insists that language is not an empty vehicle for meaning, a guarantor of universal exchange between communicating subjects, but rather is a medium that shapes and transforms any exchange.[5] In this same sense, time is not an empty territory that history can simply occupy, but is full, as Borges says of India, of its own "days, nights, deaths, and dialects" that lie beneath the narratives that are imposed on it, and which have the potential to interrupt any sense of continuity, progression, or possession.

Benjamin describes three primary errors in the conception of history as possession, also known as historicism. The first is the idea that there is a universal history, a single story that includes the multiple histories of the world: "The first blow must be directed against the idea of universal history. The representation that the history of the human race is composed of its peoples is today, when the essence of the people is obscured as much by its actual structure as by its reciprocal relations, an evasion of mere mental laziness" (GS 1.3.1240).[6] Benjamin compares the idea of universal history to the utopia of a universal language, which is an evident impossibility in our Babelic world. The second error of historicism is the representation of history as something "that lets itself be told. In a materialistic investigation, the epic moment must inevitably be exploded in the course of construction" (1.3.1240–41).[7]

The third bastion of historicism, which "is the strongest and hardest to assault," concerns the attempt to empathize (*einfühlen*) with the victors of history. The victors of history are not only the victors of individual conflicts: they are those who "inherit" a certain conception of history, a victorious version of history—one that is remembered by, and that refers to or justifies the present victors. The idea that one can empathize with the past is part of this victory. In empathy, the distance between self and other is assumed to dissolve to the extent that it is possible to "feel with" the other ("einfühlen" suggests a "feeling as one").[8] Such a conception implies a kind of appropriation of the past moment from the autonomous and sovereign standpoint of the present. The idea that it is possible to empathize with the past, to "resuscitate" a past moment for present feeling, makes that past part of the present's "cultural treasures" (I 256). A nonempathetic relationship to history requires not simply that we shift our gaze from the victors to those who are lying prostrate in history's epic narrations, but that we renounce any attempt at empathy, any attempt to "feel" the other or resuscitate—make live, return to the realm of the present—that which is apparently lost. However well intentioned such attempts may be, they cannot help but be part of the victors' attempts to return lost or forgotten moments to a picture of universal history.

Opposed to a concept of history as a chain of events that can be held within the historian's hand, Benjamin describes the past as something that can never be possessed, but can only be experienced momentarily and unexpectedly, seized in "a moment of danger" (255). He describes the past as a memory in a mournful mind that, saddened by the state that the world is in, makes room for other times, for the "echoes of history's 'laments'" and the memory that there must be justice, even as these memories flare up and disappear in a moment of (un)recognizability:

> The image of the past that flashes up in the now of recognizability is, regarding its latter determination, an image of memory. It resembles images of the past that appear in an instant of danger. These images come, as we know, involuntarily. History strictly speaking is an image that rises up out of involuntary memory, an image that suddenly appears to the subject of history in an instant of danger. (GS 1.3.1231, 1.3.1243)

The past is not an object of possession for the historian who like a bourgeois speculator wants to make it part of his holdings in the present and therefore have a purchase on the future as well—a trading in of one time for another, a "redemption" in the common economic sense of the word (the German word *Erlösung* has the same double sense of divine salvation or economic exchange that the English does). History does not appreciate, and there is no brokering of a future through the sense of a continuous and progressive present. Rather, for Benjamin, redemption involves the past as much as it does the future. It has to do with a momentary grasp or "salvaging" of an altogether ephemeral experience of history.

Knowing that the question of redemption would be the point that, as Bertolt Brecht put it, people would be least likely even to misunderstand, Benjamin is himself extremely cautious with it.[9] He asks at one point, "From what [*Wovor*] can something past be redeemed or rescued?" and at another point, "From what are phenomena rescued?" (N 9, 4). His answer to the former question is, "Not so much from the disparagement and disdain into which it has fallen, but from a certain mode of its transmission [*Überlieferung*]." He cautions that a sense of the past as an "inheritance" is more sinister than if an awareness of the past were simply to disappear. Past phenomena are not rescued to be "saved" for a present holding: "they are rescued by exhibiting the discontinuity that exists within them." They are saved to "burst open the continuum," not to form part of it or its supposed culmination.

Benjamin's sense of redemption involves a momentary salvation, a glimpse or grasp of a moment of the past that also affects the way one sees (from) the present. This difference is what blows in the wind of the dialectic: not a Hegelian dialectic that blows toward a determinate end, but a dialectic that blows in from the unknown of history. "What matters for the dialectician is to have the wind of world history in his sails" (N 9, 6). When one has the dialectical wind of history in one's sails, or in one's "words and concepts," a dialectical "image" appears, an image-flash that explodes the apparent autonomy of the present: "The dialectical image is a lightning flash. That which was must be held fast as it flashes up as an image in the now of recognizability. The rescue [*Die Rettung*] which is thus, and only thus, effected, can only take place for that which, in the next moment, is already irretrievably lost" (N 7). This glimpse of an image dialectically quivering in the winds of history reveals a history that can never be comprehended as a whole, but is comprehended only in a fleeting legibility that is like a confrontation, a "confrontation with . . . the 'now of recognizability'" (quoted in Ferris 13).

Benjamin says that a dialectical relationship with the past operates on a cyclical principle, but it is a cyclicality that never repeats anything exactly: its effect is to "dissipate the appearance of the 'always-the-same,' including that of repetition, from history" (N 9). This cyclicality that is not repetition recalls Borges's question in "Nueva refutación del tiempo": "¿No basta *un solo término* repetido para desbaratar y confundir la serie del tiempo?" ("Is not a single repeated term sufficient to disturb and confound the series of time?" (OI 177).[10] He gives as an example the sensation of déjà vu that he feels when he passes by the Recoleta cemetery in Buenos Aires: "No paso ante la Recoleta sin recordar que están sepultados ahí mi padre, mis abuelos y trasabuelos, como yo lo estaré; luego recuerdo ya haber recordado lo mismo, ya innumerables veces" ("I don't pass by the Recoleta without remembering that my father, my grandparents and great-grandparents are buried there, like I will be; then I remember having already remembered that same thing, innumerable times").

That such memories or sensations of déjà vu are not exact repetitions, "appearances of the always-the-same," is evident in the other examples he gives:

> No puedo caminar por los arrebales en la soledad de la noche, sin pensar que ésta nos agrada porque suprime los ociosos detalles, como el recuerdo; no puedo lamentar la perdición de un amor o de una amistad sin meditar que sólo se pierde lo que realmente no se ha tenido; . . . cada vez que el aire me trae un olor a eucaliptos, pienso en Adrogué, en mi niñez; cada vez que recuerdo el fragmento 91 de Heráclito: *No bajarás dos veces al mismo río,* admiro su destreza dialéctica, pues la facilidad con que aceptamos el primer sentido ("El río es otro") nos impone clandestinemente el segundo ("Soy otro"). (OI 177)
>
> I cannot walk through the suburbs in the solitude of the night without thinking that the night pleases us because it suppresses the idle details, like memory; I cannot lament the loss of a love or a friendship without meditating that one only loses what was never really had; . . . every time that the air brings me a scent of eucalyptus, I think of Adrogué, in my childhood; every time I remember Heraclitus's fragment 91: *You will not go down to the same river twice,* I admire its dialectical skill, since the facility with which we accept the first sense ("the river is another") clandestinely imposes on us the second ("I am another").

Death, memory, loss of things that were never possessed, an involuntary memory triggered by the smell of eucalyptus, the memory of the river of time: Borges says that these repetitions and others that he leaves out ("otras que callo") make up his "entire life." It is a life that he later describes as "feeling one's self in death" ("sentirse en muerte"), in which the apparent completeness and continuity of life is confronted with its limits. In a similar vein, Benjamin describes a need to pay attention to "sites in which the continuity of tradition [*die Überlieferung*] is interrupted, and whose crags and points [*Schroffen und Zacken*] oblige anything that wants to pass over it to a halt" (GS 1.3.1242).[11]

Benjamin describes such sites in which the past interrupts a continuous sense of history in the second thesis of the "Theses on the Philosophy of History," a text whose references to redemption and messianism have been particularly misunderstood in recent years.[12] The thesis begins with a quotation from Hermann Lotze, who notes that "alongside so much selfishness in specific instances," one of the peculiarities most worth noting in the conception of history is the "freedom from envy which the present displays toward the future" (I 253). Benjamin infers from this that our image of happiness tends to be based on what we already know rather than what we don't, happiness that we have already had a taste of rather than happiness we cannot quite imagine: "The kind of happiness that could arouse envy in us only exists in the air we have breathed, among people we could have talked to, women who could have given themselves to us" (I 254).

On the one hand this might seem to be a way of closing off the possibilities of the future, just another part of so much "selfishness." On the other hand it seems to suggest that we already have some idea of what a shared sense of happiness, and perhaps its correlates, justice or revolution, would entail: i.e., that it is already in us, if only in a fragmentary and ephemeral form. Yet at the same time, we do not really "know" what we know. Something indissoluble or "unsellable" (*unveräußerlich*) remains in us, oscillating in the dialectical wind of history; something that cannot be dissolved or exchanged (that is, "redeemed") without remainder.[13] The past carries inside it something that Benjamin calls a "secret index" that refers it to a different kind of redemption, one that is not an even exchange of the past for a future, of known pleasures for paradise, but which has to do precisely with what we do not know—what we may have almost known, what may have brushed against us without our full awareness, something that occurred to us that we are not (yet) able to bring into the present. In a passage that does not appear in the English translation, and of which, owing to its enigmatic complexity, I can only provide a rough translation, Benjamin writes:

> Die Vergangenheit führt einen heimlichen Index mit, durch den sie auf die Erlösung verwiesen wird. Streift denn nicht uns selber ein Hauch der Luft, die um die Früheren gewesen ist? ist nicht in Stimmen, denen wir unser Ohr schenken, ein Echo von nun verstummten? haben die Frauen, die wir umwerben, nicht Schwestern, die sie nicht mehr gekannt haben? (GS 1.2.693–94)
>
> The past carries with it a secret index by which it is referred to redemption. Does not a breath of the air that enveloped those who went before us touch us? Is there not in the voices to which we once loaned an ear an echo of those now silenced? Do not the women whom we mystify (or love) have sisters they no longer know?

With distinct Freudian overtones, what we think we know of the past bears a secret (*einen heimlichen Index*) of which only echoes and little gusts reach us. It is a relationship to this secret that endows the present with what Benjamin calls in his famous formulation a "*weak* messianic force," "eine *schwache* messianische Kraft." Pablo Oyarzún emphasizes the modifier "weak" in this formulation, and asks what a "fuerza débil" or "schwache . . . Kraft" is meant to suggest, as opposed to a strong force: "The italics—with which, for the most part, Benjamin has been very economical—lead us to think of a secret, hidden key to the force in question, a key that is called 'weakness' . . . But how are we to think a force that, without ceasing to be a force, is weak?" (30). Oyarzún writes, "How does a 'strong force' operate with respect to the past? It brings it into the present" (31). The paradoxical figure of a "weak force" describes a vulnerability with respect to the past—an openness to the breaths of air, voices or tones (*Stimmen*), and echoes that interrupt and confound any proper knowledge of the past.

In one of the fragments from the notes to the "Theses," Benjamin describes history and its secrets through the metaphors of photography and reading: "If we want to consider history as a text, then you can also say of it what a recent author says about literary [texts]: the past has deposited in them images that can be compared to those held fast on a photosensitive plate. 'Only the future [*Zukunft*] has developers at its disposition that are strong enough to allow the image to come to light with all its details'" (GS 1.3.1238). If we are to consider history as a text, it is a text that is waiting to be developed like a photograph, and whose development or revelation is always still *to* occur (*Zu-kunft*). What follows, however, suggests that the figure of photographic revelation is only partially apt to describe the reading of history. Benjamin goes on to say that there is a spot that vision cannot penetrate, a dark spot or secret that is better represented by the figure of language: "Many a page in Marivaux or Rousseau indicate a secret sense [*einen geheimen Sinn*] that contemporary readers have never been able to fully decipher." This is not the truism that a text's contemporaries are not able to understand a text produced in their own time or that genius appreciates with age. Rather the "secret sense" is something that is intrinsic to language, something that potentially can be revealed and yet is never completely revealed. It is something that always remains within the folds of language.

This brings us back to the secret or strangeness (for example, the unseen unicorn) that Borges says inhabits history, or the "reserva incalculable de sombra" that is indicated by certain kinds of writing, a reserve that historicism attempts to colonize and control. This kind of writing is full of what Benjamin describes as those sites whose "crags and points" oblige anyone who wants to pass over them to pause; points that interrupt the sense of comprehension of a given moment (the sense that "this is the way it really is or was"), or a sense of the present as the keystone of a continuum we are always on the brink of completing. It is a writing that invites moments of messianic interruption that Benjamin illustrates by citing Henri Focillon's definition of the "classic style."

> Brève minute de pleine possession des formes, il se présente . . . comme un bonheur rapide, comme *l'akme* des Grecs: le fléau de la balance n'oscille plus que faiblement. Ce que j'attends, c'est ne pas de la voir bientôt de nouveau pencher, encore moins le moment de la fixité absolue, mais, dans le miracle de cette immobilité hésitante, le tremblement léger, imperceptible, qui m'indique qu'elle vit. (GS 1.3.1229)

> A brief minute of full possession of forms, it presents itself like a quick happiness, like the *akme* of the Greeks: the arrow on the scale oscillates only weakly. What I wait for is not to see it bend again soon, still less in a moment of absolute fixity, but in the miracle of that hesitant immobility, the light tremor—imperceptible—that indicates that it [the scale] is alive.

The secrets of history, or the shadow that certain kinds of writing admit (*not* journalistic writing, for example), are secret indices of a momentary happiness, glimpses of the possibility of a world better than the one we presently inhabit. They are recognizable only by a "weak" movement—a "hesitant immobility" or a "light tremor"—that indicates that there are signs, if barely perceptible, of life.

Life here does not mean organic, individual life, but life that exceeds individuals and what we tend to think of as life. It concerns the fact that there *is* life, which also includes death and decay as well as birth and rebirth—what Benjamin has designated with the term "natural history."[14] It is not paradoxical that it is the balance that lives or indicates life. As I have already mentioned, Benjamin uses the nonorganic figures of language and other forms of representation to indicate what he means by a "natural" or vital history that is not limited to individual life and death. Animal beings, who presumably have only one life, one origin and one end, are contrasted with works of art that "live on" through a series of afterlives (*Nachleben*), and whose origins are repeated and renewed through the act of reading or translation (I 71–73). As Borges also points out, this "other" life does not necessarily occur only in subsequent versions of a work, but can be found in a single work.

The nonorganic "life" of a work of art interrupts a sense of progressive chronology. Benjamin cites Focillon a second time to describe how a work of art, "at the instant at which it is born," is a "phenomenon of rupture" (GS 1.3.1229). It ruptures a sense of continuum, of history as a progression of determinate origins and determinate ends, and the notion of the present as a point of transition in the movement from origin to end. Focillon continues, "A current expression, 'to make a mark in history' [*faire date*], makes us feel it vividly: this does not mean to intervene passively in chronology; it means to break [*brusquer*] the moment" (1.3.1229–30). The artwork ruptures not only the continuum, but also the moment; it "makes" ("faire") its moment by rupturing all sense of a single, coherent moment. This cannot be reduced to the avant-garde aesthetic of destroying tradition and installing a compulsion for novelty in place of the compulsion for preservation and continuity. Benjamin is suggesting that any artistic birth or origin shatters the sense of a "now" as epoch—what Horacio González calls "oficialismos de época," a sense of the present as manageable, archivizable property[15]—and springs out of (playing on the sense of "spring" in *Ursprung,* origin) the sense of time as a continuum in which the present is situated. The artistic inscription creates a "messianic" interruption that intervenes in the sense of continuous time, breaks it open and—momentarily and "lightly trembling" (it is a "schwache . . . Kraft")—indicates a relationship with history that does not relegate past, present, and future to official categories, but allows the dialectical wind to touch life in all its moments.

The "weak force" that opens up a sense of continuous time is a force that is latent in language, and it is a force that de Man, in one of his many unacknowledged glosses on Benjamin's writings, says is definitive of history: that it *defines* history. De Man distinguishes time from history on the basis of an interruptive power, a power to which language, with all of its "crags and points," is particularly suited. "History," he writes, "is not a temporal notion, it has nothing to do with temporality"—and here I include Derrida's parenthetical remark on this passage—"[this hyperbolic provocation, in the style of de Man, certainly does not negate all temporality of history; it merely recalls that time, temporal unfolding, is not the essential predicate of the concept of history: time is not enough to make history. J.D.], but (and this is de Man) it is the emergence of a language of power out of a language of cognition" (Derrida, "Typewriter Ribbon" 320). What de Man calls "mournful" representation opens up a sense of what is known and lets something else emerge, in the sense of an *Ursprung* or a birth that ruptures. This intervention into what Derrida calls "any continuum accessible to a process of knowledge" is what de Man understands by the term "history," which like Benjamin's messianic index or interruption does not represent anything concrete—histories of the oppressed rather than the victors, for example. Rather, its historical or messianic promise is inherent in the act of representation, the act that language or art performs in its momentary and "weak" emergence from or interruption of a cognizable continuum. Benjamin's "weak Messianic power," which enables us to hear echoes of silenced voices in the voices we hear, to feel breaths of air of past lives brush us by, to know the unknown sisters of our lovers, is also the power of language, a historical power that is intrinsic to language. It is a force that, insomuch as it cracks open the concept of history as a "continuum accessible to a process of knowledge," opens up a whole world of possibility, or the world of possibility itself.

Refuting Time

Borges's "Nueva refutación del tiempo," in addition to being a paradoxically "new" refutation of time, is also a refutation of idealism, or the idea that the world can be apprehended in ideas or concepts. The essay maneuvers a series of twists and turns through different philosophers, beginning and in some sense ending with Schopenhauer, who comes to represent an important limit-figure in Borges's thought. At first, Schopenhauer seems to represent the idealist tradition's most acceptable limit, but in the end Borges leaves him blowing back and forth like a straw man on the outer reaches of the idealist landscape.

Borges introduces the question of idealism by citing Schopenhauer's definition of the universe as divided into two basic categories, "el mundo en la cabeza" and "el mundo fuera de la cabeza" ("the world in our heads" and "the world out of our heads," OI 173). Borges questions the simplicity of this distinction by citing, "not without ingratitude," George Berkeley's provocation, which is if the world is assumed to be both in our heads and out of our heads, how do we know that that limit itself is not in our heads? Faced with this question, Berkeley fantastically concludes that the world is *entirely* inside our heads, since if we cannot tell the difference between inside and outside, the very assumption of difference, and everything it includes, must belong to us. Borges cites Hume as rejecting the category "our" here, because, in a regression ad absurdum, if the world exists only in our heads, we too exist only in our heads, meaning that there is no containing category "we" (much less Berkeley's leap of faith in an absolute containment, God), and all figures of metaphysical containment burst apart, leaving only scattered bits of confused philosophers trying to figure out how to think about the world. Hume describes the human being as "una colección o atadura de percepciones, que se suceden unas a otras con inconcebible rapidez" ("a collection or bundle of perceptions which succeed one another with inconceivable speed," 174).

But, Borges says, even this "casi perfecta disgregación" ("almost perfect disintegration") conceals a structure of containment, which is the successive conception of time. Traces of the "ergo"—translated in the Spanish as "luego"—of the Cartesian "cogito ergo sum" remain in Hume's dissolution of the categories *ego*, Spirit, and world: an "ergo" that is causal and temporal as well as logical (175). (Borges cites Lichtenberg's solution, which, instead of the authority of an absolute "yo" in "I think," proposes an impersonal "thinks" as one would say "it thunders" or "it lightnings.") He writes, "Lo repito: no hay detrás de las caras un yo secreto, que gobierna los actos y que recibe las impresiones; somos únicamente la serie de esos actos imaginarios y de esas impresiones errantes" ("I repeat: there is not behind the faces a secret 'I' that governs acts and receives impressions; we are only the series of those imaginary acts and those errant impressions"). But, he asks, "¿La serie? Negados el espíritu y la materia, que son continuidades, negado también el espacio, no sé qué derecho tenemos a esa continuidad que es el tiempo" ("The series? Having denied spirit and matter, which are continuities, and having denied space as well, I don't know what right we have to that continuity which is time").

As Derrida says of de Man, Borges's "hyperbolic provocation" does not really negate time, space, or materiality, but is rather an assertion that their conception as continuums that are accessible to cognition—continuums that we can grasp, hold in our heads—is not total. The concept of successive time does not exhaust all temporality; the "in our heads" does not exhaust the "out of our heads," even if we cannot determine the limits of such a distinction. We cannot understand, or (which may be the same thing) we cannot *but* understand the limits of our own cognition. Berkeley interprets this to mean that there are no limits, but it can also mean that there are limits to a cognitive apprehension of the world, which means furthermore that there must be ways of indicating such limits: ways of writing, thinking, being that do not assert a claim to totality (for example, "I am," "the world is," "time is") at every step. This telling that one cannot tell—telling, for example, that there are times that are not contained in the structure of a consecutive, narratable time—is the place of a mournful, materialist writing, which indicates through language that there are things that cannot be comprehensively known. It is what Benjamin says of history, that it is like reading a text in which one reads what has never been written as well as what has, in which one listens for lost echoes in the voices one hears, in which one thinks of unknown sisters of the women one has loved. Writing and reading (and hearing) indicate the incompleteness of models of containment, providing an alternative to the assertion that something is either "in our heads" or "outside our heads."

These limits appear in language's "crags and points" and also through the senses: through senses that do not necessarily "make sense" of the objects they perceive, that are not phenomenalized or apprehended as knowable phenomena. Hearing in particular is a sense often associated with disorientation and difficulty of identification (think for example of the familiar experience of hearing a noise and not knowing what it is or where it is coming from until, Hollywood style, the source is revealed to us visually). In fact, this unreliability of identification may be common to all of the senses with the exception of sight, which tends to be most closely associated with identity and identification. Borges's description of sites and sensations that interrupt him and oblige him to pause as he attempts to pass over them concerns a distinct non-specularity—for example, the sensation he has when he passes his family cemetery, his lamentation for a love or friendship, realizing at the same time that they were never his, and the odor of eucalyptus that reminds him of his childhood.

In "La penúltima versión de la realidad," after he rejects Korzybski's description of the accumulation of space and time as essential human attributes, Borges proposes the olfactory and auditory senses as "entire provinces of Being" that refute Kant's consideration of space as a universal form of intuition. Collector of absurd refutations that he is, Borges cites Spencer's observation that one only needs to "look for the left or right side of a sound, or . . . try to imagine a smell backwards," in order to refute such a claim (D 43–44). Borges then invents his own refutation, in which he imagines how it would be if the entire human race were to possess only the senses of smell and hearing.

> Imaginemos que el entero género humano sólo se abasteciera de realidades mediante la audición y el olfato. Imaginemos anuladas así las percepciones oculares, táctiles y gustativas y el espacio que éstas definen. Imaginemos también—crecimiento lógico—una más afinada percepción de lo que registran los sentidos restantes. La humanidad—tan afantasmada a nuestro parecer por esta catástrofe—seguiría urdiendo su historia. La humanidad se olvidaría de que hubo espacio . . . De esta humanidad hipotética (no menos abundosa de voluntades, de ternuras, de imprevisiones) no diré que entraría en la cáscara de nuez proverbial: afirmo que estaría fuera y ausente de todo espacio. (44)

> Let us imagine that the entire human race were only to have access to realities by means of the auditory and olfactory senses. Let us imagine the ocular, tactile, and gustative perceptions annulled, as well as the space that these senses define. Let us imagine also—it logically follows—a sharper perception from those senses that remain to us. Humanity—so phantasmatic in our minds due to this catastrophe—would continue warping (that is, weaving) its history. Humanity would forget that space existed . . . Of this hypothetical humanity (no less abundant in wills, tendernesses, unexpected occurrences) I will not say that it would enter into the proverbial nutshell: I affirm that it would be outside of and absent from all space.

This hypothetical description considers the possibility of a world that lies outside of universal forms such as space. A world in which only the olfactory and auditory sense perceptions existed would be a world that would lack a sentient relationship with space, and yet it would nevertheless still be a fully developed world. To have no sense of space, as one of the categories of the "mundo en la cabeza," does not leave us in the proverbial nutshell of our head. Rather, such a world would ultimately remain, as the vast multiplicity of existence in fact does, outside of universal categories that we use to comprehend the universe.

Borges proposes that the "warping" of history, together with human "wills, tendernesses, and *imprevisiones*," is part of this outside. This assertion that history does not exist only "in our heads" is an important assertion, considering that Borges is commonly considered to close himself off from reality. The example of a world in which only auditory and olfactory senses exist is an absurdity, but the choice of smell and hearing as examples to oppose the concept of a universal form of intuition suggests, like Benjamin's "weak force," a certain openness. The ear and the nose are literally "holes in the head," holes that are always open, vulnerable to whatever passes by. They are like the openness needed to hear the echoes, voices, and breaths of air of history; or as Borges describes, the breaths of air that touch him when he passes the Recoleta cemetery, the voices of lost loved ones that call to him, the odors that take him back to his childhood.

These memories, we will recall, are examples of what Borges calls the repetitions that abound in his life, repetitions of which he says only one would suffice to "desbaratar" a single and successive sense of time;

and which similarly seem to "desbaratar" a single, solid sense of personal identity. They are *percepi* that do not lend themselves to found a universal sense of being, to misquote the idealists ("su *esse* es *percepi,*" OI 173). As Borges suggests in his list of repetitions (which ironically includes the "repetition" of Heraclitus's maxim "No bajarás dos veces al mismo río"), the ever-changing river of existence and the perceptions and memories of it that enter us "involuntarily" not only do not allow us to identify where we are on the river ("el río es otro"), but also do not allow us to know who or what we are with respect to the river ("Soy otro"). Hume, who defined the subject as an "atadura de percepciones que se suceden unas a otras con inconcebible rapidez," seems to throw himself willingly into this uncertain stream of being, in spite of the fact that Borges suggests that he remains tied to the protective order of a sequential sense of time. Schopenhauer, on the other hand, tries to hold firmly to a rock in the middle of this swirling river. His figure appears at the end of the essay as, as I have suggested, a straw man against which Borges narrows his critique of idealism.

The end of the "New Refutation" begins with a repetition of the hypothesis, again in the form of a question, about repetition: "¿No basta un sólo término repetido para desbaratar y confundir la historia del mundo, para denunciar que no hay tal historia?" ("Is not a single repeated term enough to disrupt and confuse world history, to denounce that there is no such history?" 185). The word "historia" takes the place here of serial or sequential time ("la serie del tiempo") in the previous instance of this sentence. Borges makes it clear that a denunciation of "tal historia"—a single history of the world—involves two fundamental aspects: "Negar el tiempo es dos negaciones: negar la sucesión de los términos de una serie, negar el sincronismo de los términos de dos series" ("To deny time includes two negations: that of the succession of the terms of a series, and that of a synchronicity of the terms of two [different] series," 185). That is to say, it is to deny not only the successive and linear structure of time, but also the idea that there is a single time within which different occurrences can be lined up and located within the concept of contemporaneity, as though spatially, on a map. An example would be the idea of uneven development of colonial and colonized societies: for example, the idea that the Indians and the English colonizers lived a simultaneous time, a time which, like a natural resource, the English used to greater achievement and the Indian populations to less. In fact, as Borges asserts, the English and the native Indian populations lived in altogether different time zones, which are in the end impossible to compare, much less subsume one to the other.

The nonhomogeneity of time contradicts Schopenhauer's assertion that each fraction of time simultaneously fills the entirety of space.

> Contrariamente a lo declarado de Schopenhauer en su tabla de verdades fundamentales (*Welt als Wille und Vortellung* [*sic*] II, 4), cada fracción de tiempo no llena simultáneamente el espacio entero, el tiempo no es ubicuo. (Claro está que, a esta altura del argumento, ya no existe el espacio.) (185–86)
>
> Contrary to what Schopenhauer declared in his table of fundamental truths (*The World as Will and Representation,* vol. II, 4), each fraction of time does not simultaneously fill all of space; time is not ubiquitous. (Of course, at this point in the argument, space no longer exists.)

As in Borges's discussion of Kant, there can be no spatial mapping out of time or perception. We cannot map out in a single time or a single space what happened where, as in the familiar police tactic of trying to figure out "where everyone was on the night of—," which is a drastic reduction of the multiplicity of different times and experiences. Time, in other words, cannot be chopped up and placed neatly into a "tabla de verdades fundamentales."

In an odd addendum to this argument, and one that recalls the example of the unicorn as something strange or secret that inhabits history, Borges cites Alexius Meinong, who "en su teoría de la aprehensión, admite la de los objetos imaginarios: la cuarta dimensión, digamos, o la estatua sensible de Condillac o el animal hipotético de Lotze o la raíz cuadrada de —l" ("in his theory of apprehension, admits that of imaginary objects: the fourth dimension, let us say, or Condillac's statue or Lotze's hypothetical animal or the square root of —l," 186). The apprehension of objects that by nature cannot be apprehended (in the sense of being grasped) is an experience that could make one a little apprehensive, and indeed this appears to be the case in Borges's argument: "Si las razones que he indicado son válidas, a ese orbe nebuloso pertenecen también la materia, el yo, el mundo externo, la historia universal, nuestras vidas" ("If the reasons I have indicated are valid, to that nebulous cloud (that is, of imaginary objects) belong also materiality, the 'I,' the external world, universal history, our lives"). The "I," the external world, and universal history are things that can only be apprehended "apprehensively": apprehensive of what it is that can be grasped or understood, and apprehensive of what in those things cannot be grasped, even when we think we grasp them, like the secret strangenesses that exist in the histories we think we know.

Time and history are among the things that can only be apprehended apprehensively. Borges dips back into the skeptical-idealist tradition to consider what part or parts of time can be held on to, if any. He quotes Sextus Empiricus's observation that the past and the future, since they are already passed and yet to come, do not exist, and that the present is either divisible or indivisible. If the present is indivisible, it is not temporal but infinite. If it is divisible, it is infinitely so—that is, there will always be a part that just was and a part that is not yet (the disturbing discovery made famous for the modern era by Augustine)—and therefore does not exist.[16] This means, furthermore, that time itself cannot exist: "*Ergo* [the present] no existe, pero como tampoco existen el pasado y el porvenir, el tiempo no existe" ("Therefore the present does not exist, but since neither the past or the future exist, time does not exist"). F. H. Bradley takes up the same concern in slightly different terms: "si el ahora es divisible en otros ahoras, no es menos complicado que el tiempo, y si es indivisible, el tiempo es una mera relación entre cosas intemporales" ("if the now is divisible in other nows, it is not less complicated than time, and if it is indivisible, time is merely a relation between intemporal things," 186). In other words, if the present can be held on to, it is not time; and if it cannot be held on to, it does not exist. Such arguments, Borges suggests, "niegan las partes para luego negar el todo" ("deny the parts to then deny the whole"), suggesting that if we cannot find a piece to hold on to, time does not exist. He, on the other hand, is denying the whole (a single, successive time) to underline the fact that there are things that cannot be held on to, whether individually (the metaphysicians who want to pinpoint the present, the singularity of a here and now), or in a chain ("un solo tiempo, en el que se eslabonan los hechos," 176).

Schopenhauer is held up here as an "almost, but not quite" example. Borges quotes (this time from the *Welr als Wille und Vorstellung* [*sic*]):

> La forma de la aparición de la voluntad es sólo el presente, no el pasado ni el porvenir; éstos no existen más que para el concepto y por el encadenamiento de la conciencia, sometido al principio de la razón. Nadie ha vivido en el pasado, nadie vivirá en el futuro: el presente es la forma de toda vida, es una posesión que ningún mal puede arrebatarle . . . El tiempo es como un círculo que girara infinitamente: el arco que desciende es el pasado, el que asciende es el porvenir; arriba hay un punto indivisible que toca la tangente y es el ahora. Inmóvil como lo tangente, ese inextenso punto marca el contacto del objeto, cuya forma es el tiempo, con el sujeto, que carece de forma, porque no pertenece a lo conocible y es previa condición del conocimiento. (186–87)

> The form in which the will appears is only the present, not the past or future; these exist only conceptually or for the enchainment of consciousness, submitted to the principle of reason. No one has lived in the past, no one will live in the future: the present is the form of all life; it is a possession which no evil can snatch away from it . . . Time is like an endlessly turning circle: the side that descends is the past, the side that rises is the future; at the top there is an indivisible point that touches the tangent, and that is the now. Immobile like the tangent, that inextensive point marks the contact of the object, whose form is time, with the subject that lacks form, since it does not belong to the knowable, but is a previous condition of all that is knowable.[17]

Schopenhauer's intention is clearly to reject conventional conceptions of time as a linear and successive phenomenon. Time is not linear but circular, and the past and the future are nothing more than conceptual imprisonment. They are presented here chained and turning infinitely around an indivisible point, which is the present. Schopenhauer avoids the pitfalls that Sextus Empiricus and Bradley fear and the abyss into which Augustine famously peered. The present for Schopenhauer is indivisible but not atemporal: it is at once inextensive and unmoving and part of the continuously revolving sphere of time. Yet Schopenhauer wants to have it both ways: to live in time, and yet have a point outside of time that nothing can snatch away ("arrebatar") from subjective—albeit prerational—perception. Although Schopenhauer's conception of the Will as an unruly force that underlies the subject suggests that there is no such self-possession possible, his description of the present as a life possession that "ningún mal puede arrebatarle" suggests that there is something or someone that possesses, a self-possession that accompanies or conditions the possession of the present. The present exists as a ground for Schopenhauer's otherwise radical refutation of reassuring concepts. In the sentence that follows the passage that Borges quotes, or which Borges's citation leads up to but leaves latent, Schopenhauer writes, "Time is like an irresistible stream, and the present like a rock on which the stream breaks, but which it does not carry away"; and a little further down, "[The present] will not run away from the will, nor the will from it" (*World*, vol. 1 280).

"And yet, and yet," Borges cautions. Schopenhauer describes time as an irresistible stream that carries everything away from itself, but suggests that the present and the will are rocks in the middle of that stream, rocks that do not get carried away in the current. For Borges, on the other hand, time is the "substancia" of life, a sub-stance that, riverlike, carries away everything that is standing with it.[18]

> El tiempo es la substancia de que estoy hecho. El tiempo es un río que me arrebata, pero yo soy el río; es un tigre que me destroza, pero yo soy el tigre; es un fuego que me consume, pero yo soy el fuego. El mundo, desgraciadamente, es real; yo, desgraciadamente, soy Borges. (187)
>
> Time is the substance of which I am made. Time is a river that carries me away, but I am the river; it is a tiger that destroys me, but I am the tiger; it is a fire that consumes me, but I am the fire. The world, unfortunately, is real; I, unfortunately, am Borges.

Using the same word as he did in his quotation of Schopenhauer's description of a possession of the present, Borges states that in spite of his wishes to the contrary, the "mal" of time perpetually snatches away ("arrebata") a sense of being in the present. There is no sense of a present that the stream does not carry away. Like his previous observation about Heraclitus's maxim, the river is constantly changing ("El río es otro"), and he is changing as well ("Soy otro"). He considers this temporal nature of existence "unfortunate" (*des-gracia:* fallen from grace), but inevitable. The ambivalence of this being that is always also a not-being—a taking away from oneself, a destruction ("destrozar") or a consumption ("el fuego que me consume")—occurs in the postlapsarian form par excellence, language. Out of divine grace, where name and thing are said to coincide seamlessly, the verb "to be" does not indicate sure possession, either of the enunciating subject or of the object of enunciation. In the statement, "El mundo, desgraciadamente, es real; yo, desgraciadamente, soy Borges," the fall from grace, the "des-gracia" or dispossession is placed between the subject and its predicate like a caesura that cleaves open the copula of predication.

Ego Sum

This "yo soy" that is not a "yo soy," that takes the sense of being away from itself, is also the subject of Borges's essay "Historia de los ecos de un nombre" ("History of the Echoes of a Name"), in which Schopenhauer again makes a privileged appearance. In this essay (also from *Otras inquisiciones*), Borges recounts three repeated instances throughout history of the same "obscure declaration" (OI 161). The original occurrence appears in Exodus, in which it is told how Moses, "both author and protagonist of the book," asked God his name. God's response was, "Soy El Que Soy" ("I Am He Who Is"). Borges states here that before considering the significance of this response, it is worth remembering that for "el pensamiento mágico, o primitivo, los nombres no son símbolos arbitrarios, sino parte vital de lo que definen" ("magical or primitive thought, names are not arbitrary symbols, but a vital part of what they define"). In Moses's case, he did not ask God's name out of mere "philological curiosity," but in the interest of determining who or what God is (162). The Christian tradition interprets God's statement as an affirmation of his existence: God is what he is, there is no explanation necessary, nothing that exceeds or escapes the direct predicate God = God or Yo = Yo. He is what he is, he is that which *is,* and language, the verb "ser"—which Borges elsewhere asserts "is not a poetic or a metaphysical category, but rather a grammatical one"[19]—is supposedly equal to the task of such an "ontological affirmation" (163). For the Christians, God's statement "Soy El Que Soy," serves as a name that functions, as in the magical or primitive traditions, as a "vital definition" of God's existence. His "I am" in some sense contains his being.

Borges explains that this is not the only interpretation of God's statement. Other interpretations suggest that God's response in fact eludes Moses's question: the response does not constitute a magical name that contains God's being, but rather states that his being is something that cannot be expressed in language, or that it can only be expressed by the imprecision or inapprehension intrinsic to language. Borges cites Martin Buber, who points out that the Hebrew sentence "*Ehych ascher ehych*" can be translated as "Soy el que seré" or "Yo estaré dónde yo estaré" as well as "Soy el que soy" ("I am what I will be," "I will be where I will be"). Borges reflects, "Moisés, a manera de los hechiceros egipcios, habría preguntado a Dios cómo se llamaba para tenerlo en su poder; Dios le habría contestado, de hecho: *Hoy converso contigo, pero mañana puedo revestir cualquier forma, y también las formas de la presión, de la injusticia y de la adversidad*" ("Moses, in the tradition of the Egyptian sorcerers, would have asked God what his name was in order to have him in his power; God would have answered, in fact: Today I am conversing with you, but tomorrow I can change myself into any form, and also the forms of pressure, injustice, and adversity"). Borges follows this statement with a footnote explaining that for Buber, "vivir es penetrar en una extraña habitación del espíritu, cuyo piso es el tablero en que jugamos un juego inevitable y desconocido contra un adversario cambiante y a veces espantoso" ("to live is to penetrate a strange room of the spirit, whose floor is the board where we play an unavoidable and unfamiliar game against an adversary who is changing and at times terrifying").

Moses, as a kind of precursor to the idealists, wanted to comprehend God's existence in his name, to hold it—"tenerlo," as though in his hand. God responded that he could not be had, and furthermore, that language, the form in which Moses wanted to hold him, does not indicate presence, but only tells of its own impossibility to do so. God's answer "Ehych ascher ehych" signifies that the being that is inquired about *is,* but also *will be* (or *is* what *will be*), and also "will be what it will be": in other words, he can take on different forms or inhabit different sites in the sense of the Spanish "estar," which indicates location or state rather than ontological being, which is indicated with the verb "ser." Language does not indicate a ground of being, but rather contains a promise: it tells not what *is,* but what may be beyond its comprehension. The ontological basis of God's affirmation is also complicated, Borges suggests, when one begins to translate the statement into different languages: "Ich bin der ich bin, Ego sum qui sum, I am that I am . . ." God's "sententious name" *I Am* does not magically contain a part of him, or at least not something one can hold on to, when it begins to proliferate and transform in the multitude of languages. Or as Benjamin might say, it conveys a part of him precisely when it begins to proliferate in different languages.

It is in this history of echoes and translations that the second instance of the "obscure declaration" occurs. It concerns a minor scene in a Shakespearean comedy, in which "a loudmouth and cowardly soldier . . . has managed, by means of a stratagem, to be promoted to captain" (163). The trick is discovered and the man is degraded publicly, and here "Shakespeare interviene y le pone en la boca palabras que reflejan, como en un espejo caído, aquellas otras que la divinidad dijo en la montaña: *Ya no seré capitán, pero he de comer y beber y dormir como un capitán; esta cosa que soy me hará vivir*" ("Shakespeare intervenes and puts in his mouth words that reflect, as if in a fallen mirror, those other words that the divinity said in the mountain: *I may no longer be captain, but I have to eat and drink and sleep the same as a captain; this thing that I am will make me live*"). Here the character Parolles "bruscamente deja de ser un personaje convencional de la farsa cómica y es un hombre y todos los hombres" ("abruptly ceases to be a conventional character from a comic farce and is a man and all men"). This commentary constitutes an uncommonly radical statement on human existence. Following as an echo or repetition of God's "I am," Parolles's statement "I am not . . . but I am or I need . . ." asserts not an ontological definition of what human beings are, but defines them by indicating the horizon of justice: what human beings would be in a just world—comfort or distance from necessity (eating, drinking, and sleeping like a captain) for everyone. Parolles's statement echoes God's "I am" on the human, "fallen" level (his words reflecting as though in a fallen mirror), in a fall not only from grace but also from a social-political hierarchy that places some men over others. It is this fallen statement that Borges says is paradigmatic of the human condition: "es un hombre y todos los hombres." Being here is not an object that can be grasped, but as with Buber's interpretation of God's statement, is comprehensible only in its endless proliferation and possibility. In a slight distinction from God's "soy el que seré" (or read liberally, "soy lo que será"), Parolles's statement suggests that present being—"esta cosa que soy"—will bring about the future: "me hará vivir."

The third instance of the affirmation of personal being comes from Swift, who is reported to have uttered the Biblical declaration on his deathbed. "Una tarde, viejo y loco y ya moribundo" ("One evening, old and crazy and already dying"), Swift was heard to repeat over and over to himself, "*Soy lo que soy, soy lo que soy*" (164). Borges says that we cannot know whether he uttered this statement "con resignación, con desesperación, o como quien se afirma y se ancla en su íntima esencia invulnerable" ("with resignation, with desperation, or as one who affirms himself and anchors himself invulnerably in his intimate essence"). The use of repetition and the pronoun "lo" as opposed to the pronoun "El" voiced by God ("I am what I am, I am what I am," instead of "I am he who is"), suggests that his intimate essence did not appear to be a very stable ground in which to "anchor" himself.

Borges then tells of a fourth variant on the history of repeated echoes, which occurred toward the end of Schopenhauer's life. In his case there is little doubt as to whether he spoke with resignation, desperation, or like "one who affirms himself and anchors himself invulnerably in his intimate essence." Nearing his death, Schopenhauer is said to have declared:

> Si a veces me he creído desdichado, ello se debe a una confusión, a un error. Me he tomado por otro, verbigracia, por un suplente que no puede llegar a titular, o por el acusado en un proceso por difamación, o por el enamorado a quien esa muchacha desdeña, o por el enfermo que no puede salir de su casa, o por otras personas que adolecen de análogas miserias. No he sido esas personas; ello, a lo sumo, ha sido la tela de trajes que he vestido y que he desechado. ¿Quién soy realmente? Soy el autor de *El mundo como voluntad y como representación,* soy el que ha dado una respuesta al enigma del Ser, que ocupará a los pensadores de los siglos futuros. Ese soy yo, ¿y quién podría discutirlo en los años que aún me quedan de la vida? (164–65)

> If at times I have considered myself to be unfortunate, that is due to a confusion, an error. I have taken myself for another, for example for an adjunct who never achieves a titled posi-

> tion, or for an accused man in a process of defamation, or for a lover whom a certain girl disdains, or for a sick man who cannot leave his house, or for other people who suffer from analogous miseries. I have not been those people; they, in the end, have been the fabric of suits that I have worn and that I have discarded. Who am I really? I am the author of *The World as Will and Representation,* I am he who has given a response to the enigma of Being, which will keep the thinkers of future centuries busy. That is what I am, and who could question it in my remaining years of life?

As in the passage that Borges cites in the "Nueva refutación del tiempo," Schopenhauer asserts a sense of self-presence as a possession that nothing, not even death, can take away. If the other "echoes of a name" open the definition of self to a multiplicity of possibilities—"I am what can be"—Schopenhauer closes off the possibilities, rejecting the multiplicity of "desdichos," to remain with the authoritative identity of himself as the author of *The World as Will and Representation.*

Precisely because he *had* written *The World as Will and Representation,* Borges argues, Schopenhauer should have known that being a thinker and an author would not provide any unshakable sense of identity: "Schopenhauer sabía muy bien que ser un pensador es tan ilusorio como ser un enfermo o un desdeñado y que él era otra cosa, profundamente. Otra cosa: la voluntad, la oscura raíz de Parolles, la cosa que era Swift" ("Schopenhauer knew very well that being a thinker is as illusory as being a sick man or a disdained lover and that he was something profoundly other. Something other: will, the dark root of Parolles, the thing that Swift was"). In spite of the fact that in his philosophical writings Schopenhauer asserts that there is an impulse or life force—the will—that precedes and exceeds representation, here he insists that being is essentially contained not only by the grammatical construction "yo soy," but more emphatically by the signature of a philosophical work. Borges insists throughout these essays that on the contrary, every "yo soy," like God's, opens onto a multitude of possibilities, including that evoked by Parolles, the fallen state that is also the state of all humans. Every "yo soy" is also the being of something else, "otra cosa, profundamente," a being in otherness that involves (secretly—*heimlich*) an index to the future. A sense of self is not a possession that nothing can snatch away, but is continually and inevitably snatched away, a fact that defines its nature ("Time is a river that carries me away, but I am the river"), and which also opens to the future: "Lo que soy me hará vivir."

Terrible Infinity

God is presented in "Historia de los ecos de un nombre" as one who can name being, this "name" resonating for centuries, breaking up into bits and pieces, different languages, echoes, interpretations, verb tenses; a madman's babble, a Shakespearean declaration on what it is to be human, a nineteenth-century philosopher's assertion that he can say what he is even when he has spent his life writing that he cannot. This multifarious and fragmented condition elicits a reaction of terror ("espanto") in some observers, like the game of life evoked by Buber, or Borges's statement that life is not terrifying for its unreality, but because its reality is "irreversible and made of iron" (OI 187).

Borges cites Pascal as one who tried to put into words the terror he found at the prospect that God or existence might not have a name to hold on to. He describes this in "La esfera de Pascal" ("Pascal's Sphere"), which like "Historia de los ecos de un nombre" recounts the repetitions of a motif. The essay begins, "Quizá la historia universal es la historia de unas cuantas metáforas. Bosquejar un capítulo de esa historia es el fin de esta nota" ("Perhaps universal history is the history of a few metaphors. To sketch a chapter in that history is the objective of this note," OI 13). The essay tells of a series of spheres and spherical cosmographies written at different points in history that describe the impossible figure of a sphere that has no center and no circumference, or as Pascal's formulation has it, a sphere whose center "está en todas partes y la circuferencia en ninguna" ("is in all parts and whose circumference is in none," 16). Contrasting with this is the model of the Ptolemaic universe, "flawlessly preserved" in Western culture at least through Dante, in which the earth is conceived as the immobile center of the universe, which rotates around it. Copernicus proposed a different vision of the cosmos, out of which Renaissance humanism was conceived. Borges cites the enthusiastic declaration of one of those humanists, Giordano Bruno: "Podemos afirmar con certidumbre que el universo es todo centro, o que el centro del universo está en todas partes y la circunferencia en ninguna" ("We can affirm with certainty that the universe is all center, or that the center of the universe is in all parts and its circumference in none," 15).

This was written "with exultation, in 1584, still in the light of the Renaissance." Seventy years later, at the height of the Baroque, "no reflection of that fervor remained, and men felt lost in time and space." The Baroque was a period in which the frightening possibility was considered that the world might not be contained by some universal sense, that time, space, and life might be infinite, without determinable bounds.

> En aquel siglo desanimado, el espacio absoluto que inspiró los hexámetros de Lucrecio, el espacio absoluto que había sido una liberación para Bruno, fue un laberinto y un abismo para Pascal . . . Deploró que no hablara el firmamento, comparó nuestra vida con la de náufragos en una isla desierta. Sintió el peso incesante del mundo físico, sintió vértigo, miedo y soledad, y los puso en otras palabras: "La naturaleza es una esfera infinita, cuyo centro está en todas partes y la circunferencia en ninguna." (16)
>
> In that dispirited century, the absolute space that inspired the hexameters of Lucretius, the absolute space that had been a liberation for Bruno, was a labyrinth and an abyss for Pascal . . . He deplored the fact that the firmament would not speak, he compared our life with that of shipwrecked sailors on a desert island. He felt the incessant weight of the physical world, he felt vertigo, fear, and loneliness, and he put them into other words: "Nature is an infinite sphere, whose center is in all parts and whose circumference is in none."

Bruno asserted his figure of the universe "with certainty," suggesting that the universe is all center ("todo centro"), and that the center can be found in all of us, in every thinking human being. For Pascal, however, the center is not *in* every part: it is rather everywhere, scattered about (the expression "en todas partes" can mean both "in all parts" and "everywhere"). Borges observes that in an edition that reproduces the "tachaduras y vacilaciones del manuscrito" ("corrections and vacillations of the manuscript"), Pascal began to write the word "*effroyable*" instead of "infinite": "A *terrible* sphere, whose center is in all parts and whose circumference is in none."

Recurrent Imminence

Alberto Moreiras observes that in his description of different variations of Pascal's sphere, Borges almost ostentatiously leaves out one of the most famous descriptions of such a sphere, the rotating repetition of Nietzsche's eternal return: "In every Now being begins; around every Here rotates the sphere of the There. Curved is the path of eternity" (quoted in Moreiras, *Tercer espacio* 127–28). It is not surprising that Borges neglects to cite Nietzsche here, or cites him without citing him, as is often the case. Borges had an ambivalent relationship with Nietzsche's writings, even though, as Moreiras shows, there are points of similarity between the two.

Borges's most explicit treatment of Nietzsche's theory of the eternal return appears in a pair of essays in *Historia de la eternidad,* "La doctrina de los ciclos" and "El tiempo circular" ("The Doctrine of Cycles" and "Circular Time"), in which he mocks Nietzsche as "the most pathetic inventor or divulger" of the theory of cyclicality (HE 119). Nietzsche, who was anything but scientific in the usual sense of the word, is associated in both essays with pseudoscientific theories in which units such as atoms are said to repeat identically. Borges mocks such an idea with fantastic accounts of what such total repetition would imply: "De nuevo nacerás de un vientre, de nuevo crecerá tu esqueleto, de nuevo arribará esta misma página a tus manos iguales" ("You will be born from a womb again, your skeleton will grow again, this very page will arrive at your same hands again," 97). The idea of the eternal return is reduced to a theory based on identity, demonstrated by the example of a man who circles the earth and assumes that his point of departure and his point of arrival are exactly the same place (120), even though we know from Heraclitus's maxim that it is impossible to return to the same place twice, not only because places change with time, but the "I" changes as well. Borges asks: supposing that repetition does occur, how would we even know, if we ourselves are in an infinitely changing, perhaps repeating world? "A falta de un arcángel especial que lleve la cuenta, ¿qué significa el hecho de que atravesamos el ciclo trece mil quinientos catorce, y no el primero de la serie o el número trescientos veintidós con el exponente de dos mil?" ("Unless there is a special archangel who keeps count, what significance can there be to the fact that we are going through the cycle the thirteen thousand five hundred and fourteenth time, and not the first in the series or the number three hundred twenty-second with an exponent of two thousand?" 113).

In spite of these parodic refutations, Nietzsche's conception of the eternal return is more like the spherical infinity that Pascal finds so terrifying than the exact repetition that Borges describes. In a fallen world ("God is dead"), there is no angel that can give a comprehensive account of our "curved eternity." Rather, we must do it ourselves, with our imperfect modes of memory and representation. Moreiras describes these imperfect modes as a kind of *mourning* that acknowledge the impossibility of bringing something fully into the present, which is implicit in Borges's description of the "aesthetic act":

> La música, los estados de la felicidad, la mitología, las caras trabajadas por el tiempo, ciertos crepúsculos y ciertos lugares, quieren decirnos algo, o algo dijeron que no hubiéramos debido perder, o están por decir algo; esta inminencia de una revelación, que no se produce, es, quizá, el hecho estético. (OI 12)[20]

> Music, states of happiness, mythology, faces worked by time, certain twilights and certain places want to tell us something, or said something that we shouldn't have lost, or are about to say something; this imminence of a revelation that is not produced is, perhaps, the aesthetic act (or fact).

Moreiras writes, "The real is always in retreat" (*Tercer espacio* 125). A mournful kind of representation admits that there is much that it cannot say, that the past cannot be recuperated fully into the present. As in de Man's description of mourning, this kind of representation leaves a place for what cannot be comprehended. What cannot be brought into the present can be evoked by an aesthetic act that inscribes its incomprehension or imminence, like the breaths and secrets that brush against historical knowledge, or like the eternal return in which the here or the known (the *Aquí*) is always surrounded by a there or an unknown (the *Allí*) that it cannot fully incorporate.

Borges's fictions are full of characters who want to overcome the retreat of the real and appropriate it, either in a great work, as with Carlos Argentino Daneri in "El aleph," or in their heads, as in the case of "Funes el memorioso" ("Funes the Memorious"). Due to an accident that rendered him incapable of forgetting, Funes remembers everything down to the smallest detail. For example, he finds himself capable of "reconstructing" an entire day, a task that takes precisely an entire day. Moreiras calls this power of reconstruction a productive or reproductive memory, based on Philippe Lacoue-Labarthe's description of the Aristotelian conception of mimesis as "productive mimesis." Lacoue-Labarthe writes that Aristotle conceived of mimesis as something that supplements the nontotalizing condition of the natural world: "it supplements a certain defect in nature, its incapacity to do it all, organize it all, do it all—produce it all" (cited in Moreiras, *Tercer espacio* 126). Indeed, in a nightmarish development of this mimesis, Funes's memory soon becomes so totalizing that there is no room left for new experience. In its drive for totality, productive mimesis attempts to overcome the retreat of the real and eliminate the *re-* from representation. Funes can remember "everything," but he cannot remember that his memory is a supplement, and, this forgotten, he cannot remember that there is an outside to his head, or that there is anything that his totalizing memory cannot incorporate. Moreiras compares this memory to the Internet, where Aristotelian mimesis is achieving new extremes of totalization (189). The Internet provides the closest we have ever come to a totality of information, and yet it does not have a way of indicating that it does not include everything, which if it were to include as information, would merely repeat the idealist quandary in which the "outside of the head" appears to be comprehended by the "inside the head." The outside cannot be presented as information. We need to implement an unproductive form of mimesis: a form of representation that accepts incomprehension or the retreat of the real in order to be open to an outside—an *Allí* that is not exhausted by the *Aquí*.

Contrary to forms of representation that seek to reproduce the world they represent, Nietzsche's idea of an eternal return confronts us with things that we do not necessarily recognize as our own, but which in a kind of "now of recognizability" startle us out of a sense of what we think we know of ourselves and force us to confront the voices and breaths of air that interrogate our sense of self-possession. This is Franco Rella's interpretation of the Nietzschean return: "The time of repetition functions *schreckhaft,* terrifyingly, because it opposes to the subject parts of itself that the 'I' had thought to dominate definitively. Those parts penetrate our present existence . . . It is here that the death of God occurs" (113). Expressing the same sense of terror as Pascal, Nietzsche's figure of the eternal return describes a world in which every here ("yo soy") is surrounded by a spherical there which penetrates it in unexpected "recurrences": parts of the past that we do not know as the past, but that are a "return" of something that is never fully produced in our heads—in memory, representation, or knowledge. This formulation recalls Benjamin's description of a dialectical cyclicality in which what returns is not what we thought we knew, history as the always-the-same, as well as Borges's descriptions of the repetitions and recurrences that elicit the echoes and voices of history.

As if to narratively mimic the Pascalian sphere, Borges closes his essay on Pascal ("La esfera de Pascal") with a near-repetition of the opening sentence. He writes, "Quizá la historia universal es la historia de la diversa entonación de algunas metáforas" ("Perhaps universal history is the different intonation of several metaphors," OI 16). Moreiras stresses the fact that what distinguishes the first and the last sentences is the word "entonación," which he remarks resonates with the term *Stimmung* in Nietzsche (*Tercer espacio* 128). It is also the word that Benjamin uses in his second thesis to describe the voices or tones that echo and reverberate throughout history. Instead of a true "universal history," which would omit that which it cannot quite hear in order to record a proper account of events, Borges suggests that perhaps the history of the universe can be read or heard in the slippage of the metaphors or figures that we use to understand the world. Metaphor comes from the Greek word "to carry across," like translation (*meta-phorein, trans-latio*), and perhaps the stress on "different intonations" indicates that the metaphors that structure universal history are more a matter of translation—a moving across that is never total, that always leaves a remainder, a slight difference—than of a metaphor or figure that would transfer anything entirely, that would be able to contain the universe in its forms. This description of universal history as the repetition of "unas cuantas metáforas" recalls Nietzsche's well-known dictum that truth is a "mobile army of metaphors, metonyms, anthropomorphisms" (46). Metaphors that are taken as truth are like imperialistic attempts to reduce and subject the infinite multiplicity of the world to a few concepts and metaphors such as time, space, the autonomous "I." Borges's definition of the aesthetic act is conceived as an intervention into this form of representation in which he transcribes these metaphors in order to reveal the slippage in their translation, the *Stimmen*—voices, tones, breaths of air—that are left out of the truth claims of universal history. These *Stimmen* tell another kind of history and require that we listen attentively to what they say as well as what they do not say: to what they said that we shouldn't have lost or to what they are about to say, as Borges says of the voices evoked by the aesthetic act.

Reading, Writing, Mourning History

In response to the question posed at the beginning of this chapter as to whether Borges believes that the world can be contained in our heads, in representation, in an "I am," whether divine or mortal, I am proposing that his definition of the aesthetic act suggests that he does not. There is an *Allí* that surrounds every *Aquí,* which returns to us endlessly and never the way we think it will, always with a different intonation: echoes and voices of an "outside the head" that we will never grasp, but which we must listen to in order to avoid subjugating the universe's differences to a few small metaphors of truth. It is only when we start to do this that we can begin to destroy the hierarchies and empires commanded by the small army of metaphors. The first step involves a "mournful" repetition of "those modes of language [that] deny the whole rhetoricity of the true," that "accept incomprehension, . . . leave a place for it"; that leave a space for the "inminencia de una revelación que no se produce" (de Man, *Rhetoric* 262; OI 12).

This mournful representation concerns a form of writing that is also a kind of listening, a making space for and listening to the voices and tones of history that are not contained by the metaphors of universal history. It is also a form of reading. There is no angel who can watch over the whole of the universe and count or tell (the verb "contar" conveys both senses) the turns and returns of history, as Borges parodically describes. But there is a different kind of angel that might promise what

Benjamin describes as a kind of redemption: not a redemptive exchange of one thing for another (mortality for eternity, absence for presence), but a redemption that collects or "salvages" the echoes and breaths of history that get buried beneath the catastrophes of modern existence. This is Benjamin's description of the Angelus Novus, who stands in a position of absolute vulnerability toward the past: "His eyes are staring, his mouth is open, his wings are spread . . . His wings are turned toward the past. Where we perceive a chain of events, he sees one single catastrophe which keeps piling wreckage upon wreckage and hurls it at his feet" (I 257). Where we protect ourselves with a mobile army of metaphors, marshaled into narrative chains, the Angelus Novus sees a "wreckage" that will not be so subdued. The angel cannot escape; his wings are pinned by the winds of history, a cyclical-dialectical wind, and there is perhaps nothing to do but read this wreckage, or write it, "contando" the incomplete translation of the world's catastrophes into concepts. The angel is an illustration of Benjamin's citation from Friedrich Schlegel of the historian as a "backwards-turned prophet" (quoted in Bahti 188). A reading of the past that observes history's noncomprehension in metaphors or a rhetoricity of the true is touched by a "weak messianic force" whereby the past's secrets and shadows function as a "secret index" to the future. An openness to the difference that recurs in the metaphors of universal history "snatches one away" ("arrebatar") from an impenetrable sense of what is and pushes us toward the horizon of what can be.

Benjamin conveyed the urgency of such a project with his description of the Angelus Novus. The catastrophe of fascism threatened to leave him with nowhere to turn, and in the end he became part of its wreckage. Far from the catastrophe that was afflicting Europe, but in what he called the bad times that touch all of us, Borges describes a similar kind of history reading and writing in his story "Tlön, Uqbar, Orbis Tertius." In this story a group of playboy idealists get together and decide to invent a country, which leads to the invention of an entire planet. Their idealist schemes gradually begin to take over the real world, an eventuality that Borges compares to all conceptual schemes that try to reduce the world to a single order: "Hace diez años bastaba cualquier simetría con apariencia de orden—el materialismo dialéctico, el antisemitismo, el nazismo—para embelesar a los hombres. ¿Cómo no someterse a Tlön, a la minuciosa y vasta apariencia de un planeta ordenado?" ("Ten years ago any symmetry with the appearance of order—dialectical materialism, anti-Semitism, Nazism—was sufficient to captivate men. How not to submit to Tlön, to the meticulous and vast evidence of an ordered planet?" F 35). The seduction of idealism threatens to take over the entire world: "A disperse dynasty of solitary men has changed the face of the world," the narrator Borges reflects.

"Su tarea prosigue. Si nuestras previsiones no yerran, . . . el mundo será Tlön" ("Their task continues. If our predictions do not err, . . . the world will be Tlön," 36). In the face of this idealist imperialism, in which a metaphoric army is on the verge of corralling the world into the heads of a few men, what does Borges's character decide to do? He says he is resolved to continue "revisando en los quietos días del hotel de Adrogué una indecisa traducción quevediana (que no pienso dar a la imprenta) del *Urn Burial* de Browne" ("revising in the quiet days of a hotel in Adrogué an indecisive translation in the style of Quevedo [which I don't plan on sending to press] of Browne's *Urne Buriall*").

This reaction is not, as it might seem at first, an escapist reaction to a world in crisis. Moreiras describes this turn toward translation as a form of mourning whereby the character of Borges resists the burial of the world into a single metaphor or idealist order (*Tercer espacio* 76). He also observes that the act of writing stories such as "Tlön" is itself a kind of translation that emphasizes the disjunction between our world and Tlön. Moreiras compares both interdiegetic and extradiegetic translations to epitaphs, like those of the sepulchers described in Browne's *Urne Buriall*. He writes that Borges's "reaction is to write 'Tlön,' which is above all a translation of the Tlönian disjunction of his world, which is also ours, like epitaphs translate death and thus articulate a kind of survival." Inspired by the disinterment of some Norfolk sepulchers (in the early years of science in which bodies were first being opened and a positive form of life was not encountered inside), Browne's text recounts rituals of interment throughout history as a way of showing, in a kind of natural-historical observation of mortality's returns, how neither death nor life is contained in those structures.[21]

The figure of epitaphic translation is central to the argument this book has tried to pursue. It returns us to chapter 1 in which we considered the motif of a "sepulchral rhetoric" whereby life and death (and with them, identity, history, and progress) were believed to be contained by a particular use of language, which Borges opposed through a poetics that resists containment. In chapter 2, we looked at how the figure of biography similarly functions as a kind of tomb in which to contain life, and in chapter 3, we looked at ways in which national and regional histories are conceived as structures of containment that are based on a constitutive exclusion. These figures can all be seen as means of keeping the world securely "inside the head," a Tlönian kind of idealism whose limits Borges repeatedly emphasizes. The act of translation at the end of "Tlön" is emblematic of the ways in which he translates the metaphors on which universal history is based in order to show an excess or difference that they do not admit. In this way, he can be said to perform almost literally what de Man calls a cold enumeration, almost like death itself, of modes of language that deny the rhetoricity of comprehension. Browne's *Urne Buriall* is also such an enumeration. That Borges translates this text of disinterment as his only resource against an increasingly ubiquitous idealism is a gesture that is not irrelevant to the current state of the world in which things are increasingly contained, in a kind of neo-Ptolemaic cosmology, by concentric spheres of individualism, regionalism, and a pseudotranscendent globalism.

Even if there is no archangel who can count or tell the cycles of the universe, there are other kinds of "backwards turned prophets" who through their contemplation of history's repeated metaphors can reveal a difference that opens to a future not contained by those metaphors. This is what Moreiras calls the survival implicit in Borges's act of translation at the end of "Tlön," which also occurs in Borges's writings in general. Like his fellow translator and history writer Benjamin, Borges's task of translation seeks to open a space to live through a use of language that does not attempt to internalize a totality, but which leaves a space of in-completion—a place for the secrets of history, past, present, and future.

Notes

Introduction

1. Walter Benjamin, "The Task of the Translator," in *Illuminations,* pp. 71–73; and Jorge Luis Borges, "Pierre Menard," in *Ficciones*. Implicit in this discussion is Borges's essay "Kafka y sus precursores," which is included in *Otras inquisiciones*.

Two recent books discuss the role of translation in Borges's work in detail: Efraín Kristal's *Invisible Work: Borges and Translation* (Nashville: Vanderbilt University Press, 2002), and Sergio Waisman's *Borges and Translation: The Irreverence of the Periphery* (Lewisburg: Bucknell University Press, 2005). On the notion of life-writing in Benjamin, see Gerhard Richter's excellent book *Walter Benjamin and the Corpus of Autobiography* (Detroit: Wayne State University Press, 2000).

2. Exceptions to this include historicist criticism that seeks to place Borges's work in relationship to a historical and cultural context.

3. Throughout his life, Borges denounced Peronism as a form of populist authoritarianism. His anti-Peronism grew so rabid that he ended up welcoming the military coup of 1976, an error that he denounced several years later. For a balanced and informative discussion of this, see José Eduardo González's *Borges and the Politics of Form* (New York: Garland, 1998), chap. 11.

4. The term "landscape" is from Beatriz Sarlo's book *Jorge Luis Borges: A Writer on the Edge*. Her work on Borges (also included in *Una modernidad periférica*) sets the tone for the new historicist reappropriation of Borges, although such tendencies are also evident in Daniel Balderston's *Out of Context: Historical Reference and the Representation*

of Reality in Borges (more "new historicist" in the strict sense of the term), and the volume published from the Borges Centenary Conference, *Jorge Luis Borges: Intervenciones sobre pensamiento y literatura,* edited by Alejandro Kaufman.

5. Pablo Oyarzún pointed out the difference in tone between the two thinkers in a workshop that was held on this project in May 2002 at the University of Chile. During this workshop, Federico Galende came up with the brilliant formulation that "Borges convierte en injuria lo que es promesa mesiánica para Benjamin" ("Borges converts into an insult what Benjamin sees as Messianic promise").

Chapter 1. Origins and *Orillas*

1. Buenos Aires grew as much as 75 percent between 1890 and 1936; 53 percent of that growth occured after the start of World War I. See Sarlo, *Modernidad* 18, also 43–45. The term *criollo* in Argentina refers to a person of European descent and Argentine birth.

In a discussion following a lecture held at the Universidad Diego Portales in Santiago, Chile, in August 2002, Sarlo admitted that Borges was really more of a *reader* of *criollismo* than an unquestioning apologist. She described Borges's representations of Buenos Aires as a *ciudad moderna grado cero,* representing more a nightmarish version of *criollismo*'s ideals of purity than a favorable depiction. These comments mark a considerable change from her depictions of Borges as a defender of *criollismo* in *Una modernidad periférica* and *Jorge Luis Borges: A Writer on the Edge.*

2. Jorge Panesi considers that Borges's early writings manifest a quasi-religious—or as he says, *symbolic*—nationalism, which begins to break up in the early 1930s into something that one could tentatively call allegorical (165). I will argue along with Pezzoni that the allegorization of symbolic nationalism occurred much earlier, in the 1920s.

3. In the first edition, "La Recoleta" is the second poem in the volume. I will discuss the issue of the various editions later.

4. I have been greatly influenced by Sylvia Molloy's reading of this essay in "Flâneuries textuales: Borges, Benjamin y Baudelaire."

5. *Misteriosismo* would be translated more accurately as "mysteriousness," but this does not work well in the paragraph. I think that "mysticism" is not far from Borges's intended meaning, in the sense of a mysterious or spiritual sense of self and interpersonal relations, but without specifically religious connotations.

6. See Lagmanovich (84n) for information about the different editions of Borges's texts. He cites Horacio Jorge Becco's *Jorge Luis Borges: Bibliografía total, 1923–1973* (Buenos Aires, 1973). The main editions of *Fervor de Buenos Aires* were published in 1923, 1943, 1969, and 1974.

7. In 1945, upon receiving the Premio de Honor de la Sociedad Argentina de Escritores, Borges proclaimed that his first book of poetry, "de un modo secreto pero sensible, prefigura a los otros" ("in a secret but appreciable way prefigures the other [books]"). In his 1969 prologue to the edition that forms part of the complete *Obra poética,* he writes, "Para mí, *Fervor de Buenos Aires* prefigura todo lo que haría después" ("For me, *Fervor de Buenos Aires* prefigures everything that I would do later"; cited in Lagmanovich 92; also in OP 17).

8. "I do not set up to be a poet. Only an all-round literary man: a man who talks, not one who sings. . . . Excuse this apology; but I don't like to come before people who have a note of song, and let it be supposed I do not know the difference" (*The Letters of Robert Louis Stevenson;* cited in OP 12).

9. This is the version from the 1977 *Obra poética,* which is different from the version of the poem that Sarlo uses.

10. Just to give some idea how the revisions worked, I want to point out the slight variations between some of the different versions of the poem's end. The 1943 version that Sarlo cites ends thus: "Lo anterior: escuchado, leído, meditado, / lo resentí en la Recoleta, / junto al propio lugar en que han de enterrarme." In the 1964 version (from the *Obras completas,* vol. 1), the modifier "propio" drops out: "Lo anterior: escuchado, leído, meditado, / lo resentí en la Recoleta, / en el lugar en que han de enterrarme" (20). And in the 1977 and final version, this no longer "proper" place is designated as simply "el lugar de mi ceniza" (22).

11. See, for example, Franco (341).

12. Paul de Man discusses the history of this term in Hegel in "Sign and Symbol in Hegel's Aesthetics" (*Aesthetic Ideology* 101). Jacques Derrida discusses de Man's analysis of the term in *Memoires for Paul de Man,* 37–39.

13. Translations are mine.

14. This is Derrida's definition of allegory: a form of representation that "manifests the other (*allos*) in the open but nocturnal space of the *agora*" (allegory comes from *allos-agorein,* speaking other than publicly, other than in the *agora* [*Memoires* 37]). In another place, he describes

allegory as the "strange self-portrait of drawing given over to the speech and gaze of the other" (*Memoirs of the Blind* 3).

15. This stanza is remarkably similar to the description of Huckleberry Finn on his raft in "Nueva refutación del tiempo" (OI 175). Huck avoids the straight white line of daylight in his nighttime drift down the river. The resonance with this passage lends itself to a connection to Conrad's *Heart of Darkness*, as well, in which things—such as Kurtz or the heart of imperialism—are found, only to reveal that they can never be found again. It would be interesting to do a study of these three rivers in relation to Borges's theories on time, space, and imperialism (see chapter 4), but such a project exceeds the parameters of this book.

16. Benjamin defines aura as a "unique phenomenon of a distance, however close it may be" (I 222). The relationship of aura and prehistory is discussed in the Baudelaire essay (I 185).

17. The poetic pride that fills the first half of this poem recalls the character of Carlos Argentino Daneri in "El aleph," who is parodied and contrasted with the figure of Borges's own character.

18. It is true that these voices are of people prominent enough in either personal or national history to be remembered in photographs or in conversation, and do not include the infinite voices of the past who lacked such prominence or privilege. Nevertheless, one wonders if the opposition of visual representation, which frames the prominent figures of the past in still images, and an anguished orality that multiplies in echoes, might not be the beginning of a concern for voices that lie outside of universal accounts of history. See chapter 3 herein and the idea of the *infame* of universal history.

19. Enrique Pezzoni makes a similar point in his Lecture 16 (in *Enrique Pezzoni*). He explains that Borges presents an atemporal, ahistorical representation of Buenos Aires in this poem and "Sala vacia," but then reintroduces history ("la historia se le mete," 74). I do not agree with Pezzoni's conclusion, however, that the history that Borges introduces to the ahistorical space of the city-sala is incapable of change: "La historia que fabrica es una historia sin proceso, sin devenir, es una a-cronicidad . . . No entra el cambio" ("the history that he creates is a history without process, without future, it is an a-chronicity . . . Change does not enter," 74–75). I believe that the explosion of the past in the present has every possibility of introducing change.

20. Sylvia Molloy makes this point, but suggests that Borges's contact with alterity dissolves in the end into an empty flâneurie ("Flâneuries textuales"; also see *Signs of Borges*).

21. This is how I interpret Sarlo's reading of the line from "Fundación mítica de Buenos Aires" in which the poet remarks that the only thing missing ("sólo faltó una cosa") from the Palermo of yesteryear was "la vereda de enfrente" (OP 92; Sarlo, *Borges* 21).

22. That which endures in time and resists temporal change is attributed here to human volition, but as we have seen in some of the poems, the things that resist or run counter to time's changes are often not human and do not have a will per se, such as the dead horse in "Casi juicio final" or the past in "Rosas."

23. Interestingly enough, the first poem of *Cuaderno San Martín* is the infamous poem "Fundación mítica de Buenos Aires," in which Borges describes a childlike fantasy of the foundation of Buenos Aires in his backyard, and ends saying "This is how I tell myself that Buenos Aires began: I consider it as eternal as water and air" (OP 92). He later acknowledges that this myth of eternity is doubly false. He writes in the prologue to the 1969 edition, "This composition is . . . fundamentally false. Edinburgh or York or Santiago de Compostela can lie about eternity; not so Buenos Aires, which we have seen spring up sporadically between empty lots and dirt alleys" (89). Also of interest is the fact that the last poem of the collection, "Paseo de julio," is one of the only poems in Borges's first three books of poetry that describes modernization per se. It describes a different kind of death from that presented in "Muertes de Buenos Aires," namely, a death associated with commodity fetishism and the underbelly of capitalist accumulation.

Chapter 2. Bios-Graphus

1. Davi Arrigucci reads this parable as a call to arms for a historicist reading of Borges. He interprets the split between "Borges" and "yo" as a problem that the historically minded critic can repair, by reattaching Borges's "universalist" works to the "scenes of concrete history" (195).

2. His readings of the skeptical and the English idealist rejections of an integral and autonomous personal identity are clearly stated in texts such as "Nueva refutación del tiempo" (for example, "no hay detrás de las caras un yo secreto," OI 175).

3. The Real Academia Española offered the following explanation to me of the neologism "lirastenia" via an e-mail communication: "Sólo hemos documentado este término en Borges. Parece, por tanto, creación particular que, etimológicamente hace referencia a la 'debilidad lírica' de los poetas tradicionales" ("We have only documented this term in Borges.

From its etymological components, it would seem to be an invented word that refers to the 'lyric weakness' of traditional poets").

4. Cohen makes a useful distinction between a definable life (*bios*) and undefinable life (*zoos*). See *Ideology and Inscription,* chapter 8. This is of course the subject of much of Giorgio Agamben's work.

5. A third critic who comes from the same school of thought is Ludmer, who briefly discusses *Evaristo Carriego* in *The Gaucho Genre.* She calls it a "non-organic book" (it is a "mosaic, with aggregates and fragments," 188), but she follows the other two critics in her description of it as a cannibalistic "conversation" with an other (that is, both Carriego and Palermo), in which Borges tries to appropriate the masculine qualities that he was denied in his childhood.

6. Borges makes this point ironically in his comments on biography in "Sobre el 'Vathek' de William Beckford": "Tan compleja es la realidad . . . que un observador omnisciente podría redactar un número indefinido, y casi infinito, de biografías de un hombre, que destacaran hechos independientes y de las que tendríamos que leer muchas antes de comprobar que el protagonista es el mismo. Simplifiquemos desaforadamente una vida: imaginemos que la integran trece mil hechos. Una de las hipotéticas biografías registraría la serie 11, 22, 33 . . . ; otra, la serie 9, 13, 17, 21; otra, la serie 3, 12, 21, 30, 39" ("Reality is so complex . . . that an omniscient narrator could write an indefinite, and almost infinite, number of biographies of a man, which would emphasize different facts and of which we would have to read any number before we could confirm that they refer to the same protagonist. Let us shamelessly simplify a life: let's imagine that it consists of three thousand facts. One of the hypothetical biographies would register the series 11, 22, 33 . . . ; another, the series 9, 13, 17, 21; another, the series 3, 12, 21, 30, 39," OI 187).

7. Jorge Panesi cleverly affirms that America itself "is a Borgesian subject" (165).

8. Autobiography, which is the subject of de Man's essay, is also biography.

9. "Bastardilla" refers to italic script, but its inclusion in the list of faces behind faces behind false faces suggests the evident relation of the term to bastardy (writing in this sense would be "little bastards"—bastardillas). The allusion is suggestive of a certain illegitimacy of writing itself, as though all writing were an illegitimate mask or attempt to mask its illegitimacy. Both themes are explored throughout Borges's writings. Molloy explores the theme of masks in the first chapter of *Signs of*

Borges, although I disagree with her suggestion that the culmination of this theme ends in the construction of a "purely literary space" (14).

10. Molloy discusses this aspect of identity in Borges's text (*Signs* 13), but she does not address the implications for a notion of community. Rather, she suggests that the dispersal of identity leads to a privileging of the role of the narrator (13–14). She goes on to argue that in *Historia universal de la infamia* this tendency culminates in an erasure of both narrator and community: "the narrating subject, deliberately eclipsed as a person, blocks the passage toward a compassionate 'we'" (15). I disagree with this assertion, as should be clear from my next chapter. In spite of these small critiques, I would like to add that I have long admired Molloy's book.

11. Rainer Nägele writes, "Freud invokes the *Motiv* as an intersection of motive and motif in a letter to Fleiss on October 27, 1897, at the moment when psychoanalysis begins to take shape. 'In the determining force I divine great, general frame motif/ve/s, as I might call them, and others, fill-in motif/ve/s that change with the experience of the individual.' The motif appears as the material incarnation of the motive, the phenomenalization of a ground that opens up as an abyss" (that is, as a symptom, mentioned on the previous page) ("Poetic" 123–24).

12. In "The Image of Proust," Benjamin writes, "Fernández rightly distinguished between a *thème de l'éternité* and a *thème du temps* in Proust. But his eternity is by no means a platonic or a utopian one; it is rapturous. Therefore, if 'time reveals a new and hitherto unknown kind of eternity to anyone who becomes engrossed in its passing,' this certainty does not enable an individual to approach 'the higher regions which a Plato or Spinoza reached with one beat of the wings' . . . The eternity which Proust opens to view is convoluted time, not boundless time. His true interest is in the passage of time in its most real—that is, space-bound—form" (I 210–11).

13. I will come back to the figure of an eternal return in chapter 4.

14. Derrida's neologism of "otobiography" replaces the self of "auto" with the ear (oto-), by way of emphasizing a "feminine" receptivity in certain forms of self-writing.

15. De Man discusses Lejeune's book in "Autobiography as De-Facement" (71–72); Derrida in *Memoires for Paul de Man* (24–25). Although the contractual nature of the proper name in autobiography is more evident in autobiography than biography, I do not think it is excluded in the case of biography. In the case of *Evaristo Carriego,* it could be argued that Borges is signing for Carriego, or adopting Carriego's signature as his own, or both at the same time.

16. The law established compulsory suffrage for male natives over eighteen years of age and an electoral roll that was linked to military conscription lists. The army was given custodial duties during elections (Rock, *Argentina* 189).

17. These neighborhoods were immigrant neighborhoods near the port, not the *orillas,* which lay inland and which appeared to foster another musical preference: that of the milonga, which Borges calls an "infinite greeting" ("saludo infinito") that is related to eternity, in contrast to the tango, which is always in time, "en los desaires y contrariedades del tiempo" (EC 86–87). If the milonga is an infinite "saludo," perhaps it could be said that the sad song ("el dolorido tango-canción," 27) of the tango is an infinite farewell.

18. *Visions of Excess,* trans. Allan Stoekl (Minneapolis: University of Minnesota Press, 1985).

19. I am indebted here to Beatrice Hanssen's discussion of this in *Critique of Violence: Between Poststructuralism and Critical Theory,* 20.

20. One place where it appears is "Tlön, Uqbar, Orbis Tertius" (F 14–15).

21. This passage is an evident indication of Schopenhauer's influence on Borges. Although it sometimes appears that Borges embraced Schopenhauer uncritically, I would like to suggest (based on my reading of Borges in these pages) that he maintained an ironic distance to Schopenhauer's notion of representation and its transcendence, for example, in music. The relationship between the two thinkers is fascinating, but it is too complex to explore here. I discuss Borges's disenchantment with Schopenhauer briefly in chapter 4.

22. For example, the "campaña del desierto" of 1879 in which the last of the indigenous peoples in Argentina were decimated as the part of the final "campaign" of "civilization" against "barbarism."

23. See my discussion of this term in the introduction.

24. The wave of immigration that so drastically changed Buenos Aires in the first third of the twentieth century was largely, although not exclusively, composed of Italians. The Italians settled above all in the port neighborhood of La Boca, and had a great influence on the tango. Sarlo and Molloy both remark on Borges's apparent xenophobia in this respect, but they do not acknowledge the shift in blame that he makes from the "gringos" to the entire republic (*Borges* and *Signs,* respectively).

Chapter 3. Allegory, Ideology, Infamy

1. The (mis)representation or misrecognition of this inherent instability is key to the operation of ideology. In another essay Laclau rewrites the classical definition of ideology as the "mis-recognition of a positive essence" as "exactly [its] opposite: [the ideological] would consist of the non-recognition of the precarious character of any positivity, of the impossibility of any ultimate suture. The ideological would consist of those discursive forms through which society tries to institute itself on the basis of . . . the non-recognition of the infinite play of differences" (*New Reflections* 92).

2. This is for me a perplexing comparison. I suppose she is attempting to compare the establishment of Baroque power and the rise of the nation state, but the grounds for the comparison are not made sufficiently clear. Of course, Benjamin also discusses a nineteenth-century form of allegory, but it is one that is significantly different from that described by Sommer.

3. Rainer Nägele suggests that "origin (*Ursprung*) is the name for the absence of ground" ("Benjamin's Ground" 34).

4. I am indebted to Pablo Oyarzún for pointing out the "doubleness" of Benjamin's dialectic. The relationships between Benjamin's concept of dialectics and Adorno's "negative dialectics" have been thoroughly discussed, most recently perhaps in Beatrice Hanssen's book *Walter Benjamin's Other History,* especially in the first chapter; and most extensively by Susan Buck-Morss in *The Origin of Negative Dialectics: Theodor W. Adorno, Walter Benjamin and the Frankfurt Institute* (New York: Macmillan Free Press, 1977). Nägele gives a compelling reading of the figure of the dialectic in Benjamin's writings in "Benjamin's Ground" (27ff).

5. See Hanssen, *Walter Benjamin*, chap. 2, especially 32–33, 46–48.

6. Bahti's discussion of the *Umschwung* passage is very tempting (282–85), but I believe he is wrong that the *Umschwung* does not represent a swing away from the objectives of allegory. Hanssen's reading of the passage is more similar to my own (*Walter Benjamin* 101–2).

7. On the theme of subjectivity at the end of the *Trauerspiel* book, see Hanssen, *Walter Benjamin*, 99–100, 181n.

8. Rejection of the figure of redemption in Benjamin is so common it is almost hard to pin down. One example is Jacques Derrida's curious interpretation of Benjamin's work in his essay "Marx and Sons" in *Ghostly Demarcations* (248–54).

9. In his excellent essay "Texto-palimpsesto: Memoria y olvido textual," Nicolás Rosa describes the *infame*—"ese no-contar lo sórdido, lo cruento, lo deletero, lo animal, lo horroroso, lo siniestro, lo infame"—as part of writing's relation to the future: "se escribe *la espera* . . . No es la escritura de lo posible sino de lo imposible en estado de esperanza" (189). I am also grateful to Carlos Pérez Villalobos for having pointed out to me that this is the focus of de Man's short essay on Borges, "A Modern Master."

10. Moreiras presents a strong argument for how the story "Tlön, Uqbar, Orbis Tertius" allegorizes national allegory in "Allegory of Allegory" (227ff). I have a slightly different take on allegory, however: I do not see the need for a "post-symbolic" that is distinct from allegory.

11. The fact that Tom is from the antipodes, and passes for an English soldier, is of course significant. The figure of "el negro Bogle" as the ventriloquist behind Tom's imposturing is particularly important, inasmuch as he represents a figure that cannot be fit into the equivalential chain of the English upper class. It is interesting to note that behind Tom's "face" is the black figure of Bogle, and behind Hakim's mask there is a "peculiar whiteness." The question of race appears throughout the stories, most notably in "El espantoso redentor Lazarus Morell."

12. It is true that Pirate Ching is not killed but only deposed, returned, in fact, to her status as mere widow. In this she is like the mother of Roger Tichborne: bereaved women left to seek company in the romance of empire, or, in the case of Lady Tichborne, to find its face in the improbable mug of Tom Castro.

13. Translation is mine, but I have consulted Andrew Hurley's translation of Borges's, *Collected Fictions*). The verb *aturdir* can mean a variety of things, including to bewilder, daze, stun, rattle; to unsettle, disquiet.

14. This is where I part from Laclau. Laclau believes that all disruption is merely part of the digestive logic of ideology, which requires disturbance and heterogeneity to function ("Death" 321). I believe that the *infame,* which is related to subalternity as Moreiras describes it in *The Exhaustion of Difference,* indicates a contestatory realm to ideology's historicism. See also the theory of an "ideology critique without ground" in Cohen (*Ideology* 18–20).

15. The fact that there is not even a subject pronoun—"quienes hablan"—is significant. This absence is untranslatable in English.

16. *Anonadar* means primarily "to annihilate" or "to crush." Ironically, the hissing non-language of the Mexicans reduces Billy to nothing.

17. In contrast to the red hair and freckles that have always marked Billy above the mass of humanity ("el caos de catinga y de motas" of his birthplace), Villagrán is himself a mass: it is said that he is "más que fornido" and that he "abunda en un desaforado sombrero"—these are hard to translate, but it is more or less that he is "more than hefty" and "abounds in an enormous hat."

18. See Cohen's discussion of the relationship between Benjamin's conceptions of allegory and cinema (*Ideology* 24–25, 143ff).

19. The information on "la estatua del imaginario Falucho" comes from Andrew Hurley's annotations to his translation of the story in Borges's *Collected Fictions* (527n).

20. Two excellent discussions of music or rhythm and history appear in chapter 2 of Henry Sussman's *Afterimages of Modernity* (Baltimore: Johns Hopkins University Press, 1990); and the introduction and chapter 4 of Cohen's *Anti-Mimesis from Plato to Hitchcock*.

21. That the German word *Erlösung* means both redemption and dissolution is perhaps not entirely irrelevant.

Chapter 4. Reading History's Secrets in Benjamin and Borges

1. One example of this (there are many) is from the poem "Ajedrez": "También el jugador es prisionero/ . . . de otro tablero, / de negras noches y de blancos días" (*El hacedor* 81).

2. It is very ambiguous who these "miles de personas en Argentina" are, but there is a very strong possibility that Borges is directing his finger against the masses that were forming under the leadership of Juan Perón, who spent several months in Nazi Germany before his rise to power. That he was more of a Stalin sympathizer would perhaps have been unimportant to Borges, who considered Hitler and Stalin to be made of much the same material.

3. See Cohen, *Ideology*, 53, 105ff. The figure of materiality in de Man is also the subject of *Material Events: Paul de Man and the Afterlife of Theory* (coedited by Cohen). Coming from a different theoretical tradition, Althusser writes of the distinction between idealism and materialism "that

an idealist philosopher is like a man who knows in advance *both* where the train he is climbing into is coming from *and* where it is going: what is its station of departure and its station of destination . . . The materialist, on the contrary, is a man who takes the train in motion . . . but without knowing where the train is coming from or where it is going" (12).

4. See Agamben, *Potentialities*, 48.

5. Benjamin explains these ideas in "On Language as Such and on the Language of Man" (R 318). See also Collingwood-Selby, *Walter Benjamin*.

6. See Oyarzún (89–91). In this chapter I quote from some of the fragments to Benjamin's "Theses on the Philosophy of History," which I first encountered in Oyarzún's translation.

7. Benjamin goes on to discuss the example of Marx here, so under criticism elsewhere in these pages, as someone who (in *Capital*) successfully explodes the epic element out of history, submitting historicism's penchant for narrative to the "expandida y tensa armazón de acero de una teoría" (Oyarzún 90). Theory here can be understood, not as an armature, but as a techne that can break out of the "bewitched" spot between magic and the positivism of historicism. See Cohen on the bewitched historicism of current historicist practices (*Ideology* esp. 1–7).

8. Timothy Bahti points out that this critique is particularly directed at Schleiermacher's *Einfühlung* and Dilthey's *nacherleben* (189). Benjamin also compares empathy, or the "making present" (*Vergegenwärtigung*) of what was, to a positivistic view of history, analogous to the relationship of the natural sciences to nature: "La falsa vivacidad de la presentificación, el hacer a un lado todo eco del lamento de la historia, señala su definitiva sumisión al concepto moderno de la ciencia" (Oyarzún 73–74).

9. Benjamin did not intend the "Theses" for publication because, as he wrote, "it would open both the door and the gate to enthusiastic misunderstanding." Brecht described his reaction to the text thus: "Briefly, the little work is clear and disentangling (despite all metaphoricity and Judaism) and one thinks with horror of how small the number is of those who are even ready to misunderstand something like this" (cited in Bahti 183–84).

As with the notes to the "Theses on the Philosophy of History," I am indebted to Oyarzún's translation of "Konvolut N" of the *Passagen-Werk*, also collected in *La dialéctica en suspenso: Fragmentos sobre la historia*. I have also consulted Leigh Hafrey and Richard Sieburth's translation into English of "Konvolut N," collected in *Benjamin: Philosophy, Aesthetics, History,* ed. Gary Smith (43–83). When I quote from "Konvolut N," I will include the note indicator instead of page numbers for convenience with regard to the different translations and editions.

10. His other query, whether repetition is always exact repetition, the repetition of identical moments—"Esos idénticos momentos, ¿no son el mismo?"—is not as simple as it might appear. In the first place, he admits that there are always differences: "naturalmente, [moments that repeat] se repiten sin precisión; hay diferencias de énfasis, de temperatura, de luz, de estado fisiológico general" (OI 177). With regard to his question as to whether "fervent" readers who throw themselves into a line of Shakespeare are not literally (for a moment) Shakespeare, the story "Pierre Menard, autor del Quijote" would seem to provide a negative answer to this. Menard, who in the twentieth century undertakes the task of rewriting the Quixote line by line, is *not* Cervantes, and his not being Cervantes, the difference between him and his writing and Cervantes and his writing, is the difference of history itself. See Collingwood-Selby, "Un retrazo en la escritura."

11. Along the lines of what was discussed in chapter 1, here the ground of the past that Borges indicates is "turbulent and chaotic" (OI 179), and not at all the "posthumous efficacy" that Benjamin describes as a neurotic attempt to guard against the interruption of a continuous transmission of history.

12. See for example the discussions in *Ghostly Demarcations,* especially Derrida's essay (248ff).

13. *Unveräußerlich* means "inalienably" or "unsellably" (from *veräußern,* to sell or to alienate). Harry Zohn translates it as "indissolubly," which works well in the face of the word *Erlösung,* which has as a second or third sense "dissolution" (GS 1.2.693).

14. John McCole provides an unusually concise explanation of this term. The concept of *Naturgeschichte* concerns, in its modern as well as its Baroque manifestations, "an experience with nature that was necessarily inaccessible to classicist symbolism: the 'lack of freedom, the imperfection, the brokenness of the sensuous, beautiful physical world . . . [Nature] appears not in bud and bloom, but in the overripeness and decay of its creations . . . as eternal transience'" (135). De Man and Hanssen also provide provocative readings of the term (*Resistance to Theory* 85–86 and *Walter Benjamin's Other History,* chap. 2, "The Turn to Natural History," respectively).

15. Horacio González, "Oficialismos de época" (3–10). See also the interview with Derrida, "Deconstruir la actualidad," in the same volume, 12–24.

16. The distinction between infinities is the topic of Borges's essay "La duración del infierno" in *Discusión,* in which he compares the ideas of divine eternity and the eternity of hell, which, he says, can only be our own, that is, temporal existence. In another essay in the same volume, he explains that he does not believe in divine eternity, although he does find it to be an interesting idea: "Los católicos (léase los católicos argentinos) creen en un mundo ultraterreno, pero he notado que no se interesan en él. Conmigo ocurre lo contrario; me interesa y no creo" (174).

17. I have translated Borges's version of Schopenhauer's words, although I have also consulted E. F. J. Payne's translation of *The World as Will and Representation.*

18. Borges uses the Latinate spelling of the word "substancia" instead of the more common spelling "sustancia," which emphasizes the roots sub and stance, as if to emphasize a material substratum to understanding itself. This does not, as it may appear, contradict the figure of melancholy described in chapter 1, where Baudelaire declares that "nothing in my melancholy has moved." The fragments that the melancholic allegorist grips in the river of a progressive history are not bedrocks from which to order the rest of the universe, but are sites of resistance to the concept of progress (which is based on a firm conception of the "I").

19. Cited in Pezzoni, *Texto,* 73. Borges acknowledges that "esto Schopenhauer también lo premeditó," again suggesting that Schopenhauer functions as a limit-figure for Borges, as someone who acknowledges language and representation's limits, but in the end wants to hold on to a sense of presence and identity, grammatical though it be ("I am"), in the middle of the swirling river of temporal existence. In Schopenhauer, see *The World as Will and Representation,* vol. 2 (86–87).

20. This definition of the aesthetic significantly changes the negative connotation of Borges's description of allegory as "an aesthetic error" in "De las alegorías a las novelas." Perhaps we could reinterpret that apparent condemnation to describe a kind of "errant imminence."

21. For example, "Circles and right lines limit and close all bodies, and the mortall right-lined circle must conclude and shut up all. There is no antidote against the Opium of time, which temporally considereth

all things; Our Fathers finde their graves in our short memories, and sadly tell us how we may be buried in our Survivors. Grave-stones tell truth scarce forty years . . . To be read by bare Inscriptions like many in *Gruter,* to hope for Eternity by Ænigmaticall Epithetes . . . are cold consolations unto the Students of perpetuity, even by everlasting Languages" (Browne 45–46).

The relationship of Browne's text to the beginning of the Enlightenment (especially the surgical opening of bodies) is described beautifully in W. G. Sebald's *The Rings of Saturn* (New York: New Directions, 1998), chap. 1. Borges is also mentioned.

Works Cited

Agamben, Giorgio. *Potentialities: Collected Essays in Philosophy*. Trans. Daniel Heller-Roazen. Stanford: Stanford University Press, 1999.

———. *Stanzas: Word and Phantasm in Western Culture*. Trans. Ronald L. Martinez. Minneapolis: University of Minnesota Press, 1993.

Althusser, Louis. "The Only Materialist Tradition, Part I: Spinoza." Trans. Ted Stolze. *The New Spinoza*. Ed. Warren Montag and Ted Stolze. Minneapolis: University of Minnesota Press, 1997. 2–19.

Arrigucci, Davi. *Enigma e comentário: ensaios sobre literatura e experiência*. São Paulo: Editora Schwarz, 1987.

Bahti, Timothy. *Allegories of History: Literary Historiography after Hegel*. Baltimore: Johns Hopkins University Press, 1992.

Balderston, Daniel. *Out of Context: Historical Reference and the Representation of Reality in Borges*. Durham: Duke University Press, 1993.

Baudelaire, Charles. *Les fleurs du mal*. Paris: Garnier, 1957.

Benjamin, Walter. "Central Park." Trans. Lloyd Spencer. *New German Critique* 34 (1985): 28-58.

———. *Gesammelte Schriften*. Ed. Rolf Tiedemann and Hermann Schweppenhäuser. 7 vols. Frankfurt: Suhrkamp, 1991.

———. *Illuminations*. Trans. Harry Zohn. New York: Schocken Books, 1969.

———. "N [Re the Theory of Knowledge, Theory of Progress]." Trans. Leigh Hafrey and Richard Sieburth. *Benjamin: Philosophy, Aesthetics, History*. Ed. Gary Smith. Chicago: University of Chicago Press, 1989. 43–83.

———. *The Origin of German Tragic Drama*. Trans. John Osborne. London: Verso, 1998.

———. *Das Passagen-Werk*. Ed. Rolf Tiedemann. 2 vols. Frankfurt: Suhrkamp, 1983.

———. *Reflections*. Trans. Edmund Jephcott. New York: Schocken Books, 1986.

Borges, Jorge Luis. *El aleph*. Madrid: Alianza, 1983.

———. *Collected Fictions*. Trans. Andrew Hurley. New York: Viking, 1998.

———. *Discusión*. Buenos Aires: Emecé, 1961.

———. *Evaristo Carriego*. Buenos Aires: Emecé, 1989.

———. *Ficciones*. Madrid: Alianza Emecé, 1992.

———. *El hacedor*. Buenos Aires: Emecé, 1987.

———. *Historia de la eternidad*. Buenos Aires: Emecé, 1995.

———. *Historia universal de la infamia*. Buenos Aires: Emecé, 1954.

———. *Inquisiciones*. Barcelona: Seix Barral, 1994.

———. *Obra poética*. Buenos Aires: Emecé, 1995.

———. *Obra poética: 1923–1964*. Buenos Aires: Emecé, 1964.

———. *Obras completas*. 3 vols. Buenos Aires: Emecé, 1965.

———. *Otras inquisiciones*. Madrid: Alianza Emecé, 1981.

Browne, Thomas. *Urne Buriall and The Garden of Cyrus*. Cambridge: Cambridge University Press, 1958.

Cadava, Eduardo. *Words of Light: Theses on the Photography of History*. Princeton: Princeton University Press, 1997.

Chakrabarty, Dipesh. "Postcoloniality and the Artifice of History. Who Speaks for 'Indian' Pasts?" *A Subaltern Studies Reader 1986–1995*. Ed. Ranajit Guha. Minneapolis: University of Minnesota Press, 1997. 263–93.

Cohen, Tom. *Anti-Mimesis from Plato to Hitchcock*. Cambridge: Cambridge University Press, 1994.

———. *Ideology and Inscription: "Cultural Studies" after Benjamin, de Man, and Bakhtin*. Cambridge: Cambridge University Press, 1998.

——— et al., eds. *Material Events: Paul de Man and the Afterlife of Theory*. Minneapolis: University of Minnesota Press, 2001.

Collingwood-Selby, Elizabeth. "Un retrazo en la escritura." *Texto y poder: Las políticas del sentido* 3 (1999): 129–35.

———. *Walter Benjamin: La lengua del exilio*. Santiago: Arcis-Lom, 1997.

De Man, Paul. *Aesthetic Ideology*. Minneapolis: University of Minnesota Press, 1996.

———. "Autobiography as De-Facement." *The Rhetoric of Romanticism*. New York: Columbia University Press, 1984. 67–81.

———. "A Modern Master." *Jorge Luis Borges*. Ed. Harold Bloom. New York: Chelsea House Publishers, 1986. 21–27.

———. *The Resistance to Theory*. Minneapolis: University of Minnesota Press, 1986.

———. *The Rhetoric of Romanticism*. New York: Columbia University Press, 1984.

Derrida, Jacques. *The Ear of the Other: Otobiography, Transference, Translation*. Trans. Peggy Kamuf and Avital Ronell. Lincoln: University of Nebraska, 1985.

———. "Marx and Sons." Trans. G. M. Goshgarian. *Ghostly Demarcations*. Ed. Michael Sprinker. London: Verso, 1999. 213–69.

———. *Memoires for Paul de Man*. Trans. Cecile Lindsay, Jonathan Culler, and Eduardo Cadava. New York: Columbia University Press, 1986.

———. *Memoirs of the Blind: The Self-Portrait and Other Ruins*. Trans. Pascale-Anne Brault and Michael Naas. Chicago: University of Chicago Press, 1993.

———. "Typewriter Ribbon: Limited Ink (2)." Trans. Peggy Kamuf. *Material Events: Paul de Man and the Afterlife of Theory*. Ed. Tom Cohen et al. Minneapolis: University of Minnesota Press, 2001.

Ferris, David S. "Aura, Resistance, and the Event of History." *Theoretical Questions*. Ed. David S. Ferris. Stanford: Stanford University Press, 1996. 1–26.

Forster, Ricardo. "Borges y Benjamin: La ciudad como escritura y la pasión de la memoria." *Cuadernos hispanoamericanos* 505 (1992): 507–23.

Franco, Jean. "The Utopia of a Tired Man: Jorge Luis Borges." *Critical Passions*. Ed. Mary Louise Pratt and Kathleen Newmark. Durham: Duke University Press, 1999. 327–65.

Freud, Sigmund. "Mourning and Melancholy." *The Standard Edition of the Complete Psychological Works*. 23 vols. Ed. and Trans. James Strachey. London: Hogarth Press, 1953–74.

González, Horacio. "Oficialismos de época." *El ojo mocho* 5 (1994): 3–10.

Hanssen, Beatrice. *Critique of Violence: Between Poststructuralism and Critical Theory*. London: Routledge, 2000.

———. *Walter Benjamin's Other History: Of Stones, Animals, Human Beings, and Angels*. Berkeley and Los Angeles: University of California Press, 1998.

Jameson, Fredric. *Postmodernism or the Cultural Logic of Late Capitalism*. Durham: Duke University Press, 1995.

———. "World Literature in an Age of Multinational Capitalism." *The Current in Criticism: Essays on the Present and Future of Literary Theory*. Ed. Clayton Koelb and Virgil Lokke. West Lafayette: Purdue University Press, 1986. 139–58.

Kaufman, Alejandro, ed. *Jorge Luis Borges: Intervenciones sobre pensamiento y literatura*. Buenos Aires: Paidós, 2000.

Laclau, Ernesto. "The Death and Resurrection of the Theory of Ideology." *MLN* 112 (1997): 297–321.

———. *New Reflections on the Revolution of Our Time*. London: Verso, 1990.

Lafforgue, Martín, et al. *AntiBorges*. Buenos Aires: Vergara, 1999.

Lagmanovich, David. "Los prólogos de Borges, raíces de una poética." *Acerca de Borges: Ensayos de poética, política y literatura comparada*. Ed. Jorge Dubatti. Buenos Aires: Editorial de Belgrano, 1999.

Ludmer, Josefina. "¿Cómo salir de Borges?" *Jorge Luis Borges: Intervenciones sobre pensamiento y literatura*. Ed. Alejandro Kaufman. Buenos Aires: Paidós, 2000. 289–300.

———. *El género gauchesco: Un tratado sobre la patria*. Buenos Aires: Sudamericana, 1988.

McCole, John. *Walter Benjamin and the Antinomies of Tradition*. Ithaca: Cornell University Press, 1993.

Molloy, Sylvia. "Flâneuries textuales: Borges, Benjamin y Baudelaire." *Homenaje a Ana María Barrenechea*. Ed. Lía Schwarz Lerner and Isaias Lerner. Madrid: Castalia, 1984. 487–96.

———. *Signs of Borges*. Trans. Oscar Montero. Durham: Duke University Press, 1994.

Moreiras, Alberto. *The Exhaustion of Difference*. Durham: Duke University Press, 2001.

———. "Pastiche Identity, and Allegory of Allegory." *Latin American Identity and the Constructions of Difference*. Ed. Amaryll Chanady. Minneapolis: University of Minnesota Press, 1994. 204–38.

———. *Tercer espacio: Literatura y duelo en América Latina*. Santiago: Arcis-Lom, 1999.

Nägele, Rainer. "Benjamin's Ground." *Benjamin's Ground: New Readings of Walter Benjamin*. Ed. Rainer Nägele. Detroit: Wayne State University Press, 1988. 5–24.

———. "The Poetic Ground Laid Bare (Benjamin Reading Baudelaire)." *Walter Benjamin: Theoretical Questions*. Ed. David S. Ferris. Stanford: Stanford University Press, 1996. 118–38.

Nietzsche, Frederich. *The Portable Nietzsche*. Trans. Walter Kauffman. New York: Penguin Books, 1976.

Oyarzún, Pablo. *La dialéctica en suspenso: fragmentos sobre la historia*. Santiago: Arcis-Lom, 1995.

Panesi, Jorge. *Críticas*. Buenos Aires: Norma, 2000.

Pezzoni, Enrique. *Enrique Pezzoni, lector de Borges*. Ed. Annick Louis. Buenos Aires: Sudamericana, 1999.

———. *El texto y sus voces*. Buenos Aires: Sudamericana, 1986.

Piglia, Ricardo. "Ideología y ficción en Borges." *Borges y la crítica*. Buenos Aires: Centro editor de América Latina, 1992. 87–95.

Real Academia Española. "Consulta RAE." E-mail to Kate Jenckes. 6 June 2003.

Richter, Gerhard. *Walter Benjamin and the Corpus of Autobiography*. Detroit: Wayne State University Press, 2000.

Rock, David. *Argentina 1516–1987: From Spanish Colonization to Alfonsín*. Berkeley and Los Angeles: University of California Press, 1987.

Rosa, Nicolás. "Texto-palimpsesto: Memoria y olvido textual." *Jorge Luis Borges: Variaciones interpretativas sobre sus procedimientos literarios y bases epistemológicas*. Ed. Karl Alfred Blüher and Alfonso de Toro. Frankfurt am Main: Vervuert Verlag, 1992. 185–209.

Saer, Juan José. "Borges como problema." *Confines* 7 (1999): 79–86.

———. *El concepto de la ficción*. Buenos Aires: Ariel, 1998.

Sarlo, Beatriz. "Borges: Cultural Theory and Criticism." *Jorge Luis Borges: Pensamiento y saber en el siglo XX*. Ed. Alfonso de Toro and Fernando de Toro. Madrid: Iberoamericana, 1999.

———. *Jorge Luis Borges: A Writer on the Edge*. London: Verso, 1993.

———. *Una modernidad periférica: Buenos Aires 1920 y 1930*. Buenos Aires: Nueva visión, 1988.

Schopenhauer, Arthur. *The World as Will and Representation*. 2 vols. Trans. E. F. J. Payne. New York: Dover, 1958.

Schwartz, Jorge. *Las vanguardias latinoamericanas: textos programáticos y críticos*. Madrid: Cátedra, 1991.

Shakespeare, William. *Macbeth*. *The Complete Works of Shakespeare*. Ed. David Bevington. Glenview: Scott, Foresman, 1980. 1219–1249.

Smith, Gary, ed. *Benjamin: Philosophy, Aesthetics, History*. Chicago: University of Chicago Press, 1989.

Sommer, Doris. "Allegory and Dialectics: A Match Made in Romance." *Boundary* 2 18 (1991): 60–82.

———. *Foundational Fictions: The National Romances of Latin America*. Berkeley and Los Angeles: University of California Press, 1991.

Whitman, Walt. *The Poetry and Prose of Walt Whitman*. Ed. Louis Untermeyer. New York: Simon and Schuster, 1949.

Žižek, Slavoj. *The Sublime Object of Ideology*. London: Verso, 1989.

Index